Women in the Conquest of the Americas

D1606039

Juan Francisco Maura

Women in the Conquest of the Americas

Translated from Spanish by
John F. Deredita

PETER LANG
New York • Washington, D.C./Baltimore
Bern • Frankfurt am Main • Berlin • Vienna • Paris

Library of Congress Cataloging-in-Publication Data

Maura, Juan Francisco.
Women in the conquest of the Americas / Juan Francisco Maura;
translated from Spanish by John F. Deredita.
p. cm.
Includes bibliographical references and index.
1. Women—America—History—16th century. 2. Women—America—
History—17th century. 3. America—Discovery and exploration—Spanish.
HQ1400.M38 305.4'09181'2—DC20 92-26545
ISBN 0-8204-2043-3

Die Deutsche Bibliothek-CIP-Einheitsaufnahme

Maura, Juan Francisco:
Women in the conquest of the Americas / Juan Francisco Maura. [Transl.:
John F. Deredita]. –New York; Washington, D.C./Baltimore; Bern;
Frankfurt am Main; Berlin; Vienna; Paris: Lang.
ISBN 0-8204-2043-3

Cover design by James F. Brisson.

Cover illustration *La venerable madre Jerónima de la Fuente* by Velázquez.
Courtesy of Museo de Prado, Madrid, Spain.

The paper in this book meets the guidelines for permanence and durability
of the Committee on Production Guidelines for Book Longevity
of the Council of Library Resources.

TABLE OF CONTENTS

FOREWORD

There are a good number of reasons which have prompted me to write this book. The main one that after having taught at various universities in the United States for over fifteen years I have observed an appalling lack of information on what the Hispanic culture was in the Americas. This is truly regrettable as I believe that much of what we find in history books has been conscientiously silenced or misrepresented. It is precisely this gap that has led me to research the fifteenth, sixteenth, and seventeenth centuries of the "Encounter of two cultures" in America.

During my investigation I realized that without the presence of women it would have been clearly impossible for Spain to consolidate it's presence in America or to fashion a Hispanic Culture. During my research in Spain and America I have found this to be very well documented. Therefore my intention is to offer the reader an overall view on what their situation was at that time.

Although the importance of what they did has been superficially treated, they gave outstanding proof of their capabilities. These women came from various social and geographical backgrounds. On many occasions they play the chief role in singular feats. Surprisingly, they will remain practically unknown and unmentioned. There were military women who took up arms in battle, women explorers, women in religious orders, intellectual women, women slaves, prostitutes and also women who held a high position in public office. If we put ourselves into the historical context of that period we see that Spain, a European and Mediterranean country, was where the Islamic and Jewish presence remained the longest in Europe. It is with this in mind that I hope that this book will be read. Otherwise we might be misled in trying to understand the Spanish position in the colonization of America with that of the other European countries. It wasn't until 1492 that the Catholic King Ferdinad and Queen Isabel conquered the Iberian Peninsula and sailed to the Americas in search of a route to the Indies. Spain's ancient and rich Semitic history helped to pave the way for what was later to come. This, I believe, was the determining factor and made her better prepared for the intimate contact she would later have with the American Indians. The bitter-sweet meeting of two worlds was to culminate in a physical and cultural cross-breeding of the Iberian people with the inhabitants of America.

More than five hundred years have gone by, and these women voices have been stifled, muted. To the majority, they never existed. Just as oxygen rises to the surface of water, the same occurs with truth, which sooner or later makes its appearance. The fact is that they were always there, and not only in the background, as many wish to believe (although their voice *was* in the background), but on the front line of a nascent society. Their aspirations, desires, and dreams most often remained stifled, in the shadows of a society that was rigid in its religious principles, not very flexible with women, and little disposed to accept change in the matter of women's physical and intellectual freedom. Nevertheless, although their weak voice was deposited in dark, dusty corners of church archives and some libraries, their deeds were strong and their legacy solid and clear, in everything involved in the establishment and creation of a new society, a symbiosis of the Spanish and Amerindian societies.

It is worth mentioning, even in passing, that the information present in Spain and Hispanic America, both in the archives of private houses and in those belonging to the state, is truly formidable. The greater part of this documentation has not been catalogued, which makes it possible to assume the existence of a great amount of additional information that is still beyond our reach, which will start coming out as interest in the subject, time, and economic resources permit.

Already in the second half of the eighteenth century, Martín Fernández de Navarrete, the great Spanish scholar of the subjects of voyages and discoveries, complained of the disorder in which many archives were to be found, and of the fact that many of their documents would be sold at public auction in other countries. Not many years later, Napoleon's troops sowed chaos again in all the archives of Spain as a result of the war for independence. Despite everything, and despite the war, Navarrete carried on his work indefatigably. Sorrowfully, the scholar deplored the disappearance of documents: "With what pain did we see the accounts of voyages of some Spanish navigators, having been sold at public auction, end up in nations that emulate our glory and rival our power!" (1: 33-34). At the same time, Navarrete encouraged the investigation and organization of those that were within our reach.

> There lie the pure sources of the history of Spain in the last four centuries...which out of negligence, laziness, or lack of reflection many writers have ignored, being content to carelessly lend their credence to foreign authors, who usually write with a great deal of partiality and frequently mistake and transform not only the facts, but even the material nomenclature of our peoples and the first names and surnames of our personages (1: 33-34).

This is their story, the story of the women of both shores, the Indian women who married Spaniards, the Spanish women who arrived single and those who arrived married. And these are the voices of some of them, together with some imaginary personifications of real personages taken out of period documents:

> Leonor de Nájara, and Indian woman, says
> That she is a native of this land and that she was the legitimate wife of Pedro Moreno de Nájara, deceased, who came over to this New Spain with Pánfilo de Narváez, and found her in the conquest, by whom she has four sons and and one daughter, and she is very poor and is suffering from want; and His Majesty's officials are not carrying out for her what Your Grace ormred (Icaza 1: 124).

Leonor de Nájara personifies the mother of the modern Mexican nation, along with many other Indian women, who by marrying Spaniards created the basis of what would be the Hispanic American people.

> Catalina de Cáceres, an Indian woman, says
> That she was the legitimate wife of Pedro Borges, one of the first conquistadores of this city of Mexico and New Spain, who died and left her with many children; and very poor and suffering extreme want (Icaza 1: 125).

Catalina de Cáceres: also an Indian woman and "legitimate wife" as many other Indian women would be, marrying those who came to conquer and who were themselves conquered for life, sharing children and giving rise to a culture that would end up being racially and culturally ubiquitous. She also personifies the economic situation that many wives of conquistadores had to go through when in many cases they inherited more debts than "gold".

> Antonio de Carranza and Ana de Carranza, mestizos, say
> That they are children of Pedro de Carranza, one of the first conquistadores of this city of Mexico and New Spain, who had in encomienda the towns of Guatepec and Tepeye, and they were taken from him with no cause, and that said Ana de Carranza is thirteen years old, and they are poor, and Gonzalo de Ecija has them in his house; for the love of God he begs Your Gracious Majesty to remember them (Icaza 1: 142-43).

Antonio and Ana de Carranza, children of Spain and America, can personify the spiritual and physical union of a fusion at first violent, in which the love and hate of two races would come to bear fruit in the mestizo, their doubly legitimate heir, since "on the part of their mothers the land is theirs which their fathers won and conquered" (Miró Quesada 15).

> Isabel Gutiérrez
> Does not state where she was born, nor whose daughter she is; she is a resident of the city of Los Angeles, and was the wife of Jerónimo de Cáceres, who was a conquistador of this New Spain, and died, she married a Juan López de la Cerda, and is at present his wife; he is absent from said city; and that she has a child, and that she came over to this New Spain twelve years ago, and has people in her house (Icaza 1: 167).

Isabel Gutiérrez can personify the anonymous Spanish woman, often an adventuress, who would not hesitate to cross the ocean and undergo hardships so long as she could seek adventure, love, and hope, always together with her own in joys and adversity, but would be a fierce enemy of adversaries when they posed a risk to her kinsmen. Like many others, Isabel had to end her days poor, with children, separated from a husband who was caught up in the duties of war and was not always faithful to his vows of love.

Guiomar Marmolejo says
That she is three years old, and that she is the legitimate daughter of Antonio Marmolejo, conquistador of this city of Mexico and New Spain, and served Your Majesty in all that; and that her guardian is Alonso del Castillo.[1]

Guiomar Marmolejo can personify the product of a romance between a beautiful native woman and an unfortunate soldier who like many others lost his life fighting for a cause which, with all his heart, he considered to be just, because that was the way he was taught and because his duty was to obey orders. Guiomar would have remained in the hands of a faithful friend of her father's, who would not allow the orphaned daughter of his best friend to remain without protection and shelter.

With these brief documented quotations and imaginary personifications, we prepare the way for the history and the most salient facts about some women, who like those just mentioned, preferred to follow their dreams and ideals, even at the risk of their lives and the lives of their families, rather than to stay in Spain living a life with much more limited economic horizons. Their identity is not limited, therefore, to the most distinguished accomplishments of their fathers or husbands, as the above quotations show, but to what they did day by day for themselves, which was rarely recorded because they were women.

ACKNOWLEDGMENTS

I want to thank Dr. Rowena Rivera for her kindness in revising the whole manuscript and giving me useful ideas and suggestions. She has been always a trusty friend, a model scholar and an exemplary teacher. I want to thank my mother for going into the last details of the English translation and for her continual encouragement to finish the work as soon as possible. Thanks to my brother Hernando for his patience listening to me reading aloud some of the chapters of the book. Thanks to Lisa J. Huempfner for suggesting that I write a book about Spanish Women.

Thanks to professor Wolfgang Mieder, as well as other members of the German and Russian Department of the University of Vermont, for having stood by me during a most difficult time of my Academic career. I don't think I would have succeeded without his help and advice. I am proud of his scholarly example and friendship.

I also want to thank John G. Weiger and Donna Kuizenga for reviewing and correcting parts of my manuscript.

Without the help and expertise of Patricia Mardeusz, from the Bailey/Howe Library Interlibrary Loan, who has been always there ready to look and find the most difficult books and articles, it would have been much more difficult to finish this work. I value and respect her friendship and professionalism.

It has been a pleasure to have John F. Deredita as my translator, a fine scholar with whom I had the chance to communicate clearly and whose profound knowledge of the Spanish language and culture made things much natural and precise.

I don't want to finish these lines without mentioning an extraordinary professional, Jacqueline Pavlovic, Peter Lang's Production Supervisor, whose professionalism, kindness and promptness made the formatting of this book a reality.

INTRODUCTION

Much has been said and written about the participation of men, horses, and even dogs in the encounter of the Americas. Very little has been written, however, on the participation of women, and their extremely important contribution to all the circumstances involved in the discovery, clash, and colonization of the newly found lands. This factor has come to be ignored by many historians who have chosen to see in the encounter of Spanish America an exclusively masculine accomplishment, without realizing that in most of the expeditions and first settlements, women played a prime role. These women did not simply follow after their husbands, but like them, they sought the adventure and the hope of a better world for themselves and their entire families. "We do not believe that the history of any country has produced in so short a time such a plethora of heroic females, almost none of whom left more than a dim name hidden in the dust of the chronicles" (O'Sullivan-Beare 201).

The participation of Spanish women in their society has since earliest times been singularly important, although often when their accomplishments and activities should have been set down in writing, many of their achievements were overlooked and ignored, and the consequences of their action credited to the highest ranking family members: fathers, husbands, or brothers.

It is the intent of this book to demonstrate, through the most significant texts and documents of the "conquest", how the contribution of women was present at all times, and in what way their role in the development of events was crucial. Things would have come out much differently without the presence of women.

It would, on the other hand, be a practically impossible task to cover all those events in which women distinguished themselves, whether it was in literature, social life, or even military action. Nevertheless, the intention of this study is to awaken more interest in all those females who for so many years have remained unjustly in the shadows of the incidents that occurred. In a period so rich in historic events as the "encounter" between cultures and peoples of different continents during the fifteenth, sixteenth, and seventeenth centuries, it is necessary to look at history from other perspectives. In order to better understand the overall picture of the events, it is essential to give women the importance they deserve. In parallel fashion, some political and religious factors will be presented which have kept Spain from giving an account of the "true history of the conquest," as shall be explained later.

This passage from the letter that Doña Isabel de Guevara, a survivor of one of the first expeditions to the River Plate, wrote to Doña Juana, the daughter of the Catholic Monarchs, is sufficiently explicit to give us an idea of what many expeditions involving the direct participation of women were like:

> The unfortunate women underwent so many hardships, that it was a miracle that God chose to let them live, seeing that the life of the men was in their hands; because they took all the work of the ship so much to heart, that she who did less than another woman felt ashamed, serving as they did to work the sail, and steer the ship, and take soundings from the bow, and take over the oar from the soldier who could not row...[2]

One could even doubt if the encounter of the Americas would have been possible without such a significant female presence. It is hardly necessary to mention the Spanish queen, Isabel of Castile, for her sponsorship of the whole overseas enterprise and for leaving the cultural and linguistic stamp of the Kingdom of Castile, which was later to become one of the most universal and lasting examples of Western civilization.

Women are an indispensable measure of the cultural and economic development of a society. Through their presence, their activities, marriages, inheritances or properties, they have decisively influenced the overall development of society. The presence of women in documents and litigation is constant in Iberian sources (Boxer 9).

It was not only Spanish women and those of other nationalities who came to the Americas—Flemish, Portuguese, Italians, etc.—who showed that they could rise to the occasion. Indian women did too, sometimes on the side of the Spaniards as interpreters and allies, and other times against them, defending their own interests. They would also display acts of heroism and dedication to the causes of their peoples. The best example of these women is personified by Doña Marina, Hernán Cortés's interpreter, without whom it would have been difficult to carry out the conquest of Mexico. She was a unique woman, loved and hated for her undeniable importance to the events that unfolded, and often misunderstood when she is identified as a "traitor" to the Mexican people, when in reality the non-Aztec Indians, followers of Cortés, had as much right to be called "Mexicans" as the Aztecs themselves.

Some historians have avoided the function of women during the events that occurred in the Mexican encounter up to the capture of Tenochtitlán. Cortés mentions Doña Marina in passing in his *Letters*, at no time giving her the importance she deserved. In his *True History*, Bernal Díaz gives a more detailed, human image of her personality. The truth is that Doña Marina's presence and influence in the incidents of the contest was comparable to its most notable events. To a significant degree, the Spaniards owed a good share of their success to the contributions of that woman (Greer Johnson 66).

Julie Greer Johnson writes with words full of praise for Bernal Díaz for his "clear style" and because he included so important a personage in the encounter with Mexico (66). Unfortunately, the importance they deserve has still not been given to other chroniclers of that encounter: Herrera, Gómara, Muñoz Camargo, Torquemada, Toribio de Benavente, Tapia, and others, who supply extremely valuable additional information, although at times from a point of view differing from that of the author of the *True History*.

The Spanish people have had to accept—swallowing anything—a large amount of historical information that has been deliberately manipulated to serve the purposes of other peoples who have built up their own history at the expense of ours. As if this weren't enough, the Spaniards' capacity for self-criticism has been pretty constant since earliest times, while among other peoples, these criticisms have been most often reserved for their neighbors, a fact which brings to mind the well-known verses:

> Listening to a man, easy it is
> to know where he first saw light of day:
> if he praises England, he's an Englishman,
> if he speaks ill of Prussia, a Frenchman,
> and if he speaks ill of Spain, a Spaniard. Bartrina, "Something"[3]

Even some English-language authors, aware of this typically Spanish behavior, have commented on it: "Internal criticism, however constructive, was rarely tolerated in Elizabethan or Stuart England, and it was hard for men to believe that absolute monarchs like Charles V and Phillip II encouraged it among their subjects" (Maltby 12).

Often out of our own ignorance, we Spaniards or Hispanic Americans have admitted the validity of other "distorted" opinions, for the simple reason that they have come from countries with greater political power which have managed to "export" their version of the facts with greater ease. This is the case today of the absence of Spanish women in the Western historical context, and of the omission of them from reference works. In spite of this, several Spanish intellectuals have called attention to the fact that many Spaniards accept foreign versions because they do not know their own. Unamuno, possibly the most important Spanish thinker of this century, called such people "a few fools who do not know their own history." With reference to the Spanish history yet to be written and the misrepresentation that has been made of it, Unamuno said the following:

> Even more so now, when there is so much talk of the awareness of our backwardness with respect to the other cultured peoples; now, when a few fools who do not know our own history—which is yet to be written, first rectifying what Protestant calumny has fabricated about it—say that we have had neither science, nor art, nor philosophy, nor Renaissance (perhaps we had too much of the latter), nor anything (225).

The brilliant North American poet, Walt Whitman, had already said in 1883, a century ago, that the United States still had to learn about its past. For not everything inherited by the United States was English (Weber 1). In fact, the first women who arrived over the Atlantic to what is today the United States did not come in the Mayflower.

In this study—a survey—it is worth stressing a most important historical and cultural perspective which in the future will help to interpret from other angles those most significant aspects of the first years of Spanish presence overseas.

PART ONE: SPANISH WOMEN WHO CAME TO THE AMERICAS

SPANISH MEN DID NOT GO ALONE

I am so far from considering it improper to confess one's own ignorance, when it really exists, that, rather, I deem pretending that one knows what one does not know to be baseness of spirit; and this baseness is what has filled not only books of philosophy but also of other disciplines with infinite useless pages. (Benito Feijóo, *Universal Critical Theatre*)

The erroneous idea that the Spanish conquistadores went to the Americas without women has been perpetuated up to our time. This historical focus remains prevalent at the highest academic level, in university and high-school texts, encyclopedias, and in the public opinion of many countries. When women are mentioned, it is only in the colonizing process of the North European peoples.

In their textbook *Scholastic World Cultures: Latin America*, James A. Hudson and David Goddy state: "Unlike many early settlers of North America, few Spaniards brought wives and daughters to the Americas. They had come to explore, conquer, and seek riches, not to settle down" (34). It would seem that the Spanish conquistador and colonizer was not afforded the privilege of coming to the Americas accompanied. Fortunately, this has only been the case in the theory of some written histories.

The following quotation from Clarence H. Haring with reference to Spanish colonization in America may be seen as an example of what has been put forth by some historians who have misrepresented our history to the taste of their peoples, implying that the new Spanish colonies did not attract new immigrants, especially women: "And as the number of women among the immigrants was small, interracial unions were frequent, and a large intermediate mestizo class soon made its appearance. Immigrants, moreover, were not attracted to a community of landlords" (Haring 32).

In his book *Fire and Blood*, T. R. Fehrenbach goes even further. First he states—pulling statistics out of nowhere—that since "few Spanish women survived the voyage to the Indies," the greater part of the conquistadores had to marry native women. Spanish women were not "weak," as this author would have us believe.

> Most conquistadores had wed native women. Few Spanish women
> survived the passage to the Indies...Cortés insisted that his
> *encomenderos* marry, and this meant that almost all of them had to
> marry native women. In 1646, a century after the Conquest, there
> were still nine males to every European female in New Spain, and the
> native *criollos* were at a serious disadvantage in competing against
> *peninsulares* even for these (Fehrenbach 34).

Inexplicably, he says only a few lines later, "By the last half of the
sixteenth century, interracial marriages were officially discouraged,
though never illegal, and they virtually ceased" (235). If there were
hardly any European women to marry, as Fahrenbach asserts at first,
how could interracial marriages come to an end?

Clarence H. Haring, along with John A. Crow—as will be seen
later—and Paul T. Welty, are typical examples of those who have seen
Hispanic encounter and colonization as a second-rate accomplishment,
when compared with the English. Welty says, "In 1493 Columbus
brought about 1,500 colonists with him. They hoped to find gold
quickly so that they could return to a life of luxury in Spain"(731). The
same author also states that Cortés "burned" his ships, a legend that has
continued unchanged up to our time:[4] "Cortés burned his ships. In this
way his men had to fight to survive" (Welty 732). Welty is not the only
one, however, who gives superficial historical explanations of the
encounter of Mexico with little documentary support. In the textbook
History of a Free Nation, published in 1992, the following is said of
Cortés's encounter of Mexico: "Although Cortés's army numbered only
600, the Spaniards had luck—and sophisticated weapons—on their side"
(Bragdon et al., 42). One wonders what is understood here by "luck"
and "sophisticated weapons." On the following page, the authors say,
stressing nationality, "Most Spanish conquests in the New World were
marked by a terrible slaughter of the local people" (44). Referring to
Spanish colonization in general, these same authors say, "Generally they
[the Spaniards] were not interested in creating permanent settlements in
the Americas. Instead they flocked to the islands in search of precious
metals" (42). Within this group of textbooks, the most recent—in this
case a book teaching Hispanic language and culture to U.S. university

students—says of the Spanish conquistadores: "The Spanish conquistadores, on the other hand, arrived in the New World alone, and mixed with native women, who belonged to developed cultures that were sometimes much more advanced than European culture itself" (García Serrano 37).

Those who transmit this information in university and secondary-school texts are responsible for misrepresenting the history that young students learn, since on the one hand they exclude Spanish women and those of other nationalities from the history of America, and the other hand, they create false stereotypes of other cultures.

The only reason for excluding women from the overall picture of the encounter is directly related to the "Black Legend." The desire to present the Spaniards as a handful of men whose ultimate goal was to steal all the Indians' wealth from them, especially their gold, only to leave once the conquered cultures were destroyed, did not leave any room for the figure of women. They are mentioned very much in passing, and when they are mentioned, they appear only as "lost souls" who had no other way of surviving than to sell their "lascivious" bodies to the ardent soldiers of the conquest. The worst kind of lie is the one that carries with it a bit of truth. Therefore, in the propaganda used against Spain as regards its overseas effort, the tendency has been to omit discussion of so important a presence, and when it has been discussed, it has always been with a defamatory tone.

Professor Haring's opinion on Spanish colonization, for example, could be called the usual one. He does not go so far as to be a traditional detractor of Spain's work in America, but his prejudices against it and in favor of English colonization are clear, as can be seen in the following passage: "It remains true, however, that no other European nation could rival England in the quantity of its colonists of pure European stock, and in the 'domestic quality' of the emigrants" (34). Without digressing to discuss in detail such ambiguous terms as "pure European stock" and "domestic quality," we can say that Haring's historical orientation, from the Anglo-Saxon point of view, is clear.[5]

The reason that Haring gives is simply that of not wishing to give to the Spaniard the status of "permanent colonizer," but rather that of a "person in transit," who came only to conquer the Indians, abuse Indian women, carry off his gold and leave. This information is not limited to high-school textbooks and books at the highest academic level; it also appears in reference books as popular as this "Webster" dictionary: "Spain became overgreedy in European politics...New Spain spread its ambitious, grasping tentacles over most of Latin and South america; the names of Cortés and Pizarro head the list of zealots who brought a violent end to the Aztec and Inca kingdoms. But Spanish claims feathered far and indefinitely into North America" (Branch 356).

But things did not go exactly that way. Before the first Englishmen arrived in Jamestown in 1607, Spain already had several universities in the Americas, some of them as important as those in Mexico City and Lima, and the language and the basic principles of education were taught in schools in the north and the south of Spanish America. One year after the conquest of Mexico, in 1522, a school was established which was attended by more than a thousand Indians, where they were also taught artisan trades. In the same way, there were already schools exclusively for girls with women teachers who did not belong to religious orders. In 1535, a school for Indian girls was established, and also the first institution of higher education (Truslow 14). The first printing press was established in Mexico in 1539.

Did this type of schools for Indian girls form part of the English or French colonization of the Americas? The differences between these colonizations and the Spanish are notable. Agriculture and cattle-raising were not so deeply rooted in the French colonization as in the Spanish; for this reason, while the Spaniards maintained a population of five million inhabitants, New France did not exceed a few thousand, who in fact depended on food imports. Commerce and hunting were not enough to consolidate a permanent French colony (Truslow 23-24).

There is no doubt that there were substantial differences, not only because of the expanse of the territories claimed, but because of the way of carrying out the process of transformation of lands and people of the nations that were dominated. The stability in the social development of the Hispanic lands would not make any sense without the presence of women. This is the reason why the French were few and poor in proportion with the territories they were claiming. Although the Frenchmen did have relations with Indian women, the cultural exchange between both parties was minimal, if it is compared with the birth of a whole series of mestizo nations in the Spanish colonies which would end up having an unmistakable Hispanic stamp. The basic industry of the fur trade, which was the one that the French exploited, required great mobility and different settlements. This industries could in no way be compared with the mining, agricultural, or cattle industry, which required a much denser population, and was sedentary and stable, if one considers that it is still today the economic base of many of the peoples colonized by Spain (Truslow 24).

The idea of "race" in sixteenth-century Spain at no time implied a brake on legal marriages between Spaniards and Indians.[6] If there were obstacles between Spaniards and Indians, they were largely of a socio-economic and religious, not a racial character. This distinction existed, and still exists, among the Spaniards themselves. Perhaps the most reliable proof of this is the mestizo character of the Hispanic American cultures, with a very respectable percentage of Indians. On the other hand, if we look at what happened with the former colonies of England and Holland, we will see either a total, systematic extermination of the natives or a segregation and total exploitation of them. The cases of miscegenation between Northern Europeans and Indians were negligible. The Indian reservations in the Southwest of the United States, the treatment of natives in India, Australia, as well as countries like South Africa and colonies like Hong Kong are an example and living testimony of what has been stated. In any case, the Anglo-Saxon culture, like the Hispanic, became and is universal. The English devised a market system among all their peoples, called the Commonwealth. The Hispanics, over the last centuries have had to content themselves in some cases with a "Commonpoverty," and with hair-raising debts. It is interesting to observe the direct relation between the religion and the economy of these two respective groups: the feverish productivity of the Protestant countries as opposed to the modest economic potential of the Catholic countries. Also worth studying is the "quality of life" of both positions: "The modern man is in general even with the best will, unable to give religious ideas a significance for culture and national character which they deserve"(Weber 183). Comparisons are almost always odious, especial where "religion" is involved.

THE ENGLISH HISTORICAL VERSION

English colonization in America, in contrast to the Spanish, shows a whole series of factors which one has to dwell on in order to understand their consequences. Without a retrospective view, it would be difficult to understand the causes and effects of the interpretations that these two people have had of themselves. Today it is easier to imagine the reasons why the two most powerful Christian peoples of a past era made an attempt to mutually cancel each other out and discredit each other. It was the English people who came out ahead in this contest and imposed their economic, political, and cultural rules. In spite of the fact that the linguistic, social, and cultural contributions brought by Spanish women—a mainstay on which the structure of Hispanic America rests—the choice was to silence all of that which in any way gave credit to Spain and posed a threat to the traditional English historical version, which went over to the other side of the North Atlantic almost intact. On the other hand, the Spanish people, out of good faith, negligence, or the simple complex of having become a second-class power, has let its history be manipulated and misrepresented, often giving more credit to what comes from abroad than to what its own historians have said. There is still much to do, and many documents to research, above all in the topic that occupies our attention, which is that of the participation of women in the encounter of America.

Anti-Spanish feeling appeared in England beginning with the first religious and political differences due to common interests such as the control of the seas, which also implied control of the enormous amount of gold, silver, and consumer goods that came from the other side of the ocean.

This propaganda aimed against Spain would not have the importance that it does today if it were limited to a thing of the past, to a historical period of economic-religous confrontations. Unfortunately, this is not the case. The average student in the English-speaking world not only lacks any knowledge of the existence of Spanish women at that time of history, but is used to hearing statements like the following with regard to the colonization of the Americas:

But there was America. And for Spaniards, too, America was "the land of opportunity." By the end of Phillip II's reign it became "the refuge and haven of all the poor devils of Spain, the sanctuary of the bankrupt, the safe-conduct of murderers, the escape of all gamblers, *the promised land for women of free virtue*, and the lure and disillusionment of the many and the incomparable remedy of the few" (Crow 218).

John Crow quotes these words of Cervantes, which describe the perception of one of his characters who went over to the Americas, after having lost all his belongings in his own land. Twenty years later, this character was to return with a great fortune. "The poverty of some, the greed of others, and the madness of all cause a great exodus from the stricken peninsula to this land of free life" (218).

The most interesting thing about the passage from Crow is not the fact that it makes no positive mention of the work of Spain in the Americas, since Crow apparently does not have a very high opinion of those Spaniards who decided to cross the Atlantic, nor that it omits mention of the meticulous bureaucracy that existed—the Casa de Contratación, the Council of the Indies—expressly so that the Americas would not become what he calls the "refuge and haven of all the poor devils of Spain," but rather the unexpected reference to Cervantes. In support of his arguments, Crow makes use of no less than the most universal of all Spaniards and one who also, as is well known, wished to go to the Americas. Putting words in Cervantes's pen is a risky business, especially in a case like this, when no overall mention is made of the context, not even the work nor the Cervantes character to which the quotation refers: "These are the words in which Cervantes describes the feeling of one of his characters who went to the New World." In fact, in his work *The Jealous Extremaduran*, Cervantes alludes to a character, "Felipo de Carrizales," who after much wandering through different parts of Europe decides to go to the New World. The character in question was "born of noble parents," and does go, as many others did, seeking his fortune. The problem arises with Crow's generalization, which gives one to understand through the Cervantes passage that "all" Spaniards who went to the Americas were "poor devils." The author of

Don Quixote, however, was referring—in the speech of one of his characters—only to the "poor devils" of Seville. Cervantes does allude to the solution for the "lost souls that congregate in that city," referring to the "unfortunates" who go to Seville, and not, as Crow says, to all Spaniards. Not all the cities of Spain had the extraordinary characteristics of Seville in the sixteenth century, nor were all Spaniards "undesirable."

The truth is that the idea that the first Spaniards who arrived on the American continent were, as Crow says, "poor devils," criminals and all kinds of undesirables, is still current today. This shows ignorance, on the other hand, of the fact that almost all expeditions to the Americas had an element of private initiative, and that for this reason they were personally led by members of the most powerful and representative families of the period, who brought along with them others who were less affluent. All of them—rich and poor—risked everything they owned. There is a tendency to believe that the state was responsible for these expeditions, when at most it received a fifth of the goods conquered. These discoveries were made without prior permission from the king, who did not have to contribute any money. Once the contest were completed, they were recognized by the Crown on the basis of capitulations in which the conquistador pledged himself to observe a series of requirements and pay a portion of the profits obtained (Icaza xii).

In the same way it has been said that women did not form part of the expeditions, but this is belied by the interminable list of viceroys, governors and captains who, accompanied by their wives, were present from early on. The legislation in this regard is copious; an example is the law quoted below where no matter what the condition of the traveler to the Indies, he was required to take along his wife:

> We declare as persons prohibited from embarking for and going over
> to the Indies all married men and engaged men in these Kingdoms if
> they do not take their wives with them, even if they are Viceroys,
> Judges, Governors, or would go to serve us in any post and offices of
> War, Justice, and the Treasury, because it is our will that all the above
> mentioned take their wives; and they are likewise required to carry our

permission for themselves, their wives, and their servants (Ots 14: 367-68).

According to a Royal Order of October 13, 1554, there were exceptions; the maximum time that a married man could be in America without bringing his wife was two years, on the posting of bond (a quarter of his goods not to exceed a thousand ducats), and under pain of imprisonment if he did not hold to his promise (Ots 14: 368). Of course many women (and men) would not take pleasure in crossing the Atlantic in such precarious craft, and this was taken into account by the law in case the wife decided not to follow her husband "out of fear of the sea:" "The wife who is invited by her husband to go to the Indies should follow him; but this is a precept, not an imposition, and therfore if she claims fear of the sea, she should be respected" (Ots 14: 369). Fearful or not, there were many women who went over. With respect to these, Analola Borges says, "The emigrant women came from all social strata, although in the first expeditions it seems that the 'upper-class' sector prevailed...The repeated cases of submission and sacrifice, and also scandalous cases, appear equally throughout all strata" (Borges 394-95).

James Truslow Adams, aware that it was really the other way around and that it was not the Spanish colonist but the English who came from the less favored classes, says with respect to the first English colonists that they came not from palaces but from jails, little country houses and parishes: "The aristocracy remained in England, and with scarcely an exception, the thousands who came were from the middle and lower classes, fleeing from persecution or hard social and economic conditions" (Truslow 26).

Nevertheless it cannot be said that all Anglo-American writers attack Spain and its work in America. There are many differences of opinion, even within the Anglo-Saxon world. Every day more scholars speak Spanish and have access to primary sources of information such as the official and private archives of the Hispanic world. Some historians have even been aware of the lack of historical seriousness involved in deleting so important a female presence from history. With reference to the continuous presence of Spanish women during the first years of occupation in Peru, James Lockhart says, "In view of the old tradition among historians of ignoring them [women], the cultural and biological contribution of Spanish women to the building of a European society in Peru requires emphasis."

A. Curtiss Wilgus, in his book *Colonial Spanish America*, stresses the importance of the religious factor, as important or more important in some cases than the economic factor in the Spanish colonization. The apostolic work carried out by Spain in America was, according to Wilgus, the best of those accomplished by any nation. The reasons he presents are based, according to him, on the religiosity of the Spanish people throughout their social order from the king on down, on the seven centuries of struggle against the Moors, on the rejection of heresy, and on a jointly shared aspiration in religious beliefs.

In other studies written from the Anglo-American perspective, an objective view can be seen, since without leaving out negative aspects of both nations, in this case England and Spain, at least important fine distinctions are drawn: "If either nation could claim a moral advantage in its atrocious treatment of suspected enemies, it was Spain, where torture was at least regulated and could be administered only under official surveillance" (Maltby 41-42).

There are also some apologies for the Spanish encounter of the Americas, undertaken from the Anglo-American point of view. The most important of this group is the work of Charles F. Lummis, a U. S. historian who managed to see the Spanish encounter in a dimension that was different from the usual romantic identification with the vanquished. Recognizing that young North Americans have been simply "ill-informed" about the deeds of the Spaniards in the Americas, Lummis says, "The honor of giving America to the world belongs to Spain—the credit not only of discovery, but of centuries of such pioneering as no other nation ever paralleled in any land. It is a fascinating story, yet one to which our histories have so far done scant justice" (Lummis 17).

The root of the hatred against Spain must be understood, therefore, as the fear of an extremely powerful nation which also directly or indirectly obeyed orders from Rome. Logically, the Protestant world could hardly look favorably on the fact that a Catholic country with the most impeccable military record of the period, was threatening the rest of the European countries with religious and military conquest. The fact that Philip II attempted to conquer England through arms, which earned him the hostility of the Anglo-Saxon Protestants, did not mean that the Spanish monarch was "the cold-blooded devil of the South" but the most powerful monarch of his time, who in addition devoted himself, body and soul, to all the administrative affairs of Spain and all its overseas territories (Winks 344).

In the conclusion of his book *The Black Legend in England*, William S. Maltby says, specifically pointing to the religious aspect, that the main cause of the antagonism of the Hispanic and Anglo-Saxon peoples must be sought in two different interpretations of the Christian religion. These differences, together with geopolitical interests, made it so that our peoples lived, and still live, in mutual lack of confidence. The solution to this conflict, at first glance, would be greater flexibility in theological matters and greater tolerance when it comes time to interpret the interests of these respective peoples: "Many if not all of the writers who contributed to the Black Legend were staunch, even fanatical Protestants...Had there been no such deep religious antagonism, English, and indeed European attitudes toward Spain would certainly have been quite different" (Maltby 133-34).

PERCENTAGE OF FEMALE EMIGRATION IN THE FIRST YEARS

According to the geobiographic studies of José Luis Martínez, the percentage of female emigration that reached the Americas from Spain came to as much as 28.5% in the period 1560-79. "Of the 5,013 women recorded as having gone to America in this twenty-year period, 1,980 (close to 40%) were married or widows, and 3,024 (60%) single" (Martínez 168). The figure of 60%, representing single emigrant Spanish women, some of them accompanied by children—and this number is as a whole higher than that of married women—is not at all negligible. With respect to this fact, Richard Konetzke comments, "This can be explained by recalling that at that time there was an excess of women and for many of them it was impossible to get married" (*Emigración* 146). These figures contradict and give the lie to the idea that Spanish men had access only to native women on the recently discovered continent.

Among married women, there were many adventurous ones who did not hesitate to follow their husbands even to distant corners of the empire. All areas of Spain were represented by these women: "Those who went included the Aldonzas [of *Don Quixote*], the Celestinas, women from [the Archpriest of Talavera's fifteenth century] *Corbacho*, and Santillana's women; also the Melibeas [from *La Celestina*], the Dulcineas [from *Don Quixote*], the mystics, haughty, rowdy, or easy women, and the Beatrices" (Borges 411). All these women who played such an important role in the cultural and economic evolution of the Americas society have hardly received attention from modern historians, "not even as an economic element." Pointing out this ominous void with justifiable indignation, Borges states that any other object of mining or agriculture has been the subject of more attention on the part of Spanish American historiography than the human factor represented by women: "In the face of the glorification of the work of conquest, the silence over women settlers is offensive" (Borges 411). In the decade 1509-19, that is to say, nearly at the beginning of the encounter, Boyd-Bowman counts 308 women who came from large cities with Santo Domingo as their destination. The women rarely traveled alone: "Most of the women traveled in groups, usually accompanied by husbands, fathers, sons, or relatives. A few young single women, almost always from Seville, traveled as 'servants,' a term which may have disguised a different job" (Boyd-Bowman xviii).

Right around this specific period, from 1509 to 1519, we find a "curious fact" about one embarkation in particular on which a good number of women passengers sailed. Basing herself on the lists appearing in the *Catálogo de Pasajeros a Indias*, Ana María Ortega Martínez counts 306 women, two less than Boyd-Bowman.

> Most of them went over with their husbands, sons, and daughters. Some came completely alone. As a curious fact, we note the information listed on sheet 1910, referring to Juan Guillén, a resident of Seville; his wife María de Malaver; Isabel de Malaver, Martina Núñez Girón, Beatriz Girón, María Malaver, Catalina Guillén Girón, Lucía Girón, Eufrasia Malaver, and Juana Guillén her daughters; Leonor Rodríguez Toledano; Juana Sánchez, daughter of Pedro Sánchez...went over to the Indies on October 16, 1514 (Ortega 23).

The "different job" that Boyd-Bowman mentions is nothing other than prostitution. Continuous control of that activity by the authorities was enabled by their acceptance of it. The oldest profession was nothing new in Europe, and its importance had been recognized since the time of the Crusades. There is evidence that the Templars reckoned that the services of thirteen thousand prostitutes would be required for a year's absence. This figure gives an idea of the number of these women who participated in some expeditions (Ratcliffe 346-50). In the royal decree quoted below, issued in Granada in 1526, the first house of prostitution in Puerto Rico was authorized. "In the interest of the honesty of the city and its married women, and to avoid other harm and difficulties, there is a need to set up a house of public women there" (O'Sullivan-Beare 53). In another royal decree issued the same year, permission was granted to Juan Sánchez Sarmiento to establish a house of prostitution in Santo Domingo (Ots 14: 385). It is interesting from the sociological point of view to observe how in the sixteenth century in Spain, the fact of setting up a brothel was foreseen with some indifference out of the need to protect the "honor" of husbands, rather than the need to protect the honesty of the women who would have to work in these brothels.

The Catholic church, always accommodating to circumstances, managed, under the supervision of the bishops of Osma, the Canary Islands, and Ciudad Rodrigo, to back up this decision (O'Sullivan-Beare 53). The "honor" of the wife and daughters of functionaries was not very secure with so many soldiers on the loose.

> And the kings began then to issue extremely severe orders to prevent any functionary from going over to these lands without acquiring a legitimate wife in Spain, with the exception, of course, of the clergy...And while large doors were put on the houses, the husbands, fathers, and fiancés were beside themselves (Arciniegas 42-43).

In her study of women in Seville during the sixteenth and seventeenth centuries, Mary Elizabeth Perry points out the social importance of prostitutes and the tolerance shown toward them for centuries as "a minor evil," since, without their presence the feeling was that many men would devote their energy to seducing honorable women, to incest, to homosexuality, or to adultery (Perry 137). In spite of everything, the function of the Spanish prostitute in the Americas went beyond that of a simple remunerated physical coupling, since Spanish men had in any case easy access to Indian women. Often the prostitute represented a physical and spiritual union with the far-off homeland. This was the case of María de Ledesma in Potosí, who in addition to knowing how to sing, played the vihuela and guitar (Lockhart 161-62). Referring to prostitutes in Lima and Potosí, Lockhart states, "Spanish men found Indian women attractive, and any Spaniard could have as many as he wanted. Spanish prostitutes catered more to the need of Spaniards to be near a woman who shared their language and culture" (Lockhart 161-62).

The social function of the prostitute is not limited to a single society, or to one era in particular in the Old World; similar cases were found in pre-Columbian America. Fray Juan de Torquemada mentions in passing the existence of houses of prostitution in Mexico City before the arrival of the Spaniards:

> Cortés returned to where Motecuhzuma was, and the latter with a happy expression (disguising the distress that he had in his heart) received him. He ordered then the disbanding of a brothel of public

women, each of whom earned in Tlatelulco a small amount; there must have been more than four hundred of them, saying that because of the public sins of those women, the gods had allowed those Christians to go to his city and kingdom (Torquemada 464).

Despite everything, the idea of an "Arcadian" America full of noble, good beings, although it is completely absurd and naive, has been kept alive up to now. The only valid "Arcadia" was the one enjoyed by some Indian monarchs who not only exercised despotic control over their citizens, but in addition could take advantage of as many women as they wished. This "official" polygamy was equal to that in any other part of the world. Juan de Torquemada tells about the Mexican kings' custom of having many wives and of legitimizing the heir of the noblest woman, the ones of the Mexican caste being the most prized. The chronicler narrates that shortly after the wedding of the king Nezahualpilli with a noble Mexican woman, she had as a lady-in-waiting a sister of hers, Xocotzincatzin, who was so beautiful that the king had to ask for her in marriage too (Torquemada 184).

The first colonizers had from the beginning the support of the authorities to marry Indian women, as happened in fact. Spanish women were also encouraged to marry Indian men under the protection of the law. In an order of March 29, 1503 quoted by Ots Capdequí, we read:

Likewise: we order Our Governor and the persons named by him to take charge of said towns and also the Chaplains to seek to have said Indians marry their wives in the eyes of the Holy Mother Church; and that they also seek to have some Christian men marry Indian women, and Christian women Indian men (Ots, 14: 361).

If in the first period of colonization (1509-1519) a "good" number of women went over, in the second period from 1520-39 one can see not only an increase in the number of women who went to the Americas—more than half of them Andalusians—but also more variety in their place of origin. Sixteen foreign women showed up: 8 Portuguese, 5 Flemish, 2 Greek, and one Italian (Martínez 161).

In this second period, among 13,262 emigrants, 845, or 6.3% were women, most of them bound for Mexico and Santo Domingo. Two hundred fifty two married women traveled with their husbands and 85 went to join them. Four hundred fifty-seven were single women and girls, plus 51 widows and women of uncertain marital status (Martínez 161).

It was from that time on when that female presence begins to be noticed in a regular manner. Many of the girls and single women would be the seed of the burgeoning new society. Recognizing that the encounter of America was not only a military achievement accomplished by mercenary troops (as the campaigns in Italy and the Low Countries had been), nor just a manifestation of Spanish military power aimed at incorporating the new territories, Richard Konetzke notes the following:

> These facts are of capital importance for the understanding of the development of the American population, since not only fighting men lacking women arrived there, but from the beginning and in ever greater numbers, colonists with their wives and children went to establish themselves in the country, and married men whose families would later follow them to the new homeland (Konetzke *emigración* 124).

The same writer stresses the effort made from the beginning by the Spanish government so that men would not go over "alone." The Spanish government did not put up barriers for women to go over to the Americas, except in some special cases. On the contrary, it encouraged their presence as much as possible—an attitude that should be taken into account when the events of these first years are analyzed. "In fact coercion was almost used so that women would go to America" (Konetzke, *emigración* 124).

The traditional, romantic way of viewing history—which seeks to exclude Spanish women from the female world of the encounter-often does not correspond with the reality of the events.

> Upon experiencing the launch, the ladies would exclaim, "Is this going to be swallowed up by the sea? What a pity!" Nevertheless, they also

set sail, as has been said, but doing so the way many set foot on a caravel or ship, taking those serious, important precautions which are recommended to those who are down with double pneumonia: a good general confession and a will providing for a mass for the souls in purgatory; also, with a spirit that justified the proverb: "Would you learn how to pray? Sail away!" (Fernández duro 20-21).

Thanks to the information present in the various archives and other institutions of a period that was much more bureaucratic than we would like to imagine, all of these feats carried out by an endless number of women can be verified. Some of these accomplishments are noteworthy because of the responsibility and independence enjoyed by some women. Several Sevillian women invested their capital in businesses and even created their own companies, although the usual procedure was for them to have a male partner who represented them in their business in America (Perry 15). All this helps to confirm not only the fact that Spanish men did not come alone, but that the female presence was there, directly or indirectly in all areas of social life.

Although it is true that it was the husband who occupied center (at least in theory) in sixteenth-century Spanish society, the social function of women was not exclusively limited to secondary roles. In many cases they were on the front lines at the time when decisions had to be made, even when those decisions involved the economic life of the family. Notarized sixteenth-century documents show that women bought and sold and rented properties, arranged for the marriage of their children, and cared for the children in the absence of their husband. One example is that of Mariana de los Ríos, who in the absence of her husband Damián de los Ríos, a doctor who had gone to the Indies, signed and notarized on May 20, 1550, an authorization permitting a local merchant to represent her at the Casa de Contratación and to receive in her name everything that her husband would send her from the Americas (Perry 14).

In the financial activities of Spanish women in Peru, different facets can be observed where the active participation of women in the nascent colonial economy shows up clearly. Some women possessed significant amounts of property, both for their own use and for rent; rarely, however, were they owners of farm and grazing lands. A good propoortion of the domestic black slaves belonged to these women, and often those who were solvent participated as "silent" partners in merchandise investments and loans (Lockhart 159-60). The Franco-Argentine historian Paul Groussac left a record in his book *Mendoza y Garay* of women who had, in addition to historical importance, a direct influence on the first settlements of the future Argentina. Appearing in his work are the given name and surnames of a woman who contributed, like so many other women, not from a passive role, but from a position of power. In the same way that in his time the conquistador Francisco Vázquez de Coronado, explorer of the Southwest of what is now the United States, received a large, indispensable amount of money from his wife Beatriz Estrada to cover the cost of his ambitious expedition in search of the Seven Cities of Cibola, María de Zárate would from Spain help her relative Lucas de Zárate send a small fleet to the River Plate in 1571: "Among the relatives of both was the above-mentioned lady, Doña María de Zárate, the daughter and rich heir of the ex-accountant of the Casa de Contratación, who had in income from the Seville customs duties a principal of more than two million maravedís" (Groussac 180). Either because she wished to "do service and a good work" for her relative, as the document says, or because she saw profit in the investment, María de Zárate contributed part of that principal, "Lending to the adelantado a million and a half maravedís (exactly 1,582,496 maravedís or nearly 4,220 ducats), with the pledge of Lucas de Zárate and a mortgage on certain properties in the River Plate area" (Groussac 180).

In the same book, Groussac mentions Juana de Zárate, a somewhat legendary woman, the daughter of a Spaniard and a Peruvian princess who inherited large amounts of money on the death of her father, the adelantado Juan Ortiz de Zárate, who died on the same day he dictated his will, January 26, 1576. Doña Juana, "the mestiza daughter of the adelantado Zárate" ended up marrying Juan de Torres y Vera, by whom she had a son, Juan Alonso de Vera y Zárate.

> Save for a certain peculiarity deriving from her situation as an exceptionally rich and spoiled orphan, Doña Juana would

resemble—because of similarities in their education, tastes and habits—her women peers in the "tiny social group" in the River Plate or Potosí, which on the other hand differed little from its like in Lima and even Seville or Madrid (Groussac 228-29).

These women pioneers, whether in the social or financial area, from the first years in the Indies, can be compared with no disadvantage to those women who would arrive years later from the English-speaking world. Melveena McKendric specifically compares the pioneering enthusiasm of the English women who colonized North America with that of the Spanish women who crossed the Atlantic with their husbands and fathers, or the single women who went under the guardianship of an illustrious woman with the intention of starting a family. Their work varied from physical labor to exclusively political and administrative tasks (McKendrick 42-43).

Doña María de Toledo governed the West Indies as vicereine. Doña Juana de Zárate was name Adelantado of Chile by Charles V. Doña Isabel Manrique and Doña Aldonza Villalobos were governors of the Venezuelan island of Margarita...Doña Catalina Montejo succeeded her father as Adelantado of Yucatán. The wife of Hernando de Soto governed Cuba during her husband's absence (McKendrick 42-42).

Passing mention has been made of Doña María de Toledo, a great woman who helped her husband Diego Colón to obtain the privileges and property that he should have inherited upon the death of his father Christopher Columbus (Cristóbal Colón). In order to obtain those privileges, Diego had to file a lawsuit, which he won, thanks to the influence of his wife's family (Acosta 141). Although she belonged to one of the most noble families of Spain, María de Toledo did not hesitate to go over to the Americas with her husband, who had been named governor and viceroy of the island of Hispaniola (Acosta 142). During Diego Colón's absence from Hispaniola from 1515 to 1520, the now vicereine, María de Toledo, took on the duties of governing the island: "They set sail in June, 1509, taking with them a veritable court: the new Vicereine was accompanied by many ladies from noble families and other families that were not noble but were distinguished for their virtues" (Acosta 142).

Doña María was the mother of five children, and she showed herself to be not only an intelligent woman, given the influence she had in Santo Domingo, but also valiant: "Aunque me da pasión el destierro de mi casa y las fatigas de mi pleito, siéntome por otra parte consolada con el favor y merced que V.M. siempre recibo..." ["Even though the banishment from home and the hardships of my litigation disheartens, I feel consoled by the favor and mercy that I always receive from Your Majesty..."].[7]

Upon learning of the death of her husband Diego in Spain, she herself asked permission to put herself at the head of a fleet and to go colonize the mainland, a permission never granted to her (Acosta 143).

Information also exists about Aldonza de Villalobos, the first colonizer of Margarita Island, Venezuela. When the Spaniards tried to set up a colonial establishment on the island of Cubagua, they took women there, whose names are not given by the chroniclers. We do however know the name of the first colonizer of Margarita: she was Doña Aldonza de Villalobos, whose father, Don Marcelo Villalobos had asked permission to build a fort on the island. Upon his death, it fell to his daughter to carry out her father's project, in 1526 (Acosta 153).

There are several records and names of "the first women" who settled territories such as Panama or Peru, as in the case of Inés Escobar, who in 1512 was the only white woman in the city of Santa María la Antigua in Panama: "She was married to a certain Caicedo, and she had a kind of inn, so that the honor of primacy was hers. The couple possessed extensive lands and slaves" (Borges 418).

In the case of Peru, it has been established that the first married woman was Inés Muñoz, Francisco Pizarro's sister-in-law, and also that the first single woman was Juana Hernández, an expeditionary who acccompanied Hernando de Soto's troops from Nicaragua (Borges 418). There is also evidence of an attempt at falsification, with the intent of passing for "the first woman." "In 1537, the City of Kings of Lima initiated its population with three hundred eighty Spaniards and only fourteen women, but in 1560, a certain Isabel Rodríguez, with evident deceit, added to her signature, 'first conquistadora of these kingdoms of Peru'" (Borges 418).

It is said of Inés Muñoz that she was the first to import and grow wheat in Peru; others say that it was María Escobar in the same year and also in Lima. Gonzalo Pittaluga says in this respect that there is a possibility that both women had the same concern at the same time: "Or they did the same thing by chance and went about sowing the scarce seed—seemingly in flower pots on the terraces of their houses—to see if it would manage to grow shoots" (77-78). In reality, the importance of these events does not lie in finding out who was the "first woman" who planted this or that. Of course for many, this information represents documentary evidence of the first order, but these accomplishments should be seen on a metaphoric level as the "sowing" of a new seed in a different soil. Without this planting undertaken by some of these women, the "growth" of a new society would have been very different or simply would not have been possible in permanent fashion.

As for the social conditions of these women, Lockhart states that it was as varied as that of the men, going from sisters of fishermen to daughters of counts (Lockhart 157). The most influential women in Peru were the wives of the encomenderos, who in many cases had as much influence as their husbands (Lockhart 157). Many were the women who improved their living conditions by going over to the Americas; not everything was hardships and suffering. Many women who in Spain would not have imagined "a better world" were able to make their dreams come true in the newly discovered lands. Some of these "nouveau riche" women enjoyed comforts and authority that they had never had in Spain: "The marriage was held with great pomp and ostentation, as if they were in the most opulent court in Spain" (Pinto 397).

The stereotyped image of passive and submissive Spanish women which is held in the Anglo-Saxon world, has not left much room for those thousands of adventurous women, who alone or with their husbands, decided to try their fortune with valor and genrosity of spirit, even with the knowledge that death could be present at every step: "And so there came unpretentious, honorable girls, those of high lineage, and some predestined to be the wives of conquistadores" (Pinto 397).

In fact it was women who many times had the initiative to go in search of adventures, without waiting for a handsome gentleman to come looking for them. As Analola Borges says, there is a "reversal of values" in the concept of love: "Now it is not the lady who waits in the castle for the knight-errant to return, but the maid is the one who, risking her life, goes out to find the unknown hero" (395-96). The recently-arrived woman would share the same dangers with men, from the severity of the climate of the most remote regions, to the pain and horror of wars and illnesses: "But also they alone had the pain of bearing children, feeling in their own flesh the wrenching sense of the premature and violent deaths of those same children to whom they had given birth in sometimes Dantesque circumstances" (Borges 395-96).

Perhaps the most gripping aspect of all this is not the interminable list of hardships that these women had to go through, but the fact that even with the knowledge of what could await them, they kept on going over to the other side of the Atlantic in ever greater proportions, although not great enough to satisfy the needs of the populations founded in the first years: "Despite the suffering, the exodus did not come to a halt, but rather increased as the years went by. The lands to be populated and the towns or cities already founded were very far from having the inhabitants needed for urban development, and the requests calling for women settlers kept coming" (Borges 396).

There is a need to look at the history of the first years of encounter with a different perspective. To leave in oblivion, or to skim over such a significant number of women, significant for their quality as well as their quantity, can only lead us to have a distorted view of reality. In his article on women in the conquest of America, Jaime Delgado summarizes in a few lines the difficult and often risky role played by the Spanish women who participated in the encounter of America, whether it be as nurses, soldiers, or cooks: "Many times, thanks to them, the incursions turned out to be victorious and the peoples and cities were maintained in order and good governance, as in the cases of Doña Isabel Manrique and Doña Aldonza de Villalobos, who ruled the island of Margarita, or that of Doña Beatriz de la Cueva, who governed Guatemala until she died" (Delgado 105).

In his work on the emigration of women to America, Richard Konetzke confirms their unequivocal presence, asserting that they must have come over in a high proportion, since twenty years after the

Spaniards had arrived on the American continent, no scarcity of women was noted. Also, Konetzke writes, in the middle of the sixteenth century there was a surfeit of women in Mexico City, and it was difficult for many of them to marry (147-48).

> In 1542, the solicitors of Mexico City received an order to petition the emperor to found two convents, since in Mexico City and in all of New Spain there were a great number of girls, legitimate daughters and illegitimate daughters of distinguished, honorable Spaniards who were not able to marry (Konetzke 147-48).

The difficulty in marrying off the young women even came to involve the viceroy himself, who had to intervene in the matter. "In addition, Viceroy Antonio de Mendoza informed his successor that there were in New Spain many young women, the daughters of good families, and he recommended that, by taking a real interest, he do something about marrying them" (Konetzke *emigración* 148). This surfeit of women was not confined to New Spain; a very similar situation existed in Peru. Although it is true that in the first thirty years of the encounter there was a certain lack of women, because of the emigration and the large number of female births, this situation was reversed (Konetzke *emigración* 148).

In 1553, the solicitor Fernández informed the Council of the Indies that in Peru there was an excess of women who had been born in the country or were immigrants (Konetzke, *emigración* 148). Similarly, solicitor Castro wrote in 1565, stating that in Peru the number of women was so great that, in consequence, there was a demand for them to bring high dowries to marriages, for which reason the girls were unable to marry (*Gobernantes* 3: 36). In the early times of the encounter of Peru it did not seem advisable to allow the foundation of convents, so as to encourage the development of the population. But "Later so many women have been born here, and every hour more are born, that they could be taken out to settle another kingdom" (Konetzke, *emigración* 148).

For its part, the language transmitted by these first women settlers would be a most important element when the cultural identity of the new Hispanic American nations was to be fixed.

IDENTIFICATION WITH THE CONQUERED

The absence of the female element in the overall picture of the encounter obeys the generalized notion of brutality and pillage with which the Spanish settler has been depicted. Nevertheless, as we shall see in the course of this study, Spanish women occupied important posts in Hispanic American society, with much more significance than has traditionally been believed.

In the propaganda created against Spain during her expansion in the Americas there has always been a will to exclude Spanish women from everything connected with the discovery, conquest, and colonization of the newly found lands. The reason is simple: the traditional image of woman has always inspired respect, fondness, love, comprehension, and identification with a being who has been gifted by nature to conceive and raise the children that we have all been. Cesáreo Fernández Duro says, in reference to the women of the encounter, "Glory to them, glory to their memory; for everywhere their presence was a stimulus in the risks they took, an example in their hardships, toughness in danger, a balm in adversity, a perennial seed of historical achievements" (Fernández Duro 22).

Men, on the contrary, simbolize the violence and cruelty of beings who are capable of annihilating entire peoples for the sole purpose of satiating their ambition and gaining power. The automatic identification with the Indian, with the weak, the defenseless, with the mother and with the child, makes it much more difficult to see the situation from an impartial point of view. Almost never mentioned in the histories of the Americas, however, are the sufferings and infinite hardships that Spanish women and children had to go through when they crossed the ocean to be at the side of their fathers, husbands, and lovers. The Spanish Crown considered it an indispensable basis for lasting rule over and economic exploitation of the Americas that colonial establishments be created there in which the emigrant would settle permanently and live off what the country would produce. In order to achieve this, there was an effort to encourage, through different measures, marriage and family life in the colonies; and with this very purpose, the Crown regulated the emigration of women to America. No matter how defectively this was applied in practice, it cannot be denied that even so, no small influence was exercised on the maintenance and development of the Hispanic-European population in the Americas (Konetzke, *emigración* 150).

Mention has already been made of how easy it always is to put oneself on the side of the weak, the exploited, those persecuted for some cause. In our Western society, this point of view always means, one way or another, taking women and children into account as beings less favored by nature when they have to defend themselves. This behavior, whether it has its origin at the beginning of time or, especially, in the last two thousand years, since the appearance of Christianity, has prevailed up to now. During the nineteenth and twentieth centuries, a socioeconomic doctrine appeared, with a dialectic very similar to the Christian—except for spiritual and material differences—to the extent that it represents the uplifting of the less favored classes and the just distribution of wealth among all humankind. Christian philosophy tells us that "We are all equal in the eyes of God;" the Marxist or communist proclaims a fair distribution of goods among the proletarian classes, with no dominant, exploitative hierarchy. Although the doctrine of Jesus Christ through the New Testament, and the New Testament through the Catholic church, has endured for two milennia, the same is not true of communist ideology, which having a materialist, and therefore objective basis, has failed completely because the economic theory of its manifestos has not corresponded to the practice of them. Nevertheless, we are not "common," we are not "equal;" nature has made us different. We are not better nor worse, just different. When a lion brings down a zebra and gives it to his whole pride to eat, is not exploiting a "lower" class, but rather maintaining his own survival and that of other zebras, along with the equilibrium of the ecosystem of a specific place. The same happens with birds, which feed on insects, or with big fish who eat small ones. The desire to see history and society always from the point of view of the "conquered" or the "weak" does not always reflect events objectively.

These is nothing new in the way of thinking: we always search for that ideal, utopian island where we can all enjoy all the benefits possible within our existence. That search very often is focused on the past, with the intent of seeing in remote and exotic cultures that imaginary place. The greatest exponent of the Humanist movement in England, Thomas

More, explained this in his book *Utopia*, at the beginning of the sixteenth century. Unfortunately, this free-thinking Englishman was decapitated in 1535.

The Spanish colonizers distinguished themselves very markedly from other Europeans by entering into contact with the Amerinds. In this way a "total" encounter, Castilian style, was displayed throughout the entire process of the engagement. It was a continuation of the process of "reconquest" of Christian Spain on another soil and with other people. Miscegenation in the Americas was the most significant factor in this whole process. It is this factor and no other that has distinguished the Hispanic people from others who arrived at American lands.

> The Spaniard, on the other hand, might have had this or that attitude toward aboriginal women, but fundamentally he lacked racial prejudice; on the one hand because the long struggle for Reconquest had accustomed him over several centuries to exogamic relations, particularly in border areas, and on the other hand because of the noble egalitarian sense and the sense of a common dignity of man, evident in both church sermons and in the will of Isabel, the Catholic Queen, and reinforced in Charles V's imperial concept of the "universitas christiana" (Miró 10).

Logically, prejudices existed with respect to taste and to the social, economic, and religious distinction of Indian women; the same was true regarding Christian women. Thus, cohabitation with Indian women could confer status if they were chieftains or the daughters of nobles. From the first years of the encounter, marriage with baptized Indian women was authorized by law. It is interesting to verify that this process of miscegenation was not confined to marriages between Spanish men and Indian women, but was extended to and approved for Spanish women, so that they could marry Indian men.

> Richard Konetzke quotes a 1504 order issued to Fray Nicolás de Ovando which simply states that "if they wish to marry Indian women, let be out of the free will of the parties and not through force." Another order to Ovando, also cited by Konetzke, perhaps can be seen to establish the basic reason for this authorization: "and in like manner

let him make sure that some Christian men marry some Indian women and Christian women marry Indian men, so that they will communicate with and teach each other" (Miró 11).

There are not many documented cases of Christian women married to Indians. Nevertheless such unions existed, even among women of "well-known" families, such as Doña María de Esquivel, from a distinguished Extremaduran family, who married Carlos Inca Yupanqui, a grandson of Huayna Capac (Miró 13).

These unions were favored in theory and practice. Different degrees must be distinguished in them, since there were notable differences among the various Indian groups and in the circumstances they found themselves in. On this point, Aurelio Miró Quesada writes that the situation was reversed, and the person who rose in social status upon marriage with an Indian woman, was the adventurous conquistador, unknown in Spain, who would marry an Indian woman of "markedly superior social and material condition (11-12)". In any case, permission for mixed marriages was included in the Laws of the Indies, Book VI, Title 1, Law ii (Miró 11).

Very significant examples could be cited to illustrate a miscegenation with no prejudice about inferior status, during the first two centuries of encounter. There must have been very few of the first conquistadores who did not leave mestizo children in the Americas. Miró Quesada expands on this point:

> And there is an even more striking proof that there was at that time no prejudice about inferior status in the fact that amid the whirlwind of civil wars, the first rebel governor of Peru was Diego de Almagro the younger, the mestizo son of Captain Diego de Almagro and a Panamanian Indian woman (12).

The relations betwen native women and Spaniards, as can be expected, did not follow an established pattern or any existing ordinance in this regard. Many of these unions came about spontaneously, with no direct intervention from the church or the monarchy. In Peru, the reasons were more political and social than economic, since the best-known Spanish captains married native women of the highest castes:

"The marriage of Martín García de Loyola, Saint Ignacio's nephew to Beatriz Clara Coya, the daughter of Sayri Túpac, gave cause for official rejoicing; from this marriage was born the mestiza daughter who was later married in Spain to Juan Enríquez de Borja, the son of the Marquess of Alcañices and a relative of another illustrious Jesuit figure: Saint Francisco de Borja" (Miró 13).

The most important aspect of this entire process, as has already been mentioned, was not simply biological, but cultural miscegenation, which occurred in all spheres. As Miró Quesada says of Peru, the Indians did not only suffer the hardships of war, but through Spain they also discovered writing, the book, horses, oxen for tilling the soil, the grapevine, wheat, sugar cane, the right to travel and think and the longing for freedom: "Beyond kings and laws, this was the fundamental and decisive event in the land that was no longer the Tahuantinsuyo, nor New Castile either, but was baptized with the unforeseen, mestizo name of Peru" (Miró 14).

It was precisely this unique identity that, once the conquest was consolidated, began to make some royal officials nervous. The logical fact that many mestizos did not feel "love" for the kings of Spain made some people look warily at these "new Spaniards," and not exactly out of racial prejudice. This fear was based on the possibility that the mestizos would ally themselves with the descendents of the Incas to attack the Spanish authorities and end up controlling the land, "since their possible common ground of intention was based on the fact that these mestizo rebels considered 'that on the part of their mothers the land is theirs, and their fathers won and conquered it;' that would be a double right to it" (Miró 15).

The mestizos' opinion was not in the least mistaken. If anybody had a right to the new territories, it was precisely they. Much more right than the "cold bureaucrats," merchants and "second-round colonizers" who arrived later. Both mestizo men and women had to meet certain barriers when they wished to acquire "employment, honors, and dignities." Nevertheless, good judgment almost always prevailed:

The Third Provincial Synod of Lima ruled in favor of the mestiza women, 'since before the Lord virtue is prized, not lineage.'

Illegitimacy itself remained in the background with respect to the quality of the person; thus the Inca Garcilaso, for example, had no trouble obtaining a commission as a Captain of His Majesty in the campaign against the Moriscos in the Alpujarras of Granada (Miró 16).

Another interesting point worth stressing is the nature of the name "mestizo," chosen by themselves, which at the beginning had a positive connotation, giving a unique identity to those who formed part of that social category. One of the most emotional writings on this topic came from the brilliant mestizo writer of that period, the Inca Garcilaso de la Vega:

> We children of Spanish men and Indian women, or Indian men and Spanish women, are called mestizos, to show that we are a mixture of both nations; it was imposed by the first Spaniards who had children in the Indies, and because it was a name imposed by our fathers and because of its meaning, I call myself by it in full voice and I am honored by it. Although in the Indies if you say to one of them you are a mestizo or he is a mestizo, they take it as an insult (*Comentarios* 373; bk. 9, ch. 31).

It can be seen that there was more awareness of miscegenation, or mestizaje, in the Indies than in Spain itself. With an attitude such as that of the Inca Garcilaso, a writer and historian of the highest order, a remedy could be found for many racial and social problems that affect our societies today and that have no other possible solution than to accept proudly and without complexes the bloodline of each one of us.

MAYAN WOMAN DEVOURED BY DOGS

In the context of the encounter of America, we have a very significant case of "identification with the conquered." The renowned Bulgarian literary critic Tzvetan Todorov published his book *The Conquest of America* in French in 1982, in an attempt to analyze some of the most significant details of the encounter. It is worth quoting the critic Antonio García Berrio on Todorov's book on the conquest, where García Berrio states that he considers "its methodological arguments disproportionate," taking into acount the magnitude of the text described therein on the encounter of Mexico: "It is his recent, irrelevant semiotic version of the most hackneyed topics of the by now tedious Black Legend" (García Berrio 356 n.).

In the work in question, Todorov displays a direct identification with the sources defending the position of the weak. But despite everything, on some concrete points, he gives a quite complete, objective view of the encounter, within the limits of his own ideology. Todorov dedicates his book to a woman, a woman belonging to the group of the weak and conquered. "I dedicated this book to the memory of a Mayan woman devoured by dogs" (dedication). There is no harm in identifying with the martyr of a people who have been invaded by force of arms. Indeed, anyone not identifying with this poor woman can bracket his or her moral status as a person. There is no other way. Nevertheless, this Mayan woman, sacrificed by the Christians who arrived in her lands, represents nothing more than the same process that occurred under Roman dominion, when the Romans would sacrifice Christian men and women, who at that time were a minority, to beasts for the amusement and relaxation of Roman citizens. The only question in this case is whether there are really "good people" and "bad people." According to what history has taught us up to the present time, most military conquests and campaigns have had economic and political purposes, which have been shrewdly supported with religious and moral goals in order to carry them out. This procedure is not privative to any particular Eastern or Western culture; rather, it seems common to all those who have exercised power over others in a given moment of history. Todorov is aware of this reality; nevertheless, he maintains his Manichean point of view, giving the Spanish settlers the role of

"villains." Martín Fernández de Navarrete, referring to the importance
that the historian should give to original documents and not to critics or
apologists of one side or the other, says, "Nothing can correct and direct
the historian's judgment as well as authentic, original documents, which,
produced by the circumstances of the moment, are free of prejudice and
partiality, and sometimes, because of their consequences, can be of
greater help and usefulness than would seem from their simple content
and the reading of them" (75: 44).

How would the Mayan people have treated its enemies?
Unfortunately, Todorov bases a good deal of his book on the
exaggerations of Father Las Casas, the archetype par excellence of the
defender of the weak, and therefore the most famous of all chroniclers
of the Americas. Todorov himself nevertheless recognizes that unlike
Sahagún and other members of religious orders, Las Casas did not take
the trouble to master the language of the native peoples: "Even Las
Casas never masters a native language" (219). Although it is true that
the first laws defending the Indians were promulgated in 1512 (the
Burgos Laws), after the second voyage of Columbus in 1495, only three
years after the discovery, the Catholic Monarchs were already aware that
the treatment that should be accorded to the inhabitants of the new
continent had to be just and in keeping with the doctrine of Christ.

> After the second voyage of Columbus, the Admiral had sent a shipment
> of Indians of which the Crown authorized sale in April, 1495. But on
> the next day, it was ordered that the proceeds of the sale be held,
> because the Monarchs were troubled in their conscience, and they
> wished to learn about the morality of their action from the mouths of
> theologians. It was at that moment when the process began of putting
> what was being done on hold (Morales 305-06).

Todorov seeks to give his work a historical, "true" character, as if
his information and the interpretation given of it were the only ones
possible. Todorov himself falls into the fallacy of all those who see their
way of thinking as the only correct way, failing to realize that "truth" is
a subjective thing that can admit infinite points of view.

But the most interesting aspect of all this information, which appears in the documentation and the manuscripts of many chroniclers of the period, both secular and ecclesiastic, is precisely that fact "that it appears.": "So outspoken were these informers, particularly ecclesiastics, that Spain's enemies seized upon their accusations to create the 'Black Legend' of Spanish cruelty and obscurantism" (Hanke 135-36). Thanks to this information, today research can be done more conscientiously and from different angles, on the motives and causes related to Spanish presence in the Americas. "Only recently has it been brought out that the widespread criticism allowed, and even stimulated, in America by the Spanish government really constituted one of the glories of Spanish civilization" (Hanke 135-36). In any case, Todorov, with evident naveté regarding human behavior in extreme situations such as wars, thinks that simply because of the fact that we are "informed" about some events, they will not occur again. He says in the last pages of his book:

> I am writing this book to prevent this story and a thousand others like it from being forgotten. I believe in the necessity of "seeking the truth" and in the obligation of making it known; I know that the function of information exists, and that the effect of information can be powerful. My hope is not that Mayan women will now have European men thrown to the dogs (an absurd supposition, obviously), but that we remember what can happen if we do not succeed in discovering the other (247).

It is a praiseworthy attempt to "warn humanity" about what can happen if we do not discover the "other." In this case, the events narrated are nearly five centuries old. One may ask if it is a matter of "recalling" our history in order to "discover the other" and not to fall into the temptation of exploiting and dominating those whom destiny has put in our way. Is it enough to discover the other? The Aztec people went from being the exploiter of their neighbors through arms, taxes, and other ways—it is reckoned that 50,000 were sacrificed annually by the Aztecs at the time the Spaniards arrived, a higher figure than of those executed by the Spanish Inquisition throughout its history—to being conquered by the Spaniards. Today we see and "discover" how the horrors of a very recent past are being repeated on the same scale by peoples considered "civilized." Perhaps it is necessary to look at humankind not as the "other" but as one's self, and to see that all of us, to a greater or lesser degree, are capable of the highest acts of good or evil, according to the moment and the circumstances.

LINGUISTIC INFLUENCE OF SPANISH WOMEN IN THE AMERICAS

Being the more conservative element that maintained tradition in the family, Spanish women would make possible the continuation of Spanish culture in the most remote regions of the Empire up until surprisingly recent times. Still today this assertion can be proved in the language and religious traditions in force in southern Colorado and northern New Mexico. The Spanish language spoken today in those lands in the southwestern United States, is the second oldest form of Spanish in the world after Sephardic or Ladino, which is still spoken in some parts of the eastern Mediterranean. Boyd-Bowman's geobiographical studies show that Andalusia was the region that gave character to the Spanish of the Americas, while Seville was the province with the largest number of emigrants, both male and female. "By region, the distribution for the decade 1509 to 1519 is the following: Andalusia provided 37% of the total of colonizers but an enormous 67% of the women" (Boyd-Bowman xx). This 67% of the total of the women, who came from Andalusia, were to leave an indeleble mark on both the language and all types of customs and traditions. "White women in early colonial society must have exercised a linguistic influence that was much greater than their number would suggest. In linguistic history, women have traditionally played a conservative role" (Boyd-Bowman xx). The first of colonization having been the most important with regard to fixing the language in America, Andalusian women deserve the distinction of being the first to linguistically "mark" the Spanish language spoken on the American continent:

> At that time, conversation was even more than today the preferred amusement for women, and those Spanish women, more than half of them Sevillian, must have contributed forcefully to the formation of the early Spanish-Antillean dialect, serving as a mode, both in their language as in their social bearing, for the more numerous Indian women of the island colonies (Boyd-Bowman xx).

Thus the old polemic between Pedro Henríquez Ureña and Amado Alonso over the supposed Andalusianism of American Spanish can be closed off: "It turns out to have a solid demographic base during those first hundred years when the foundations of Spanish culture and language were laid in America" (Boyd-Bowman v). Indeed, American Spanish has its most representative roots in Seville, and it was Sevillian women who made it last and pass on generationally for centuries. These assertions, firmly supported by Boyd-Bowman's detailed demographic studies, are confirmed over and over again in many chronicles of the period.

In her own study on this matter, Analola Borges says, quoting J. Rodríguez de Arzúa, "Cold statistics tell us that in the time between 1509 and 1538, that is, for twenty-nine years, one thousand forty-one women set out for the Indies, of whom three hundred fifty-four were married" (Borges 6). She also adds an observation that should not be ignored. This is her supposition that the number of these women who went over to the Americas must have been much higher than the "cold statistics" tell us.

> But we must suppose that the number was very much higher, if we recognize that the statistics do not list all the passengers and if we consider the settlement already carried out by this time, and even the orders forbidding families to leave from the Canary Islands because it would harm the region. Jaime Rasqui's well-known expression "Those married in the Indies were those who perpetuated the Indies" is fully borne out in the exodus of women settlers. From the mother country, the project of female emigration was carried out as something that produced children for settlement (Borges 6).

It would be naive to think that there were no women in the illegal traffic carried out by sailors and merchants during those first years, no matter how much control the authorities exercised in this matter. The difficulty lies in forming an approximate notion of the number who arrived.

The onetime bishop of Santa Marta, Lucas Fernández de Piedrahita (1624-88), says with respect to the language spoken by the inhabitants of Cartagena de Indias, "The natives of the land, poorly disciplined in the purity of the Spanish language, generally pronounce it with those bad habits that are always present in the people of the coasts of Andalusia"

(149; bk. 3, ch. 149). The same author says the following of the women of Santa Fe de Bogotá: "The women are generally beautiful, with a good bearing, and keen, with a courtly wit, especially the noble ones, and they outdo men in the conscientiousness of not breaking their word" (Fernández de Piedrahita 133; bk.6, ch. 4).

This attribution of more value to the word of women is worthy of praise, not because they did not deserve it, but because traditionally women have been considered "frivolous" when it comes time to give credit to what they have said. This statement takes on even more force coming from a representative of the clergy.

In his *Historia general del Nuevo Reino de Granada*, Piedrahita complains—he considers it "worthy of criticism"—that in what was to be Colombia, many Spanish men preferred to marry Spanish women instead of native women, as had been done in other parts of America. The reason for this, the chronicler says, had nothing to do with "inequality of blood," since many of these Indian women were noble—daughters and sisters of kings and chieftains—but rather with the fact that they were "pagans" and "prisoners." On the other hand, this confirms the unequivocal presence of Spanish women in these regions (297-98; bk. 12, ch. 9). Whether the reasons driving this group of Spaniards to marry their compatriots were religious or of another nature, what is certain is that the majority were Andalusian women, and among Andalusian female emigrants, no province had so high a percentage as Seville. This is confirmed today not only in the language spoken, but in the architecture, and of course in the religious customs—festivities, pilgrimages, "Holy Week," devotions, and so forth. The Andalusian theory of the Spanish spoken in Hispanic America was proven by Boyd-Bowman in his linguistic studies of the 56,000 settlers identified, who went to the Americas. Making a chronological division from the first embarkation from Spain, he points out the decisive demographic importance of the Andalusians and above all the Sevillians, in the first century of Spanish presence in America (Boyd-Bowman v). This strong Andalusian presence was to continue in subsequent years. All this serves to confirm what was until recently the Andalusian *theory* about America.

Once again, Boyd-Bowman's statistics call attention to the fact that Andalusia had the greatest influence on the first happenings and on the settlers of Ibero-America. Nevertheless, "Proportionally Old Castile provided three times more early governors and captains than Andalusia" (xxii). This linguistic connection between different parts of the Iberian peninsula and the Canary Islands with Ibero-America is obvious, but in some cases, there is even more affinity between overseas regions and Andalusia than between Andalusia and other regions of Spain. The most noticeable case is that of Canary Islands Spanish and that of the Caribbean.

Signaling the importance of the contribution of Andalusia and especially Seville in the literary and therefore cultural area of the first years in Hispanic America, Menéndez Pelayo states, with reference to the good taste and tradition of linguistic correctness which some prominent Spanish minds left in Peru and Mexico, some of them being women, "Nearly all of these poets were Andalusian, and most belonged to the Seville school, of which the early poetry of Spanish America can be considered a branch or continuation" (92-93).

As will be seen later, among these minds Menéndez Pelayo was thinking of "Amarilis," a poet born in Peruvian territory in the sixteenth century, whom he was to call a "phenomenon of literary history." Meanwhile it is shown that the gate of entry to and departure from Spain throughout the entire sixteenth century was to be Seville. Its importance did not lie only in its commercial and political, but also its cultural ascendency, especially in its later diffusion throughout the world, to the extent that even today if one asks about Spain outside of its borders, the most likely thing is that mention will be made of some type of music, dress or characteristic stereotype of the Andalusian region.

Seville was the recruiting center for the later expeditions to the Americas. It was also the most important river port of its time, the site of the Casa de Contratación, a chamber of commerce, and of the Council of the Indies, and the most popular Spanish city among the colonizers. The whole tide of persons of all social classes and trades, both Spaniards and foreigners, passed through this city. Seeing the febrile activity of Seville, many set up permanent residence, especially bankers and businessmen who to a large extent financed many of the expeditions that were carried out during that century. Many others—artists, mariners, soldiers, nuns, monks, shipbuilders, prostitutes—would seek their material and spiritual fortune in that great gateway open to a new and different American world, full of hope and adventure, which this great city offered (Boyd-Bowman xxiii).

As we have managed to see, Spanish women did indeed "survive the Atlantic crossing" from the first moments, and they arrived in ever greater number, leaving their presence deeply rooted in all facets of American social life. The transplantation of Spanish society to the overseas terrritories would have had a much more transitory and provisional dimension without so fundamental a female presence.

PART TWO: WOMEN IN THE FIRST TEXTS OF EXPLORATION

FIRST NOTICE OF WOMEN IN THE OVERSEAS ENCOUNTER

Solomon reigned in days of peace,
and God gave him rest on every side,
that he might build a house for his name
and prepare a sanctuary to stand for ever.
How wise you became in your youth!
You overflowed like a river with understanding.
Your soul covered the earth,
and you filled it with parables and riddles.
Your name reached to *far-off islands*,
and you were loved for your peace.
(Ecclesiasticus 47.14-18)

The first women who went over to the Indies were probably the thirty women who went with Columbus on his third voyage (1497-98) (Boxer 35). Cesáreo Fernández Duro is of the opinion, however, that they appeared beginning with the second voyage (1493). He bases himself on the information given to us by Christopher Columbus's son, Hernando Colón, in Chapter 50 of his *Historia del Almirante*: "After Caonabo left, he set fire at night to the houses where the Christians lived with their women; for fear of which they fled to the sea, where eight drowned and three perished in uncharted territory" (172; ch. 50).

It is not entirely clear which women are being referred to, Indian or Spanish. In any case, the existing information unquestionably points to the presence of Spanish women on the third voyage. Silvio A. Zavala once again elaborates on the relevant documentation by saying that the idea of a strictly military and gentlemanly Spanish colonization is false. Artisans and laborers arrived from the very first:

> Christopher Columbus received authorization to take 330 salaried persons to America: 40 noblemen, 100 foot soldiers and laborers, 30 sailors, 30 ship's boys, 20 gold washers, 50 farmhands, 20 officials of all positions, and *30 women...the women would only have a right to 12 maravedís per day* (*Estudios* 185-187).[8]

From that time on, the number of women increased progressively. Already in 1502, Knight Commander Ovando took over prominent families with their households. A few years later in 1509, Diego Colón—a son of Christopher Columbus—arrived with his wife, Vicereine

María de Toledo, a niece of Ferdinand the Catholic King, together with a full entourage of ladies and young women who arrived with them. This is where the first signs of social life showed up in a nascent colony.

> They were all unmarried women—Gonzalo Fernández de Oviedo writes—and they married rich men, "because, in truth, there was a great lack of such women from Castile, and although some Christians married prominent Indian women, there were many others who would under no circumstances take them in marriage, because of the unfitness and ugliness of those women" (Fernández Duro 14).

It is clear that to the author of the above quotation, Fernández de Oviedo, Indian women were not the first choice for marriage. What is not demonstrated at any time in the accounts of the time is the "unfitness and ugliness" of which Oviedo speaks. Obviously, each individual must have had his own tastes and prejudices. It would be interesting to know what the Indian women's opinion of some Spaniards was.

From the first trip around the world, carried out by Magellan and Elcano in 1519—an expedition that began with 237 men, of whom only 18 returned—we have some information about the natives of the lands they passed through. Nevertheless, on this voyage, after all men had confessed, Magellan did not permit any woman to join the fleet "out of respect."[9] Magellean wife's name was Beatriz Barbosa and she received the sum paid to her husband during that voyage.[10]

It would be incorrect to think that it was in the sixteenth century that "Europe" discovered the "Orient." It would be more accurate to say that the "Orient" had already discovered Europe many years before. During the Islamic occupation of the Iberian peninsula, this occupation kept up continuous contact with other peoples of the same religion, such as that of far-off India, with whom a thriving commerce was maintained. They managed to take advantage of the technological and industrial advances of other, conquered peoples, disseminating their knowledge throughout the world. They were even known in the Moluccas and on the remote islands of the Indian Ocean, where there still remain proofs of their influence (M. Fernández de Navarrete 75: 8).

But the first concrete name of a Hispanic who arrived in China, more than one hundred years before Marco Polo, is that of the Spanish Jew Benjamín de Tudela.

The Jew Benjamín de Tudela went in the year 1160 to visit his brothers in the Orient, believing that he would find his people there in good standing and in great prosperity; and going from Spain to Constantinople he crossed over to Tartary China and different provinces within India; he traveled to many islands of the Indian Ocean, and returned to his homeland after thirteen years with much news of his own and news acquired from others, which introduced a part of our globe up to that time unknown to Western peoples (M. Fernández de Navarrete 75: 9).

The Latin naturalist Pliny speaks of the Amazons in his *Natural History*, a true encyclopedia of science from antiquity. There were many variants of the these supposed tribes of women that were to appear over the first years of exploration. Columbus himself, through the information that Bartolomé de las Casas give us about him, mentions the supposed existence of these women. "The Admiral believed that these women must have the customs that are told of the Amazons, because of things that he says he saw and learned of there when the Indian women were questioned" (433; ch. 111).

It is worth looking further into the supposed veracity of the existence of those women.[11] Although it is true that from the most remote antiquity there had been speculation about these mythological fighting women, it is also the case that after the exploration of the river called "Amazonas" by the explorer Francisco de Orellana, true accounts were given, even by eyewitnesses, of the existence of said women. This and no other must have been the reason why Orellana was to baptize the river with that name. A lieutenant-general of Gonzalo de Pizarro (1541), Orellana crossed the South American continent from Quito to the Atlantic Ocean, in one of the most impressive exploits of American exploration. The Andean Mountains, with their snow-capped peaks and the chilling gorges through which they had to pass did not break the will of those valiant visitors. As Roberto Levillier recounts, basing himself on old references by conquistadores, chroniclers and rulers of those regions, the roads from Quito to the Napo River were the worst imaginable. When the rivers overflowed, bogs would form that forced the explorers to make large detours, so that eighty leagues' distance would become two hundred: "The snow-capped peaks—Cayamburu, Sincholagua, Antisana, and Cotopaxi—let loose a good share of their snow in the summer, and this swells the volume of the river currents, unforeseeably; for that

reason the Indians traveled about only in certain months of the year"
(116).

Not content with these barriers, Orellana's men and "women"
decided to travel along the world's largest river with all sorts of threats,
from the terrible, devouring piranhas to alligators and giant anacondas.
Many of the Indians who lived along this river rubbed their arrows with
curare, a deathly poison that made encounters much more fearsome. The
fever, hunger, and desperation of some members of the expedition did
not discourage Captain Orellana from pushing onward. Fray Gaspar de
Carvajal was a member of that expedition and an eyewitness of the
presence of the women mentioned above. The physical description of
these women, their valor and boldness in battles against the Christians,
in which Carvajal lost an eye pierced by an arrow, is striking. The
chronicler says that when the Indians found out about the arrival of the
Spaniards they went to ask the Amazons for help, arriving in a group of
ten or twelve. These Indian women fought in front of the Indian men
with such spirit that the men did not dare run away, and if one tried to,
he was beaten to death right there, this being the reason why the Indians
defended themselves so well. As to the physical description of the Indian
women, Carvajal tells us:

> These women are very white and tall, and they have very long hair,
> braided and put up around their head; and they are very stocky and
> they go around naked, with their shame covered, with their bows and
> arrows in their hands, making as much war as ten Indian men; and in
> truth there was one women of these who put a span[12] of arrow through
> one of the brigantines and others less, so that our brigantines looked
> like a porcupine (80-81).

Carvajal also records the details of a thorough interrogation that
Captain Francisco de Orellana conducted with an Indian man about the
characteristics and customs of those formidable women.

> The Captain asked him who those women were [who] had come to help
> them and fight with us: the Indian said that they were women who
> resided inland seven days from the coast, and because this man was
> their subject, they had come to guard the coast...The Captain asked if
> there were many of these women: the Indian said yes, and he knew of
> seventy villages by name, and he counted them off before those of us
> who were there, and he had been in some of them (Carvajal 85-86).

According to the type of questions that the Indian was asked, it seems that the Christians were already strongly predisposed to believe in the Classical stereotype of the Amazon in ancient texts. Continuing the interrogation as to whether these women had children, the Indian said yes, and when Orellana asked how it was possible to become pregnant without the presence of a man, the Indian answered that these Indian women "at times, when they have that longing," would declare war on a chieftain who is their neighbor, taking male Indians by force to have them for the time they consider convenient, until they were pregnant, and they would return them to their land. When the time came to give birth, if it was a male they would kill it and send it to the father; if it was a female they would bring it up "with great solemnity" and educate it in the art of making war. Referring to the chieftain of these Indian women, the Indian said, "that among all these women there is one lady who controls and has all the other women under her hand and jurisdiction, which lady is named Coñori" (Carvajal 86).

The information given by the Indian in question coincides with the generalized, Classical idea that if a male child was born, the women would kill it. In any case, this information is not easy to believe; nor is the fact that the name of the chieftain of the Amazons, Coñori, begins with the term vulgarly given in Spanish to the female sexual organ. Carvajal insists in his chronicle that everything he says is true:

> And everything that this Indian said and more had been said to us six leagues from Quito, because there was a great deal of news about these women there, and many Indians come downriver one thousand four hundred leagues to see them; and so the Indians farther up had said to us that the person who went down to the land of these women would go a boy and return an old man (87).

Fray Gaspar de Carvajal is the most direct source we have about these women, but there were later expeditions that ended up confirming what he said to some extent. The German soldier in the service of Spain Ulrico Schmidl (1510-67) says the following about them in his *Relación del viaje al Río de la Plata*:

> These women have a single breast and they get together and have carnal relations with their husbands three or four times a year. If they become pregnant then and a little male is born, they send it to the husband's house; but if it is a little girl they keep it with them and burn

off its right breast so that it does not grow and in that way it can use
their arms, the bows, for they are warrior women (Schmidl 182).

In his popular work *El Paititi* (1976), the Argentine researcher
Roberto Levillier ends his chapter on the Amazons saying that these
women could survive so long as no people superior to them came on the
scene. Levillier says that because of the presence of the white race they
had to take refuge in the vast, remote expanses of the Amazon region
where "according to some researchers, their descendents—the
Wauras—live, retaining their primitive characteristics in open clearings
of the Xingú jungle" (159).

If these statements were true, we would have in these women not
only an unusual example of a matriarcal society, but also a feminism put
into practice in one of the most primitive societies.

Francisco de Orellana "discovered" the Amazon River in 1542, the
same year that the Portuguese began to trade with Japan. The river in
question had been known on earlier Spanish maps with the name
"Marañón." Within a short time, Orellana returned to Spain and asked
the King for the privilege to conquer and pacify the Amazon River. The
Crown offered him the title of adelantado and captain-general of those
lands, although despite his insistence he was deprived, among other
things, of a prime tool of war for the conquest of such an immense
territory: artillery. Orellana was to return to encounter the Indians at
a disadvantage, given that they were much more adept at handling canoes
and were capable of shooting their arrows from the water at much
greater speed than the Spaniards needed to load their blunderbusses and
crossbows. This courageous captain paid with his life for the incredible
boldness of returning to the Amazon to gain control of such a huge
territory in order to increase his reputation and the lands of the Spanish
Crown, despite the fact that the Crown did not provide the minimum
needed for the expedition to be brought to a successful conclusion. But
this exceptional man was not alone. Through the historians Herrera y
Tordesillas and Fray Pablo de Torres we are aware of a person who was
always at his side: his wife. Almost nothing is known of this formidable
lady, who was always overshadowed by her husband yet had to go
through the same hardships. In the following fleeting passage of Herrera
y Tordesillas we can find a sporadic mention of her:

> These Castilians sailed downriver, until they came out at la Margarita,
> where they found the wife of Captain Francisco de Orellana, who said

that her husband had not managed to take the main branch of the river, and that, determined to return to the land of the Christians, because he was sick, occupied with searching for food for the journey, the Indians shot seventeen of his men with arrows, and from this grief and from his illness he died in the river, *and she, who had always gone with him*, had returned there in the brigantine, with the people who had been left (Herrera 254; década 7, bk. 8, ch. 9).[13]

The Chilean essayist José Toribio Medina, one of the greatest Hispanic American scholars, expanded on the information regarding the biography of Ana de Ayala, as the Adelantado's wife was named. Apparently Francisco de Orellana married over the strong resistance of Fray Pablo de Torres, later the Bishop of Panama, who did not wish for him to marry a woman who was not not going to contribute "a single ducat" in her dowry. The problem was not just that Ana de Ayala was poor; the Adelantado also wished to take along two of his sisters-in-law on the expedition:

Your Majesty knows that the Adelantado married, over my objections, which were many and legitimate, because he did not receive any dowry, I mean not a single ducat, and he wishes to take his wife over there and even one or two sisters-in-law: he maintained, for his part, that he could not go without a woman, and instead of going and cohabiting he wished to marry; in everything I answered him appropriately, as a Christian should answer, and told him that it was in the interest of this enterprise not to burden the fleet with women and the expenses for them (*Descubrimiento* cxcix-cc).

The exact number of women who traveled on this expedition is not known. As for the men, it is reckoned that about 450 "more or less" went along (Medina, *Descubrimiento*, cciii-iv n. 192). There is, however, one reference to the number of women. A letter from Father Pablo de Torres written to the King on March 19, 1545, states, "May it please Our Lord to protect their souls first of all, and give them time for penitence, for they are in great danger everywhere; and they have already commenced to give out one pound of biscuit among three men , and no wine or meat; and the stern of the main ship, where the Adelantado sails, is full of women" (Medina ccxi).

Not many people survived this voyage. "Of the expeditionaries, only 44 persons escaped, as Peñalosa and Doña Ana de Ayala attest" (Medina, *Descubrimiento* ccxx n. 204). But the Adelantado's expedition and death led to failure, not because women were taken along, but because no kind of help was received from the Crown which would have allowed him to set out well-equipped. Medina says in this regard, "Orellana's wife, with a notable practical sense, as someone who was able to see things up close, gave to understand—to our mind rightly so—that her husband's enterprise failed because he did not receive the help he needed from the Crown, which would have succeeded in saving the enterprise" (*Descubrimiento* ccxiii n. 198).

Medina mentions in passing the good service that these Spanish women provided on expeditions such as that of Pedro Meléndez de Avilés to Florida or Pedro de Valdivia to Peru and Chile (*Descubrimiento,* ccxii-xiii, n. 197).

So ends the story of a man who died in the river that made him famous, having had to navigate in his life against factors even more severe than the current and the dangers of the Amazon: religious intolerance and official indifference—like Hernando de Soto, who was buried in the Mississippi River. In spite of everything, Francisco de Orellana could have said proudly that although he had everything against him and it cost him his life, he married the woman he loved most and crossed the greatest river in the world. It is known that Ana de Ayala was still alive in 1572.

> The historians do not say what the woman's name was, nor her station, although Father Torres asserts that she was "most poor." We have managed to find out that her name was Ana de Ayala…After having seen her husband die on the brigantine on which he was traveling on the Amazon, she came into harbor with the remaining survivors at Margarita Island, from where she went to Nombre de Dios and then to Panama, probably for the purpose of claiming the property that her husband had left in Guayaquil. She was still living there in 1572 (Medina, *Descubrimiento* cxcix-cc, n.189).

His wife, of whom we know very little, deserves the same fame as Orellana, for she was capable of following her husband to what could be called without much exaggeration the "very jaws of hell." The name of this extraordinary woman, Ana de Ayala, should remain in the memory of all of us as one of the most important among those of the singular women who went over to the Americas.

One of the first chronicles with tremendous dramatic potential is the story of the Spaniard Juan Ortiz, which appears in the chronicle

Expedición de Hernando de Soto a la Florida, by the Portuguese Fidalgo de Elvas, a member of that expedition of Hernando de Soto. In this case it is the true story of a Christian who had the sympathy of a chieftain's daughter. Juan Ortiz had gone with Pánfilo de Narváez's expedition to Florida and was one of those who stayed on the ships and were able to return to Cuba. Later he returned to Florida with "twenty or thirty" others in search of the Christians they had left. Within sight of an Indian village, they saw a kind of sign with a map. Ortiz went to land with another Christian. All at once some Indians came out and took them captive. Juan Ortiz's companion, who had sought to defend himself, was killed right there, and Ortiz was taken prisoner. At this point the chieftain's daughter appeared. When Ortiz was in captivity, she interceded to save the life of the Christian, telling her father that a single Christian could do him neither good nor ill, and that it would be more honorable to hold him captive: "Ucita ordered that Juan Ortiz be tied hand and foot on four stakes, on top of a bar, and underneath he ordered a fire to be lit, so that he would be burned there. And a daughter of his begged him not to kill him" (Elvas 51-52). Three years later an enemy chieftain named Mocoço set fire to the village, and Juan Ortiz lost his former privileges with Ucita, since apparently the chieftain Mocoço felt sympathy toward him. Juan Ortiz managed to find out through Ucita's daughter that Ucita intended to sacrifice him on the next day. The Indian woman counseled him to go with the chieftain Mocoço, since the latter was always asking about him; and in that way he could be saved: "And at night, since he did not know the path, the Indian woman went half a league out of the village and put him on it" (Elvas 51-52).

The Indian woman who on two occasions saved Juan Ortiz's life appears in the chronicle printed in 1557, in the Portuguese city of Evora. This historical work may well have been the inspiration for a whole series of dramas with similar features which appeared later in Europe.

On the same Florida expedition of Hernando de Soto, through Herrera y Tordesillas's *Historia general de los hechos de los castellanos en las islas y tierra firme del mar océano*, an incident is mentioned in which Hernando de Soto himself benefited from the kindness and generosity of an Indian woman chieftain. The same Juan Ortiz mentioned above functioned as an interpreter between Hernando de Soto's men and the natives of those regions, once he was rescued by De Soto's men. Like his captain-general, Juan Ortiz ended his days in Florida, and was unable to return to his place of birth, Seville. The courtliness and refinement displayed between the Spanish conquistador and the Indian woman are worthy of a pastoral novel or a romance of chivalry. The truth is that, according to the passage in Herrera y Tordesillas, the Indian woman chieftain assisted the Spaniards so they would not die of hunger. The chronicle says that the Indian lady was a "young woman ready to wed," who approached in a canoe, accompanied by seven or eight women, with six Indian men in another canoe. She told the Adelantado that she very much regretted the deprivation that the Spaniards were experiencing, and that she had two houses with sufficient provisions to aid the needy. She offered him one of these and said that if he wished, she would leave the whole village to him. To which Hernando de Soto replied:

> in good grace and courteously, thanking her and saying that he would be content with what she chose to give him. and while the Adelantado spoke, the Indian woman took of a string of pearls that she wore around her neck and gave it to the interpreter Juan Ortiz so that he would give it to the Adelantado, saying that her hand did not offer it so as to preserve her woman's honesty. The Adelantado rose up and received it most graciously and presented her with a ruby, which he wore on his finger, with which peace was established, and the Indian woman went away, and everyone wondered at her beauty and good deportment (Herrera 27; década 1, ch. 15, 27).

On that same expedition of Hernando de Soto's to Florida, the courage of Indian women managed to shine forth on more than one occasion. Herrera y Tordesillas recounts a much more inauspicious incident than the above, but which once again brought out those women's capability of fighting to the death alongside their people. Once when the Spaniards had arrived at an Indian town, the Indian men and women came out to fight, and were ultimately taken prisoners or killed because they refused to surrender: "And when Francisco Reinoso Cabeza de Vaca went into a house, five women who were hiding there came at him and would have strangled him if two soldiers had not finally come in. To take him out of the women's hands it was necessary to kill them all"(Herrera 43; década 1, bk. 1, ch. 7).

As can be seen, it is not an exclusive trait of the Iberian peoples to carry out defenses like the one against the Romans at Numancia. It is clear in the previous note that no one among these Florida Indians "chose to submit." On both sides there were courageous men and women who preferred to give their lives rather than to surrender to their enemies.

AMERICAN WOMEN AND THE CONQUISTADORES

It would be naive to dismiss the enormous attraction exerted by native women on the Spaniards who landed on their shores. I refer not only to the need to have sexual relations after spending months at sea, but also to the great beauty and grace of many of the women, who captured many Spanish hearts. The Spaniards did not take long to discover the human quality of those who would become the mothers of their children and the beginning of a new people. The same could be said of the effect that those men had on Native American females. It could of course be argued, and in fact has been claimed, that Spaniards, because of their genetic and climatic background, are more passionate, "hot-blooded" as it were, than other European peoples. It is, however, unjust to attempt to see in this bond a merely physical component. The union took place on a spiritual plane as well, and on all levels. This assertion lacks a scientific basis, since one would first have to define what is understood by "Spanish." Nonetheless, it is true that the Spaniards, and to a lesser degree the Portuguese, were the ones out of all the Europeans who most visibly gave substance to that "magnetism" in the form of a new "race." The greater part of Hispanic America is of mixed blood, and not only in a racial sense, but also spiritually: in its music, in its art—in short, in its culture. Bearing the unequivocal stamp of Spain, Hispanic America possesses as well that grace and colorfulness furnished by five centuries of contacts between the Amerindian, European, and African cultures. One has also to recognize that the racial mixture can vary from 55% Indian in Guatemala or 45% Indian in Peru to 98% European in Argentina, or 60% black and mulatto in Cuba, but that none of the groups for that reason lacks cultural blending. This fact should not be seen as something that Spain can boast about, nor much less regret: it is the historical effect of the sixteenth-century European people that was most apt to consummate that union. As the most "mixed" people of Europe, Spain, especially on her southern fringe, was able to more easily accept the aborigines, and transmit and unite its culture to them, simply because it had been undertaking that sort of cultural fusion since the earliest times that the Iberian peninsula was inhabited.

Descriptions of American and Asian women appear from Columbus's first reports to our time. Many descriptions are full of admiration, curiosity, desire, even surprise at the beauty of these women, who in some cases are called better-looking than those of Europe. Pedro Fernández de Quirós's account describes Polynesian women in this way:

"And everyone who saw them state that they are beautiful of leg, hands, lovely eyes, face, waist, and figure, and that they are more beautiful than Lima ladies, although the women of Lima are very much so" (82). Peter Martyr D'Anghiera offers us a "succulent" example in the welcome that the thirty women of the chieftain Beuchio on the island of Hispaniola gave to the adelantado Bartolomé Colón and his men:

> ...dancing, singing and playing music by order of the king, completely naked except for their private parts, which they cover with a kind of underskirt made of cotton. The virgins, on the other hand, wear their hair down over their shoulders, and a ribbon or band around their forehead, but they do not cover any part of their body. Our men say that their faces, chest, breasts, hands, and other parts are very beautiful and of the whitest color, and that they imagined that they were seeing those most beautiful Dryads or nymphs that came out of fountains, of which the ancient fables speak. All of them, bending their knee, presented the palm fronds that they carried in their right hands to the Adelantado, while they danced and sang in competition with each other (Martínez 202).

María Teresa Villafañe echoes the thinking of the Portuguese Don Soarez de Sosa, who points out not only the beauty of native women but also their faithfulness, submissiveness, and other qualities that "captivated" those who were going to conquer: "There are beautiful women who would have nothing to envy from those of the Rua Nova in Lisbon" (128).

Despite what has been mentioned above, there were also commentaries on the freedom of Indian women as compared with Spanish. Pero Hernández, the secretary for the explorer and governor of the River Plate, Alvar Núñez Cabeza de Vaca, observed in his *Comentarios* how the women of the Guaycurú Indians had the power of freeing a prisoner who had been captured by the men of the tribe with the intention of killing him. These freed prisoners, if they wished to stay among the Indians were treated just like the Indians themselves: "And it is true that the women have more freedom than was given by Doña Isabel, our queen, to the women of Spain" (Villafañe 128).

On the contrary, not many opinions of women about men exist. Nevertheless, there are some formulated by men themselves about Indian men. In this case, the great Portuguese navigator working for Spain, Pedro Fernández de Quirós, describes a thirteen-year-old youth:

He was white in color, handsome of neck and build, sharp-featured and fair of face, somewhat freckled and flushed, his eyes black, attractive, good forehead and eyebrows, the nose, mouth, and lips very well proportioned to the whole, with well-set, white teeth. In short, he was mild in his laughter and affections, with extremely good manners. Because of so many good features and graces he was taken for a beautiful young woman; however, he was a boy seemingly thirteen years old (226).

This description of masculine beauty is poetic in the extreme, a rare occurrence in the routine severity of the travel accounts of that period. It appears that this Polynesian boy was engraved on the memory of the Portuguese sailor, this being the most lyrical description of his entire account. Another appears in the same work, regarding a girl about fifteen years of age. It is worth mentioning even though it is not so effective as the one above.

...and also an upright, graceful, sprightly lady, very elegant, her neck and breasts high, very slim of waist, her hair very blond, long and untied, all of her very pleasant, and very white as far as color is concerned. And because she was so pretty, this woman shocked us more than the sight of us did her; for with a manly spirit and swift steps, her semblance happy and smiling, she came out to greet them and with her own hand gave Gallardo a new blanket, which she was carrying folded under her left arm, and then with great affection and both arms open she embraced him and in their way she gave him a kiss of peace on his cheek (Fernández de Quirós 229).

The Spanish men were not always the ones to take the initiative when intimate relations with native women were entered into. It is not risky to state that after gold—and for some, before gold—the most attraction was exercised by the image of the American woman, who was in many cases free of all the inhibitions and social and religious taboos that Spanish women had with regard to sex. In the following case it can be seen how the Indian women were used as bait to take the Spaniards.

In a later encounter of the territories comprising Yucatán and Guatemala, General Ursúa warned his soldiers about the sexual provocations of the Indian women, since on some occasions they had been used to strategic and military ends. The chronicler Juan de Villagutierre relates a notable event, when the Spanish troops were awaiting an ambush by the Indian chieftain Canek, who did not come, but nevertheless sent women alone in canoes, while he stayed with his squadrons on the land, and it was impossible to find out what ruse moved him to do this. The Spanish general had people armed and ready: "Over all these three days the infidel women were received, dainty, elegant, decked out and their hair braided by the Indian servant women...And the barbarous women, seeing the little attention paid to them, for the purpose for which they must have been taken away from their honorable fathers and husbands, began to incite with crude, provocative demonstrations" (Villagutierre 429; ch.5).

The Indians must already have known the weak side of the Spaniards. Nevertheless, on this occasion, the long-suffering soldiers had to abstain, when they saw that behind the generosity shown by the Indian women there were ulterior motives. These "motives," however, were not those of the Indian women themselves, but of the chieftain who forced them to carry out those demonstrations in order to achieve his own ends.

There were many love affairs between Spanish conquistadores and native women, some of historic proportions, such as the one between Doña Marina and Cortés. The descriptions of the "beauties" of the Americas are very numerous: Polynesians, Guaranís, Mexicans, Peruvians, and other women who captured the hearts of the Spaniards. Among the most notable cases one could cite that of Anayansi, with whom Núñez de Balboa lived, or Sinca, the Indian woman of the province of Chicarona, with whom the conquistador Espinosa fell in love and "it was necessary to tear him away after a year of staying by her side" (Villafañe 128).

Also Don Pedro de Aldecoa, one of the thirteen who accompanied Francisco de Pizarro and followed him, after his stay on Gallo Island, to the coast of Trujillo, fell in love with an Indian woman chieftain. Pizarro refused to let him stay, and he had to be taken prisoner and sent on board. He had fits of madness, all that is known of him is that his name appears in the grants given by the Queen to Pizarro, in which she conferred titles of nobility on the Gallo Island thirteen, and golden spurs on those who were already nobleman (Villafañe 128-29).

Spanish men were not the only ones to take pleasure in the games of love. Apparently, some Spanish women must have taken similar pleasures, and some information is available on this subject. As for the "crude" provocations that the Indian women made toward Spanish men, much the same occurred with the provocations of some Spanish women toward some Indian men—there being no need to confirm the "crude" practice on one side or the other. It should be remembered that many of these accounts were written by fathers of the church. For single women to go over to the Indies, they need a letter of good conduct. Even so, according to Ana María Ortega Martínez, some of poor reputation must have been smuggled through: "Mendieta complained about the bad behavior of some Spanish women: '...because once out of church they go naked among the Indians, worse than the lewdest fishwives...' And Oviedo says, 'I have seen many naked Indian women who are more modest than many clothed Christian women'" (Ortega 13).

Here not only are some Spanish women seen in a bad light because of their "evil behavior," but also the poor fishwives, who, having nothing to do with the matter, are called lewd.

It is known that the emperor of Mexico, Moctezuma, had three thousand wives, among ladies, servants, and slaves. Very interesting because of the timeliness of the topic is the information given about the abortions produced by some of these women so as to "be free of pregnancy." These Indian women, "the daughters of gentlemen," practised abortion to keep their emperor and other nobles happy. The timeliness of the topic makes this point more interesting, when we consider that this practice has been engaged in for many years, probably since the beginning of humanity. From the quotation one can infer that the Aztecs had nothing against this procedure, just as in the same quotation Fray Juan de Torquemada takes it for granted that these actions were carried out through the "persuasion of the devil:" two different ways of judging the same action:

> Motecuhzuma took for himself, especially those that he liked best, the ladies, daughters of gentlemen, who were many and well treated, and he gave the others as wives to his servants and to other gentlemen and nobles; and they say that there was a time when he had one hundred fifty pregnant at one time, and they, persuaded by the Devil, took action, taking things so they could get rid of the babies and be free of pregnancy, so as to give in to Motecuhzuma's lust (230-31; bk. 2, ch. 89).

There was a notable disparity of values and opinions regarding the behavior of women among the different native groups. To attempt to judge the values of the "Indians" as a monolithic group is a great mistake. One of the tribes that attracted most attention from the earliest times was the "Caribs," a people scattered over some of the islands of the Caribbean Sea. In the case quoted below, it is interesting to observe how it was specifically women taken captive by these Indians who gave information and described to the Spaniards the Carib Indians' custom of eating human flesh and of cutting off the "members" of the sons they had with these women and waiting until they became "men" in order to eat them. Seemingly, the flesh of children and women was not so tasty. This information was gathered during Christopher Columbus's second voyage, on which they managed to rescue twenty "young and beautiful" women whom the Caribs had kidnapped from other islands so as to have them as concubines:

> These women also say that those men exercise a cruelty that seems incredible; they eat the sons they have with them, and only bring up those that they have with their natural wives...They say that the flesh of men is better than any other thing in the world; and it would seem so, because on the bones that we found in these houses everything that could be gnawed they had gnawed, nothing was left of them but what could not be eaten because it was too hard. In one house there we found the neck of a man cooking in a pot. They cut off the member of the boys that they capture, and they make use of them until they are men, and then when they wish to have a celebration they kill them and eat them, because they say that the flesh of boys and women is not good to eat. Three of these boys came fleeing to us, all three of them with their members cut off (M. Fernández de Navarrete 75: 186).

It is therefore unfair and inaccurate, in referring to the encounter of the Americas, to judge the actions of Spanish or native women and to put them into the same pattern, in the same way that it is inaccurate to refer to the different groups of the recently discovered continent as if they were a single group. Many of these women, either because they were captives as in the case of the "Caribs" or because they were following the orders of their males, were not directly responsible for their actions. It is not a question of attempting to absolve the women from their responsibilities, nor much less to blame them when they are being judged by the mentality of fathers of the sixteenth-century church, but rather of attempting to understand the circumstances in which their actions took place. Both Spanish and native women shared attitudes and customs, each group being adapted to its own circumstances.

DISTORTION OF SOME WOMEN THROUGH THE ENCOUNTER TEXTS: THE "BOBADILLAS" AND BEATRIZ DE LA CUEVA

The conscious disinformation circulated about some notable and extraordinary female personalities of the Hispanic world with respect to events that occurred in the Indies at the end of the fifteenth century and in the first half of the sixteenth, merits some attention. The devices used to discredit valid information pose an enormous risk in a society such as ours that is so saturated with information and so culturally polarized. The information presented about the events connected with 1492 has led many to examine their conscience and to look at so complex a period from different points of view. In spite of the controversies surrounding the topic, some have managed to analyze the events in a scholarly, dispassionate manner. Others, however, have carried their passions to the limit. The demythification of the figure of Columbus and the identification with the conquered have in many cases been the canon to follow at a time of political correctness. Some of the books written on the encounter serve as models of this disinformation, treating historical personages from perspectives that today could only with difficulty be considered "contemporary." Here is one example: "Modern scholars have concluded that the Spaniards who came to impose their civilization on the Americas were men whose traditional heritage of cruelty had been given new impetus by quickly changing historical circumstances" (Varner xiii).

To take as fact all the stereotypes and false beliefs about the actions of a people without having reliable proof of them distances us from a serious historical approach. In order to create a "valid" de-forming discourse it is necessary to support it with a series of semantic elements capable of penetrating the conscious barriers of common sense. This is what has happened in the case at hand. In the quotation above we observe a series of words such as "modern," "Have concluded," "impose," "traditional heritage," "cruelty," which go about shaping an ideological mosaic, pro or con, in the reader's mind as he or she goes on reading. It is a game that is dangerous, but highly effective. When the authors of the book in question allow themselves all the freedom in the world to say, "Modern scholars have concluded," they are only displaying a lack of an understanding of the subject that would permit them to analyze the context in depth. On the other hand, it would be a much more difficult and laborious task for them to take the trouble to quote sources and the names of those "modern scholars" who have decided that the Spanish conquistadores had a "traditional heritage of cruelty." The reason for this is simple: a generalization such as the one quoted leaves no room for any type of reflection. One does not know the intellectual quality, nor the number, nor the nationality, nor the ideological bases of those "modern scholars" who have reached that conclusion. It is, on the other hand, easier to utilize a pseudo-informative discourse that operates with the same effectiveness. The result of the dis-information leads to the creation of permanent stereotypes of persons and peoples, in this case the Hispanic, which accumulate in traditional information banks as a false, but highly contagious message is transmitted. It is the beginning of a cultural epidemic with unexpected results.

In the book quoted above, *Dogs of the Conquest*, there is also passing mention of some Spanish women of the sixteenth century. But the commentaries made do not do justice to the human quality of those women. With hardly any historical or documentary basis, one of them is accused of being "lax" with men, and another, "blasphemous." This book is not an isolated case, but rather one more example of a profusion of studies carried out by otherwise respectable persons who, even though they know a language and culture, deform and misrepresent it. The authors of the book in question are referring in the first case, to Christopher Columbus's first voyage to the Canary Islands and the stop he made on the island of Gomera. Out of mere speculation, basing themselves exclusively on a brief commentary by Michele de Cuneo, a writer who accompanied Columbus and who had "a particular propensity for storytelling and gossip," they voice their of a possible amorous adventure between the famous navigator and Beatriz de Bobadilla, the lady in question (Cioranescu 148).[14] The basis for this "romance" has its origins in a letter preserved at the University of Bologna "the authenticity of which is not wholly certain" (Cioranescu 147).

> Doña Beatriz naturally would have found the blue-eyed and fair-haired Genoese attractive, though he as yet was not a man of proven significance. But suspicion of a brief affair betwen the two rests on the known moral laxity of the lady and on the casual statement of Columbus's boyhood friend, Michele de Cuneo, that the admiral was "tinto d'amore" with her (Varner 3).

This kind of hypothetical romance would fit better in a Hollywood film or a supermarket novel than in a book of historical criticism. In fact, the physical description of the Admiral has yet to be proven. If Beatriz de Bobadilla, a widow at that time, had or did not have amorous adventures, no one has a right to judge her, much less when the evidence is so poor. Therefore, this is an incomplete opinion that must be filled out with additional information. The Varners' text is worth observing as an informative model which, although it has applied the conventional filters of historical verification, must also apply, albeit in retrospect, a series of suppositions that cleanse the evidence set forth. Since the authors have as a critical basis an underlying "morality" and "religion," the reader shall have to remain in a narrow area of dissent with the arguments set forth, since this dissent could imply a break with established moral canons. Moral authority resides—who can doubt it?—with those who are in possession of the "word of God."

In his book *Christopher Columbus*, the Italian author Gianni Granzotto takes up Cuneo's words where he says that the Admiral "had taken a fancy" to Beatriz de Bobadilla and adds something of his own besides: "With all his sailing, they saw each other no more than a few days out of the year. A few days and a few nights, and no doubt Columbus spent a few more this time around with the lady of Gomera" (201).

Alejandro Cioranescu, who devotes a whole chapter of his book *Colón y Canarias* to Beatriz de Bobadilla, concludes, after having studied this figure in detail along with all the possiblities of a supposed romance between these two personages:

> It is gratuitous to imagine that Doña Beatriz responded lasciviously to a love affair that we only imagine; and that the Admiral would have forgotten his projects and his obligations and traveled around the ocean in search of his beloved. The legend of the Admiral's Canary Islands love affair may be attractive, but it belongs to literature (151).

Another author, Mauricio Obregón, also takes up Cuneo's information with reference to Beatriz in particular and the Bobadilla family in general, whom he calls a "mafia." Again referring to the stop Columbus made at Gomera, Obregón says:

> Cuneo tells us that there he was *tincto d'amore* for his second Beatriz, Beatriz de Bobadilla, the daughter-in-law of Inés de Pedraza and widow

of the first governor of the island. She was a relative of the future governor of Hispaniola, who would do so much damage to Columbus, and also of Isabel, the wife of Pedrarias, the man who decapitated Balboa. Another mafia. The gossip was that Queen Isabel married her to Pedraza, whom she appointed governor of this island at the end of the earth, to get her away from Fernando's vigilant eye. She must have been good-looking...(66).

In the question of "mafia," Obregon would be right if he aimed this criticism at Francisco de Bobadilla for what he did to Christopher Columbus, or at the man who caused the death of Vasco Núñez de Balboa, Pedrarias, the husband of Isabel de Bobadilla. But this criticism is unfair and incomplete if it is directly extended to their female relatives. The way the information is presented, Obregón leaves no doubt that both Beatriz and Isabel de Bobadilla were participating members of that "mafia." But considering that the latter did everything possible to avoid Balboa's death, this label loses its force.

Fortunately, supplementary information exists on Beatriz de Bobadilla, "the lady of known moral laxity," and her family. She belonged to the dynasty of the Bobadilla women, a whole line who were of vital importance from the earliest time of colonization. It is worth mentioning a few of these women. Hernando Colón, Columbus's son, makes passing reference to Beatriz in connection with a ship that Christopher Columbus had the intention of taking with him: "The people of that region were awaiting Doña Beatriz de Bobadilla, the ruler of the same island, who was at Gran Canaria and who had with her a ship belonging to one Grajeda, from Seville, a forty-ton ship; which, since it was appropriate for his voyage, he could take" (Colón 97). It is not at all strange that this woman would attract the attention of many men of that period if she was as attractive as is claimed:

The widow of the ruler of Gomera, still young and having the reputation of having been one of the most beautiful ladies of the Court and of having attracted the attention of the Catholic King [Fernando], might well have attracted that of the discoverer of the Indies; but the source indicating that is worthy of only limited and circumspect confidence (Cioranescu 151).

Beatriz was related to Isabel de Bobadilla, the wife of the founder of Panama and settler of Nicaragua, Pedro Arias Dávila or "Pedrarias."

Las Casas calls Isabel a "notable lady:" "Pedrarias's wife was a notable lady named Doña Isabel de Bobadilla and also de Peñalosa, niece of the Marchioness of Moya...[she was] a faithful servant of the Catholic Monarchs" (3: 32). Doña Isabel, the mother of eight children, followed her husband to the remote corners of the Americas, although she was aware of the hardships that everyone expected on these voyages.

> She was one of the first women who helped colonize Acla, Nombre de Dios, Panama, and Nicaragua. No hardship daunted her and her huge spirit managed to adapt to all circumstances. That lady brought up in the court of the kings of Spain managed to suffer without complaint a fierce climate and great want; moreover, she set an example for the other women and even the soldiers, who at times despaired, anticipating hunger, horrors, epidemics—during which hundreds of Spaniards would die—dangers on sea and on land, and above all the plagues typical of those countries where the white man cannot live serenely. The historian Herrera is right to say that she was called the Excellent Woman (Acosta 150).

Perhaps the most notable event in the life of this lady was her attempt to resolve the difficult situation between her husband Pedrarias and the discoverer of the South Sea, the Pacific Ocean, Vasco Núñez de Balboa:

> Doña Isabel wished to calm her husband's hatred with respect to Vasco Núñez de Balboa and arranged to have her oldest daughter, Doña María, brought from Spain, to marry her to the Discoverer of the South Sea, confident that in this way the quarrels between Pedrarias and Balboa would come to an end. But that sacrifice did not have the effect she desired, for when Doña María arrived at the Darien the unfortunate Balboa had already died, beheaded by order of that most cruel governor (Acosta 150).

One of the great scholars of the sixteenth century, and above all a person familiar with everything that was happening in the Americas was the Italian who had settled in Spain, Peter Martyr d'Anghiera. Among others, Peter Martyr knew Christopher Columbus personally. In his work *Décadas del Nuevo Mundo* (1511), he left a record of a most valuable letter written by Isabel de Bobadilla to her husband Pedro Arias Dávila. The letter reads:

Beloved husband, it seems to me that as young people we were united with the marital bond to live together, not separately. Wherever fate leads you, whether among the raging waves of the ocean or in horrible dangers on land, know that that I shall accompany you. No danger can threaten me so cruelly, no manner of death can befall me that would not be much more bearable to me than living apart from you over such an immense distance. It is preferable to die once and for all and be thrown out to sea for the fish to eat me or to the land of the cannibals for them to devour me, rather than to be consumed in continuous mourning and perpetual grief, waiting, not for my husband, but for his letters. This is my decision, made not rashly, nor on the spur of the moment, nor on a woman's whim, but maturely thought out. Choose one of the two things: either you cut my throat with your sword, or you agree to what I am asking (Mártir 140; decade 2, ch. 140).

This letter speaks for itself of the stature of this woman. As to having her "throat cut" by her husband, I do not think it was a joke, since Don Pedro was not a man of excessive scruple—Núñez de Balboa could testify handily to that. In his *Historia de las Indias*, Bartolomé de las Casas also mentioned this woman, calling her a "manly matron": "Thus this Isabel de Bobadilla, Pedrarias having decided to go on that voyage without her, she, as a manly matron, did not wish to stay behind on any pretext, but rather to follow her husband on sea and on land" (3: 32). If any woman had to be credited for being most involved in the whole enterprise of the Spanish encounter in the Americas, Doña Isabel would have to take a first place. Her husband was the founder of Panama and the settler of Nicaragua; her daughter Isabel married Hernando de Soto, conquistador and explorer of Florida; her daughter María was intended to be the wife of the discoverer of the Pacific, Vasco Núñez de Balboa; and her other daughter, Leonor, traveled through all of the Americas, and was widowed on two occasions. On the island of Cuba was Isabel de Bobadilla, daughter of the other Isabel and of the mighty conquistador Pedrarias Dávila, Count of Gomera. She was the wife of the governor of Santiago de Cuba, Hernando de Soto, who at that time was exploring the lands of Florida. She married Hernando de Soto in 1537. When De Soto left Santiago de Cuba to go to Florida, he left interim control of the government to his wife, who had to face great difficulties. This lady, the first woman governor of Cuba, died a few years after Beatriz de la Cueva, who was the governor of Guatemala (1541). Inca Garcilaso de la Vega in chapter 13 of book 1 of his

Historia de la Florida calls this great woman, "who was beautiful in the extreme," shortly before the Adelantado Hernando de Soto left for Florida, "a woman of great virtue and discretion" (1: 261): "And, as the time when he was able to sail was approaching, he named Doña Isabel de Bobadilla, his wife and the daughter of the governor Pedro Arias de Avila, a woman of great virtue and discretion, governor of that great island..."(1: 168) Isabel de Bobadilla never saw her husband again after his departure. When Diego Maldonado and Gómez Arias went to meet him at the appointed place in October, 1540, the Adelantado did not show up. They did the same for three consecutive years, leaving messages on the trees and hiring Indians to take letters inland, but Don Hernando never appeared again. When Isabel de Bobadilla found out about her husband's death, it seems that the life was went out of her forever. Later she returned to Spain with a white slave woman named "Isabel," whom she freed so that she could marry the fisherman Alberto Díez (Torre 269).

There is valuable information showing how women of the most diverse social classes—slaves and aristocrats—set sail for the Americas. Garcilaso tells us that Doña Isabel's beautiful sister, Leonor de Bobadilla, would marry Hernando de Soto's second-in-command, Capt. Nuño de Tovar. It seems that they married in secret (Garcilaso 1: 267; ch. 8). Leonor became a widow upon the death of her husband in the conquest of Florida and was married again in Peru, to Lorenzo Mexía, who was violently assassinated by one of Pizarro's followers. She was married for the third time to Blas de Bustamante (Borges 440). Analola Borges calls her the "symbol of a woman settler" and also informs us of some events in Doña Leonor's later life:

> Fifteen more years of life in the Indies had given her two husbands and two brothers who had violent deaths. She had been in Cuba, in Panama in Peru...; she had witnessed the decimated armies of Florida, the fleets destroyed in the Antilles, the intrigues of governors and conquistadores on the mainland, the civil wars in Peru...At thirty years of age, Leonor de Bobadilla was a woman settler who bore the life of the Indies grafted onto her own flesh (440).

Another contemporary author, Ricardo Majó Framís, already some years ago (1963) wrote a bulky study of the lives of the Spanish navigators, conquistadores and colonizers. In his book Majó also mentions the Bobadilla family and gives some detailed descriptions of some of these women. Referring to the governor and captain-general of the Darien, Pedrarias, this author indicates that one of the reasons why Pedrarias received this appointment was that he was married to Isabel de Bobadilla:

> Pedrarias managed to go there as captain and governor thanks to his old friends at the Court; to his being known for a long time at the Court with the nickname of the *Jouster*; and to his marriage with the Bobadilla lady, who was the sister of that other woman with whom, for so many years, Queen Isabel had soothed her sorrows and her tears (2: 188).

Displaying an outdated anti-Semitism, Majó presents a portrait of Pedrarias that denies him Spanish citizenship: "He was not strictly speaking a Spaniard; he was *Jewish*; his class was that of the converted Jews" (2: 129). Further on Majó attempts to explain what a "Jew" is, implying some connection between Pedrarias's wickedness and his status as a converted Jew:

> Jews have no more homeland than their skin. Their true homeland, that of their heart, is their *hatred in motion, their hatred that walks*, like that of the tragic Asahuerus. They see physical profit; they have a fine mental grasp of that. But where there are material goods to be won, there is the homeland. Thus Pedrarias goes to the Indies, happily, like a farmer who goes to measure his harvest and profit from it (2: 129).

Referring to Isabel de Bobadilla, Pedrarias's wife, he mentions her origin: "Also from a family of Hebrews, or near Hebrews, was his wife, the Bobadilla lady, the niece or cousin of tht Marchioness de la Moya, who was Columbus's fairy godmother and was married to Andrés Cabrera" (Majó 2: 130). He also mentions Isabel de Bobadilla, the daughter of the other Isabel of the same name and the wife of the governor of Florida, Hernando de Soto: "He entered into marriage with a daughter of Pedrarias, named Elvira or Isabel, for it could be no other, according to the daughters of Pedrarias mentioned in the will that the old captain, who was from a line of Jews turned Christian, dictated before he set off for Castilla del Oro" (Majó 2: 929). Majó goes on to describe Pedrarias's daughters in   unflattering terms: "Doña Elvira and Doña Isabel, children when Pedrarias went off to the Indies, who in

1536—twenty-two years later—would be dull spinsters in a misty spinsterhood" (2: 929). Further on, when the same author describes the marriage between Hernando de Soto and Isabel de Bobadilla, he again displays his clear prejudices: "It was an artificial marriage, well thought out by old people, into which entered both calculation and a reflection of the twilight of this passion called love. Fame has portrayed Pedrarias's daughters as lanky scarecrows, veiled in black, persistent in prayer and celibate in life" (2: 290).

Note should be taken of the construction "Fame has portrayed…". Paradoxically, we have here the opposite example from the Varners' Beatriz de Bobadilla: "the lady of moral laxity." There is no escape for these women: they are either sanctimonious or very frivolous. Later Majó again labels the Isabel de Bobadilla mentioned above with the terms "austere spinster," "haughty," "stubborn spinster." It is a sad fate for these women to be prejudged for their religious belief or the actions of their forebears.

The Varners accuse another of the great women of the encounter of "blasphemy," indirectly implying that her death was brought on by the wrath of God over her evil ways. Although in this case Beatriz de la Cueva, the wife of the deceased governor of Guatemala and captain of Cortés Pedro de Alvarado, had some detractors who could not stand to see a woman in charge of governing Guatemala, she gave sufficient proof of courage and nobility throughout her life to be remembered with respect and veneration. Nonetheless, the Varners refer to her in these terms:

> When he [Alvarado] died on July 4, 1541, his widow, Beatriz de la Cueva was made gobernadora of Santiago de los Caballeros. This grief-stricken woman, approached by a priest with words of consolation broke into blasphemy against God. When on the following night a great flood swept her and six hundred others to their death, many blamed the catastrophe on her profanation. Though some thought her cadaver should have been cast to the many hungry dogs roaming the city, she was spared the ignominy (78).

It is a great injustice to run through the life a woman of this character, mentioning only a few words of desperation she spoke over the death of her husband, and condemning her forever as a "blasphemer" and the cause of the flood that took the life of a great number of persons in the region. It is a superstitious, inquisitorial accusation, linking weather phenomena to human actions. Nevertheless, this type of thinking, worthy of a medieval mentality—which is to say a closed one—has had other interpretations. Fortunately, historians with greater mental clarity and less dependence on fanatical religious manicheism give another perspective on the woman who was the first lady governor in the Americas.

If we go back to the sources of this information, it can be seen that not even Gómara (1511-59), nearly 500 years ago, dared to issue a condemnatory judgment of this woman when he explained the events that occurred. On the contrary, he was to excuse her words and actions, saying that they were said "without heart or sense:"

> Doña Beatriz behaved rashly and even spoke like a madwoman when she found out about her husband's death. She painted her house black inside and out. She cried a great deal; she did not eat, she did not sleep, she would have no consolation; and thus it is said that she answered anyone who consoled her that God had no more evil to do to her; blasphemous talk, and I think she said it without heart or sense (286).

Further on, during the dreadful storm that shook Guatemala in 1541, in which 600 persons died, among them Beatriz de la Cueva, Gómara laments the death of this woman, who would have been able to save herself if she had not left her room:

> Doña Beatriz got up at the sound and out of devotion and fear entered into a chapel of hers with eleven serving women. She went up to the altar and embraced an image, giving herself up to God. The force of the water grew and hit that room and chapel like many other rooms of the house and flooded them: it was a great pity; because if she had been in the room where she was sleeping, she would not have died (286).

Gómara recounts that during that storm all kinds of stories were heard. During the flood a cow was seen passing, carried along by the current. It had a broken horn and on the other, a rope. An "unknown" black man also went by on that street. Some said that the black man was the devil and that the cow was the daughter of a woman "whom they had flogged in Córdoba as a witch and procuress." Gómara comments on all this with a much more modern mentality than that seen in some of the previous examples: "They also tell the story that they saw in the air and heard very fearful things. That may be; but out of fear, everything is seen and understood in reverse" (286). Superstition was therefore one factor worth taking into account during these occurrences, but there were other factors worthy of consideration, such as the envy that many had toward Beatriz de la Cueva because she became governor, the first woman governor in the Americas.[15]

In his *Historia de Guatemala o recordación florida*, Francisco Antonio de Fuentes y Guzmán, defending Beatriz de la Cueva from the criticism of many who did not wish to see a woman in a position of such authority, compares the governance of Guatemala to that of the nascent European monarchies. Both the one and the other were at some time governed by women:

> And if in such ancient kingdoms, where there were men to spare, and men that they call great, such high-born women governed, what does it matter that in Goathemala, a recently founded kingdom, a woman should govern who was not of the lowest order? And more than Mexico and Lima, Goathemala will be able to count among its glories, that which the monarchies of France, England, Spain and Flanders had when the government of women governed and maintained them; this glorious occurrence in Goathemala was exemplary in our Western Indies, for, from the beginning of its infancy, it began to be on a par with the greatest monarchies of Europe. And, finally, sometimes it is better to be governed by a heroic woman than by a cowardly, weak man (286; bk. 4, ch. 7).

Still today there is resistance to accepting women in positions of high responsiblity. The texts of the encounter, as we have seen, run the risk of being judged and transformed, often in a very different way than is indicated in the original sources. The cases of these great, unknown women are only one lamentable example of the injustice and deformation that can be performed on such outstanding personages from our history.

INDIAN WOMEN ON THE EXPEDITIONS OF PÁNFILO DE NARVÁEZ AND FRANCISCO VÁZQUEZ DE CORONADO TO FLORIDA: 1528-1541

And the other women, I do not remember all their names, and it is not necessary to name some of them; but these were the first Christian women that there were in New Spain. (Bernal Díaz del Castillo, *True History of the Conquest of New Spain*, ch. 36.)

In Alvar Núñez Cabeza de Vaca's *Naufragios*, an account of Pánfilo de Narváez's failed expedition which tells of the odyssey of Alvar Núñez and his companions during an eight-year pilgrimage through North American territory—one of the most exciting "chronicles" of the encounter—mention is made in the last chapter of a group of ten women from this expedition who did not manage to go inland with the group of Governor Pánfilo de Narváez and Cabeza de Vaca. These women, of whom Cabeza de Vaca was to receive news several years later, are noteworthy not only because they formed part of one of the first formal expeditions to Florida, but for the ease and independence with which they married and became lovers of other men, seeing that their husbands had already given them up for lost. It should be noted, however, that a large part of the information presented in this work is taken from the imagination of the author himself:

At that time when they had gone back onto the ships, they say that those persons who were there saw and heard very clearly how that woman said to the other women that, since their husbands were going inland and putting their persons at such great risk, they should by no means take the husbands into account; and that they should then see whom they were going to marry because she was going to do so, and so she did. She and the other women married and became lovers of those men who stayed on the ships; and after the ships left there, they set sail and continued their voyage (220-221; ch. 38).

It is clear, once again, that when the conquistadores and settlers had the even the least hope of carrying out their intentions, they sailed with their wives. The event narrated above took place in Florida in 1528.

There is also information about a fact that would be repeated successively and involuntarily throughout the encounter: double marriages. The concern of women in those first years was as great as the uncertainty of duration of the unions, since there were many conquistadores who died in the line of duty. Many women, giving up their husbands for lost, entered into marriage again. This was the case when Gonzalo de Salazar, who had remained in command of New Spain while Cortés made his expedition to Las Higueras, publicly announced the failure of Cortés's journey and his death. Many of the wives of the absent soldiers, believing themselves widows, married again (Fernández Duro 17).

Alvar Núñez Cabeza de Vaca's work *Naufragios* is important, among other reasons, because it informed us, for the first time about the different Indian tribes of the Southwest of the present-day United States, although I repeat that many times the information may not necessarily be reliable.[16] In any case, mentioned on numerous occasions are different groups of native women that are worthy of attention, among other reasons, because the protagonist spent—there is no doubt of this—nine years in the Southwest of what is today the United States and in northern Mexico. These Indian women show up on several occasions in Alvar Núñez's work, always in an impersonal but nonetheless meaningful way. They are the women who on more than one occasion functioned as interpreters between Cabeza de Vaca's "group" and some tribes. The small group of surviving Christians therefore depended on the mediation and communication that these women undertook with the different tribes: "Because women can make contact, even though a war may be going on" (187; ch. 30).

> When we wished to take our leave of them, some women from other Indians who lived farther on arrived; and informed by them where those houses were, we set off for that place, although they begged us to stay that day because the houses where we were going were far off, and there was no path to them, and those women were tired, and when they had rested they would go with us the next day and guide us, and so we bade them farewell; and shortly thereafter the women who had come with other women from the same village came after us (175; ch. 27).

The attire and clothing of these Indian women caught the attention of the explorer from Jerez. "These people go entirely naked, in the fashion of the first ones we came across. The women go around covered with deerskin" (190; ch. 30). A bit further on he mentions other Indian women, "the most decently attired women than we had seen in any part of the Indies...They wear cotton shifts that reach their knees, and half-sleeves over them, and skirts of shaved deerskin that touch the ground; and they soap them with some roots that get them very clean, and so they keep them very well; they are open in front and tied with straps; the women wear shoes" (Núñez 194; ch. 31).

Chapter 18 provides another description of the dress of the Indian women of that area. "The women cover their private parts with grass and straw." Referring to the "Iguaz" women, he says, "The women are worked very hard and long, for of the twenty-four hours that make up day and night, they have only six hours rest" (145).

The female image is not always positive in Alvar Núñez's narration. Quite violent situations come up that say very little of the "humanity" of the Indians they meet. It is this balance in the view presented of the natives, sometimes worthy of the greatest respect, others of the greatest repugnance, that makes it possible to appreciate overall in the work its sense of "reality." Many times these Indians are imbued with drama and a novelesque character, but they are made to seem not beings with extraordinary attributes, but just another extension of humankind.

> And they told him how they had had Esquivel there, and how when he was there he sought to flee because a woman had dreamed that he was going to kill one of her children, and the Indians went after him and killed him and showed Andrés Dorantes his sword and his beads and other things that he had. They do this because of a custom they have, and that is that they kill their own children because of dreams, and when daughters are born they let dogs eat them, and they throw them out there (143; ch.18).

This passage is an example of what has been mentioned above: far from giving a stereotyped image of the natives, it offers a whole range of situations in which their virtues and defects are presented. The most paradoxical thing about this information presented by Cabeza de Vaca is that he himself, years later, on his second voyage to the Americas, this time as Adelantado and Governor of the River Plate, was to give an example of his own cruelty with the Christian slave women that he took with him.

The sexual element does not appear at any time as Cabeza de Vaca's work unfolds. Nevertheless, a few lines below the reference to the Indian women mentioned above, there is a possible allusion, in which the "paternity" of the events is not entirely clear. "It happened very often that some of the women who went with us gave birth" (195; ch. 31). One would have to ask if the first mestizos of the southwestern United States appeared here or whether on the contrary, the three Spaniards and the Moor, survivors of the expedition, maintained a strict sexual abstinence over the nine years that they traveled around lost. The fact is that upon arriving in Mexico, none of them mentioned any illegitimate child, mor any responsibility of that type. Logically, if the image that Alvar Núñez wishes to leave in his work is that of a "spiritual father," it would be through purification, work, and suffering—which would raise him to a "higher" moral level. When the Indian women would give birth, the "fruit of their womb" would be offered to the Spaniards to be touched and blessed: "And then when it was born they would bring us the baby to touch and bless with the sign of the cross. They would always go with us until they left us with others, and among all these people there was a strong belief that we had come from heaven" (195; ch. 31).

The "Mariame" Indians mentioned above had the custom of giving their daughters to the dogs to eat (143; ch.18), because if the daughters married the other Indians—all of whom were enemies—the latter would multiply in such a way that in a short time the Mariames would become their slaves, for which reason it was much safer to kill recently born daughters so as to avoid such an upheaval. The solution that the Christians proposed to these Indians, according to Alvar Núñez, is itself hardly orthodox: "We asked them why they did not marry them among themselves. And among themselves they also said that it was an ugly thing to marry women to their relatives and that it was much better to kill them and give them to their enemies" (143; ch. 18). Here one can see a clear allusion to incest as a solution to the problem. For their part the Indians solved the problem by "buying" women from their enemies, although "the marriage does not last beyond the time when they are content, and they undo the marriage with an amulet" (Núñez 143; ch. 18).

In Chapter 19, Alvar Núñez presents another scene that could very well have taken place in one of the typical Hollywood western saloons. The fighting among Indians forced the Christians to separate for a year, during which time the author of the *Naufragios* had to flee his masters three times because of hunger and "because of the bad treatment that I received from the Indians," as Alvar Núñez puts it: "The Indians we were with fought each other over a woman and punched and thrashed each other and beat each other's heads; and with the great anger that they had, each one took his household and went to his place" (148; ch. 19).

As Alvar Núñez's testimony seems to indicate, women in these native societies did not always have the advantage. In some circumstances, the Indians "became intoxicated with a smoke, and they give everything they have for it," (172; ch. 26). and when they drank a substance taken from trees, which they prepared over a fire, shouting during the procedure, if any woman moved about in that situation they would rape and beat her. They threw out the substance they were drinking because they said that something evil would enter their body and make them die. These Indians' opinion of the female sex was quite negative, even when the Indian women were having their menstrual period: "And when the women are in their time, they search for food only for themselves because no other person will eat what they bring" (173; ch. 26).

Some years later, due to the account given by Alvar Núñez Cabeza de Vaca upon arriving in Mexico, a very large expedition was organized: some thousand Indians, 336 Spaniards, 250 of them on horseback, not counting their women and children, and more than a thousand horses and mules for provisioning. At the head of the expedition marched Francisco Vázquez de Coronado, who with the support of Viceroy Antonio de Mendoza and that of his own adventurous spirit, managed to set out on what was expected to be another conquest of Mexico or Peru. Coronado crowned his ambitions by marrying the rich and beautiful Beatriz Estrada. There are some data on the amounts invested in the expedition: 60,000 ducats by Viceroy Mendoza and 50,000 more from Coronado, most of this raised thanks to the mortgages taken out on Doña Beatriz's properties. The rest was contributed by gentlemen who participated in the expedition. Doña Beatriz de Estrada was therefore an indispensable and most valuable element in the realization of this enterprise. The history of the encounter, whether in Mexico, Peru, or any other place in the Americas, is full of exemplary women who contributed to the extent of their possibilities to the most arduous, self-sacrificing tasks. They spurred the men on to combat and cared for the wounded, giving an example and inspiration to those who were at their side (Boxer 48-49): "In a *cédula real* addressed to the citizens of Arequipa on 19 September 1580, Philip II expresses his gratitude for the way in which they, and more especially their wives, had answered his appeal for a voluntary contribution to meet the vast expenses of his wars against Turks, infidels, and heretics in Europe" (Boxer 48-49).

One of the most notable institutions on Coronado's expedition on which we have information is that of the "soldaderas," women who accompanied their husbands and sons to the end of their endeavors. Some of the names of these women included the following: Francisca de Hozes, the wife of Alonso Sánchez; María Maldonado, the wife of the tailor Juan de Paradinas; and Señora Caballero, the wife of Lope Caballero. As for María de Hozes, the American historian Herbert E. Bolton, who devoted most of his life to studying the Spanish expeditions in the United States, comments the following: "She had both mind and tongue of her own. María Maldonado, an early Florence Nightingale, nursed sick soldiers, mended their ragged garments, and was generally regarded as an angel of mercy" (Bolton 62).

Around that same time, 1541, somewhat farther south in Guatemala, as we have seen, Beatriz de la Cueva, the wife of Pedro de Alvarado, Cortés's captain, took charge of governing Guatemala when her husband died. Thus, only twenty years after Cortés's conquest of Mexico, in 1541, the first woman governor in the Americas appears, and Beatriz de Estrada helped to finance an expedition to what would later be United States territory.

There are numerous isolated cases of women, Indians and Spaniards, who in one or another place of the remote regions of the American lands would be involved in an event worthy of mention.[17] Elizabeth Salas gives an example of Indian women defending their territory during the Castaño de Sosa expedition to the village of Pecos (New Mexico). In this case the Spaniards saw that the Indians were armed on the roofs of their adobe houses and on the ground. When Lieutenant Castaño went to demand the surrender of the town, all he received was the ashes that an Indian woman threw down at him from one of the houses (Salas 20-21).

The immense geographic difficulties present in the most remote areas were not enough to break the spirit of these women. In 1569, the Spaniard Catalina Plasencia de Bazán, accompanied by her daughter María Bazán and her grandchildren, had to go through the Humahuca Gorge in order to meet her husband. When the caravan she was traveling in was attacked, she managed to flee and arrive at Talavera after a long, difficult journey (Villafañe 136-137).

If we were to look for specific precedents, equivalent women who fought to defend their lives and that of their families even in situations where defeat seemed imminent, we could go to the origins of humanity, but the Crusades are a good example. In the battle of Dorylaeum (1097), close to the city of Eskisheir, the Christian troops, accompanied by women, met the Turkish troops: "Although we had no hope of resisting them or of bearing the pressure of such superior force, yet we persevered steadfastly there with unanimity. The women who accompanied us assisted our forces greatly on this day by bringing drinking water to the warriors and at all times shouting encouragement to those who fought and defended them" (Tudebode 34-35).

There were not a few acts of heroism among women who participated in the encounter and in the defense of the Americas, just as there were not a few cases of courage among women in the history of Spain. Several chronicles recorded evidence of the valor of some women who in many cases encouraged and accompanied their husbands and male companions in launching the riskiest enterprises.

WOMEN AND SLAVERY

> For liberty and also for honor one can and should risk one's life; and
> on the contrary, captivity is the greatest evil that befall men.
> (Cervantes, *Don Quixote.*)

The relationship between Spanish women and slavery can be divided into
two parts: first, the Spanish women who were in charge of Indian male
and female slaves, generally because they inherited an encomienda, or
some repartimiento, and secondly, those Spanish women who were
themselves taken as slaves from Spain to the Americas. Not so much
has been written about this latter group, as will be seen a bit further on.

From the outset, those Spanish men who moved to the newly
discovered territories with their wives had more privileges than the rest
in the sense of receiving a greater number of Indians. The following
case exemplifies the benefits of those who would arrive in the Indies with
their own wives. In the time of Diego Colón, Christopher Columbus's
son, the proportion varied between the hundred Indians who were to be
given to the fortress commanders and oficials who were married, and the
thirty that were given to farmhands who came with their wives (Zavala,
La encomienda 834). Likewise, there is documentation that mentions
women as owners of "Indians" on their encomiendas, as was the case of
Doña Catalina de la Cruz (Zavala, *La encomienda* 834).

Contrary to what some historians choose to believe, the Spanish
government made laws for the protection of the Indians. As Silvio A.
Zavala tells us in his exhaustive study on the topic, "The encomendero
had to defend and shelter the Indians and could not allow them to be
mistreated. He had to provide them with instruction" (Zavala, *La
encomienda* 834). Once again a kind of parallelism can be seen with the
traditional Medieval structure: the master's role as protector vis-à-vis the
serf's vassalage and service. From existing information one gathers that
at the very least serious thought went into the treatment that should be
applied to the Indians, and in this particular case, Indian women.

As the encounter went on, the legal process in favor of the Indians
went on; they had ever more defenders in both the civil and the
ecclesiastic sphere. In 1528, Emperor Charles V dictated other
ordinances in Toledo, in which the natives were protected against
possible abuse by their encomenderos in the matter of transporting cargo.
As for Indian women, he ordered: "that they not have the wives of the
encomienda Indians making bread for the slaves who work in the mines,

nor in other services without giving them a salary" (Zavala, *La encomienda* 54).

Unfortunately, the laws protecting the Indians arrived too late in the Antilles, where the Indians were practically eliminated. On the other hand, these initiatives favoring the natives of the lands discovered were applied on the continent.

Within the second group of women, that is the Spanish women who went over as slaves from the Iberian peninsula, some observations are in order. The general idea exists that during the period of the encounter slaves were exclusively black or Indian. This idea is erroneous, since in Spain itself—as in many other European and Arab countries—slavery existed. Slavery is as old as humanity itself, nor was it anything new for the inhabitants of what would be called the New World, either. With regard to the number of slaves existing in Spain at the end of the sixteenth century, Domínguez Ortiz estimates their number as 100,000. The majority of them were located in Andalusia and also in the Madrid and Valladolid courts. Only the Basque country was free of slaves. Their price ranged around one hundred ducats (Ubieto, Reglá, Jover, and Seco 324).

This information gives an idea of how slavery was not exclusive to the encounter of America. On the other hand, it is interesting to verify that this practice also included "white women" and also Christian women, who were taken to the Americas together with their masters. The treatment accorded these slaves could vary considerably from one country to another. In his article "Esclavas blancas en las Indias occidentales," published in 1927, Jose Torre Revelló extracted a series of very valuable documents on the subject from the Archivo General de Indias in Seville. He begins his article by saying that some of these white slave women "were branded with hot irons." The strangest thing is that one of the most famous explorers of the encounter, considered by many as a "saint," was in his time responsible for the decision to do this. The always polemical explorer from Jerez, Alvar Núñez Cabeza de Vaca, by both word and deed, was responsible for one of the most ignoble actions of those carried out in the Americas, although in this case, unfortunately, it was generalized practice in Europe. Once he was named adelantado, captain-general, and governor of the River Plate, Alvar Núñez, the supposed "Messiah of the New World," issued a proclamation that royal officials should have an iron made to brand slaves brought from Spain.[18] It is known that there were white Christian women among these slaves, and that some were branded on their faces (Torre 263n.). "Some white slave women were branded with hot irons, a procedure also followed with the Indians, and which in the case of blacks was abolished in the eighteenth century" (Torre 263). In one of the documents quoted in this article, a series of reasons was presented, worth our attention, justifying the importation of white slave women.

It was said that the arrival of white slave women in the Indies would fill the need for women in those places where the conquistadores were marrying Indian women, "people so distant from reason."[19] Since "Indian women are people so distant from reason," serious consideration was given at the beginning of the encounter to the white slave trade so that these slaves could be married to the conquistadores. Taking into account the fact that the conquistadores were already getting married, many of them to Indian women, one has to conclude that the "lack of reason" must be attributed not to race but to the lack of Christian indoctrination. The importance of religion must have carried much more weight than we can imagine today. On this point, there is another document displaying this assertion. It is said that if Spanish men had to choose between a Castilian woman who was a *conversa* and a white Christian slave, they would always opt for the latter.[20] Evidence of this can be seen in a letter from the Catholic Monarch Ferdinand:

> Likewise you say that the Admiral and the officials who have written you from Hispaniola that white slave women should not be sent to that island because there were many young women from Castile there who were conversas and in order not to marry them they would marry said slave women, from which much disserves to us would result and harm to said island and since I have ordered an inquiry and discussions and it is found that there is no obstacle impeding the sending of said slave women, see to it that what I have ordered you about this matter of sending slave women to said island be carried out and be thorough and diligent in the matter, for I am depending on you... Logroño, on the tenth day of the month of December of the year fifteen hundred and twelve...The King (Torre 266).

It is important to note the date of the document, 1512, and the fact that the king himself states that by this time there were many Castilian women who were conversas in the Indies. This information serves, once again, to point up the early and substantial presence of Spanish women in the Americas.

In another document dated 1528 and signed by the king, reference is made to the bishop of Fernandina island (Cuba), Fray Miguel Ramírez, who had asked permission to bring two white slave women over to that island to serve him.

> Inasmuch as you, the venerable and devout father and teacher Fray Miguel Ramírez, bishop of Fernandina island told me that you went over to that island and you should like to take two white slave women there and you petition and request that by my grace I order license to be given to take them freely without paying any fees or whatever shall be my will, and I looked favorably upon it, and by this letter I give you license and permission so that from these kingdoms of ours you can take over and will take over to said island these two slave women, and we order the officials who reside in the city of Seville in the Casa de la Contratación of the Indies that they allow and permit you to take these two slave women freely and unhindered without putting any hindrance or impediment up before you and that they and our officials on said island not ask of you or require any fees. Madrid, on the twentieth day of March of the year fifteen hundred and twenty-eight (Torre 267).[21]

Also preserved is another official document relating to the slave trade, signed by the queen ten years later, to the effect that three white slave women could be transported to Cuba. The most important aspect of this document is the fact that the request came from Isabel de Bobadilla, the daughter of the other Isabel with the same name and Pedro Arias Dávila, mentioned above. The quoted document also says tht these three slave women are "Christians and women of good life and reputation" (Torre 268). It reads:

> To you, our officials who reside in the city of Seville in the Casa of the Indies: Doña Isabel de Bobadilla, wife of the adelantado Don Hernando de Soto, our governor and captain-general of the province of Florida, has told me that she has three white slave women who are good Christians and women of good life and reputation, whom she would like to have with her to serve her person and house on the island of Cuba, and she petitioned me to give her license for that or whatever shall be my will; therefore I order you to make inquiries and find out who the above-mentioned slave women are and to make sure that they were Christians before they were twelve years old and that they are servants of said Doña Isabel, and when she takes them with her to said

island of Cuba you allow and permit them to go over there for her and
that you neither put up any impediment nor allow any to be put up...In
the city of Valladolid, on the sixteenth day of the month of February
of fifteen hundred and thirty-eight years. The Queen (Torre 268).

This is not the only information concerning these three slaves. It is
known that one of them was married in Havana in 1538 and had two
daughters. This slave, named Isabel, returned to Spain with her
daughters, and the by then widow Doña Isabel de Bobadilla, leaving her
husband, "the fisherman Alberto Díez," on the island of Cuba. It
appears that back in Spain, at the time that the slave Isabel wished to
return to her husband in Cuba, the members of the Casa de la
Contratación in Seville put up barriers to her return. Then Isabel de
Bobadilla asked for help so that her slave could fulfill her desire and go
back to her husband. Thanks to this, we have the following document
signed by then Prince Philip in 1546. The prince would become the king
of Spain, Philip II, ten years later in 1556:

> To you, officials of the Emperor and King my lord who reside in the
> city of Seville in the Casa de la Contratación of the Indies: I have been
> told by Doña Isabel de Bobadilla, the widowed wife of the Adelantado
> Don Hernando de Soto, that at the time when she and her said husband
> went over to the Indies, among the other people they took with them
> was *a white slave woman branded on her face* born in that city, whose
> name is Isabel and that after her husband died, she freed her; in
> Havana said Isabel married Alberto Díez, a fisherman, by whom she
> now has two daughters...I order you to allow and permit said Isabel to
> go over to said city of Havana to live with her husband and to take
> with her the children that she may have and that you neither put up any
> impediment nor allow any to be put up. Dated in the city of Madrid
> on January 13 of the year 1546 (Torre 269).

This is a most precious document which gives us more information
about the situation of some of Isabel de Bobadilla's slave women and
also of Philip II, when he judged that the rights of the morisca
(converted Moorish) slave woman "Isabel" took precedence over the
Council of the Indies bureaucracy. The Sevillian slave mentioned, who
was "branded on her face," was probably bought to serve in the house
of the then adelantado and governor of Florida, Hernando de Soto. It is
usually thought that since these persons had had a different religion, in
this case Jewish or Islamic, they did not belong to the group of

Spaniards. Lockhart, however, stresses the facility that these groups had for adapting and being accepted by the majority (Lockhart 151).

The "conversa" slave women were Spanish by birth and most of them were of Caucasian origin. The "moriscas conversas" were in reality as Spanish as the Christian women, and their integration into Christian society was no novelty. It was a process that went on throughout the entire Christian reconquest in Spain. There were also mulatto women born and educated in Spain who spoke Spanish as their first language. They often gained their freedom, and when this would occur, they would occupy positions equivalent to those of Spanish Christian women, and would even marry Spanish men (Lockhart 151). There was in principle no reson not to put them on an equal social level with other Spanish women. Even King Ferdinand decided not to have more slave women sent, since there were already enough "conversa" women.

The most moving thing is to observe how Isabel de Bobadilla, as soon as she was widowed, freed her slave woman so that she could "live with her husband," the fisherman Alberto Díez. She likewise helped her again when "Isabel" wished to return to her husband in Havana and was not being allowed to do so.

GUIOMAR THE SLAVE: FIRST QUEEN OF AMERICA

One cannot go through the history of the Americas without mentioning incidents that attract attention more for their strangeness than for their historical dimension. This is the case of the proclamation of the first queen in America: Queen Guiomar. The event occurred near the Venezuelan municipality of Barquisimeto in 1552. It is the unusual case of a black slave woman who was the lover of the intrepid black man Miguel, who managed to free himself from the power of his Spanish masters and organized a mass uprising in the mines where he worked, losing his life in the effort. This black slave was not only capable of freeing himself, but he time and again stood up to the Spaniards with a bravery and an impact rarely seen in the events of the encounter.

When the municipality of Barquisimeto had been founded and the settlers saw the profits they could make, they decided to put more than eighty blacks in the mines to help the salaried miners, who would be in charge of "keeping them in line." One of those miners, Pedro Barrios, decided to punish one of the black men by whipping him. When the black saw that he was surrounded, he seized a sword and defended himself, escaping into the mountains. This charismatic black, who spoke Spanish as well as his masters, was able to hold the entire Spanish garrison in check (Fernández de Piedrahita 91-92; bk. 11, ch.7). Miguel successfully convinced twenty Indians and blacks from the settlement to follow him and thus be able to enjoy the freedom that their Spanish masters denied them. Some of the fugitives managed to take some weapons when they fled, using them some days later at night in an attack on the mines. During the attack they killed, and severely tortured, those miners from whom they had received lashes and took the others prisoner; later they freed them so they could go to Barquisimeto and recount what had occurred. The men freed went with the message that Miguel intended to destroy Barquisimeto and was informing them so that his victory would be even more resounding (Fernández de Piedrahita 91-92; bk.11, ch.7).

When the slave Miguel had managed to gain the complicity of other blacks and many of the Spanish-speaking Indians who wanted freedom as much as he did, and who respected and feared him, he proclaimed his lover Guiomar "queen" and the son he had had with her "prince." With the approval and applause of his subjects, he proclaimed himself king and named ministers and officials. But the bold Miguel was not content with this; so as not to leave untended the spiritual part of his ephemeral kingdom, he even named one of the blacks who was with him "bishop." A church was built for the new prelate to preach to his new congregation (Fernández de Piedrahita 92-93; bk. 11, ch 7).

A man capable of fighting for his freedom in this way is worthy of respect. The bias of the chronicler of this event, Fernández de Piedrahita, does not do justice to the figure of a person who, being neither Indian or Spanish, had sufficient ability to lead and courage to proclaim himself king and fight his oppressors on an equal basis. Queen Guiomar and her son returned to slavery once Miguel and his men had been defeated by the Spanish troops. The story of this extraordinary occurrence ends with the following words of historian Piedrahita:

> Thus attacked by our men, the adversaries did not lose their spirit, for following their king, who encouraged them with his voice and his example, they began to defend the entrance, where despite their resistance the Spaniards drove them back to a short distance from a place where Miguel, pressed hard together with his people, did everything befitting a valiant king, until, falling to the repeated thrusts of two blades, he dismayed with his death the spirit of those remaining (93; bk. 11, ch.7).

Once Miguel was dead, the Spaniards imprisoned "Queen" Guiomar and her son, returning them to their original slavery, putting a tragic end to that unprecedented, ephemeral kingdom. Life is worth sacrificing if it is reduced to a sterile, humiliating, unfree existence.

LA MALINCHE AND GUADALUPE

Many thinkers of world stature make judgments that go beyond simple and sometimes arbitrary geographic-political borders. One example is the Mexican thinker Octavio Paz, who explains in simple fashion the complex and often painful subject of Mexican national character.

> We twentieth-century Mexicans, even those of pure Indian descent, look on the pre-Columbian world as a world on the *other side*, not only distant in time but across the cultural divide. Clearly—although official opinion due to an intellectual and moral aberration does not accept it—that there are greater affinities between independent Mexico and New Spain than between them and pre-Hispanic societies (Paz *Sor Juana* 25).

The direct result of this complex Mexican way of thinking is the personage of Doña Marina, "La Malinche," Cortés's companion, whom Mexicans and foreigners have written a great deal about, idealized, and demonized on numerous occasions. To begin with, it is worth mentioning the connotation given to the term "malinchista." In his book *El laberinto de la soledad*, Octavio Paz complains that for some time the press has put the term "malinchista" in circulation as an equivalent for anything that betrays the Mexican people on account of being "corrupted" by outside, foreign influences.[22]

Octavio Paz goes on to discuss the constant bipolarity in which Doña Marina is presented. Like Christopher Columbus or Hernán Cortés, she has been pulled back and forth between the status of heroine and that of exterminator. Cortés's "tongue" has been called a "traitor bitch" (*chingada traidora*) and a "faithful lover." Octavio Paz says, "Doña Marina has become a figure who represents the Indian women fascinated, raped or seduced by the Spaniards. And in the same way that the child does not forgive his mother who abandons him to go seeking after his father, the Mexican people does not forgive la Malinche for her betrayal" (Paz 77-78).

Was Doña Marina ever conscious of the concept of a "Mexican people?" It seems too much to place all the weight of responsibility for the conquest of Mexico on a single woman. On the other hand, this has its advantages. From the national-indigenist point of view, it is much easier to blame a defeat on the person of one woman than on that of a whole people. There is nothing new in this. In Spain, the "one to blame," according to the popular ballads or *romances* for the entry of

Muslim troops into the Iberian peninsula was another woman: Florinda, known as "La Cava." In order to avenge the rape committed against her by the last Visigothic king, Rodrigo, she told her father Count Julián to open the doors to the Arab invasion and consequently to the "loss" of Spain. There is no need to dwell here on the incalculable value of the contribution of Islamic culture to Spain. If we go back a bit further into Classical literature we shall see how in the wars between Greeks and Trojans, Princess Helen was the one who "provoked" the conflict between those two peoples. It is hardly necessary to say that there are many other cases like those already mentioned, where the woman is used as the scapegoat, the best-known being those of Ariadne—the daughter of King Minos, who provided Theseus with the string which helped him out of the labyrinth to then kill the minotaur, and who was later abandoned by him—or Tarpeia, who gave the citadel of Rome over to the Sabines and was later killed by them. Some of these legends have their origin at the beginning of our civilization, as in the case of humanity's oldest epic, in which Ishtar, the Babylonian goddess of fertility who helped the legendary hero Gilgamesh to make his conquests, was later rejected. Nor is it necessary to mention that the person responsible for the fact that the earthly paradise cannot be enjoyed in the Judeo-Christian world was Eva, who tempted the innocent Adam to eat the prohibited fruit, according to the Old Testament. All of which shows that it is much easier to blame a defeat or calamity on a woman than to accept the enemy's victory.

As for La Malinche, it is worth presenting, even if only in passing, some biographic facts which will help to draw the real portrait of the person in question:

> Malintzin was the daughter of the nobles and chieftains of a village called Painalá, eight leagues from Coatzacoalcos, who possessed several other villages in that area. Her father having died when she was very young, her mother was married again to another chieftain, by whom she had a son, who promptly replaced the future Marina in the affections of her mother. The latter and her new husband agreed to make their son the heir of the chieftainship, and since the girl was in the way, they decided to hand her over to some Indians from Xicalanco and they announced that she had died. Later the people from Xicalanco turned her over to those of Tabasco and they turned her over to Hernán Cortés (Díaz 61; ch. 37).

It is difficult to call this woman the "traitor of the Mexican people."
It was rather she who was betrayed by her people. The same happens
with the legend of Quetzalcatl, when it is stated that in a certain way the
Aztecs were already predisposed to being defeated. There appears to be
a strong necessity to expiate the guilt for a people's defeat through
defenseless beings or myths that somehow justify the events that have
occurred. Paradoxically, the events in history often occur inversely from
the way they are presented: "As Carlos Pereyra wrote, the Indians made
the Conquest and the Spaniards the independence. Malintzin-Doña
Marina symbolizes in exemplary fashion the fascination felt by the
Amerindians in the presence of the invaders, in the same way that Cortés
himself constitutes the paradigm of the contrary phenomenon: the
conquistador conquered by his conquest" (Delgado 109).

The opposite pole from "La Malinche" in Mexico would be the
"Virgin of Guadalupe," one of the most important institutions within
Mexican popular culture. The Virgin of Guadalupe is a perfect example
of the cultural and religious syncretism undertaken by the Catholic
church when it entered into contact with other cultures. In 1531, only
ten years after the conquest, the Indian Juan Diego swore that he had
seen the Virgin of Guadalupe in the same place that had previously been
devoted to the worship of the Mexica goddesses Toci and Tonantzin
(Salas 24).

The Spanish image of the Virgin of Guadalupe is found in the village
of the same name: Guadalupe (Extremadura). It is interesting to
observe how even in the name there is an implicit union of two hybrid
Arabic-Latin words: River of wolves. There is no exact account of its
origins, although the legend takes them back to St. Luke the evangelist:
"Almost all the famous images of Christian iconography retain a kind of
vestige of melancholy and taste for the primordial and mysterious"
(García and Trenado 23). The image conserved today in the monastery
of the Extremaduran village is a seated wooden figure made out of cedar,
in the Romanesque style, not earlier than the eleventh or twelfth
centuries.

The Virgin of Guadalupe was in fact the first image that Columbus
visited after his first voyage, the same way that King Philip II and Cortés
and many other explorers passed through Extremadura for that sole
purpose. Nevertheless, in spite of all the popularity that this image
acquired in Spain, above all in the sixteenth century, it never reached the

extremes that it did in Mexico. Even today, many Mexicans are Guadalupans before they are Mexicans.

Fortunately in present-day Mexico, ever more people have opted to accept both the pre-Columbian and the Hispanic past, since to deny one of them would be to deny their own identity; the same would happen if a Spaniard should deny his Semitic past.

In fact, a parallel phenomenon has occurred in Spain with the Muslim past. In its teaching over the centuries, the Catholic Church has depicted non-Christian cultures as foreign, non-Spanish, when in reality the Spanish national character cannot be understood without its Latin, Jewish or Islamic heritage. For some time now, fortunately, that interpretation of our past has been to a large extent corrected. It would be as absurd to accept La Malinche's guilt in the defeat of the Aztecs as to accept the defeat of the Hispanovisigothic troops as the fault of the sexual excesses of Don Rodrigo with "La Cava."

In short, in one or another case, the women were there. Whether they were Spanish or Amerindian, a new society was being created in the Americas:

> A complete world, made to last and with aspirations of perfection, which is born and develops in America as a result of the Spanish presence and action on that continent. A world whose birth would have been impossible without the collaboration of the Amerindian woman and without the humanistic and universal sense of the Spaniards, free of the racial prejudices that limited other peoples, and the creators of an authentic trans-humanism, in which they gave place and equal status to all people on earth (Delgado 111).

It was the accumulation of hatred and intrigue among the different European economic interests on the one hand, and the lack of vision of the Spanish government with respect to overseas policy on the other which in many cases gave rise to animosity among the Spaniards themselves born on one or the other side of the Atlantic and precipitated the independence of these peoples from Spain. Still today it is possible to see this animosity in a country so beloved and so similar to Spain as Mexico.

The female presence was, as can be seen in the following quotation from Analola Borges, a key factor by which this whole social meshing began to take shape.

We do not doubt that the charater of the settler women, accepting their destiny, almost always heroic, provided that "illumination" and "modernization" that has had historical, sociolgical, and vital repercussions in the formation of the community of Hispanic nations with a unique style that was given to it by the women of that time. The firmness and solidity of the home with which the Spanish woman imbued her family, the basis of American settlement, makes them the real founder of the Indies. Had it not been so, the discovery enterprise would have remained an exploitative colonization or a commercial agency, within a territory having a hybrid, frustrated population (Borges 410).

That hybrid, frustrated population which Borges speaks of is obvious, above all, in those colonizations where there was no racial mixture nor cultural adoption of any type of the cultures that were conquered. Spain took to America a multinational and multiracial culture with heroes, heroines, and traitors, united by a multitude of successes and mistakes, but ultimately united by a language and blood that was in many cases common.

PART THREE: WOMEN-AT-ARMS IN LITERATURE AND HISTORY

WOMEN IN LITERATURE AND LITERARY LIFE OF THE PERIOD: LAURENCIA AND AMARILIS

Women have always been present in Spanish literature and history, from their beginnings. Castilian queens like Doña Urraca (1080-1126) or María de Molina (1265-1321) showed, from the inception of the history of the kingdoms of the Iberian peninsula, what a woman is capable of. Doña Urraca did not have an easy life. In 1107, she lost her husband, and one year later (1108) her brother, Sancho, and the year after that her father Alfonso VI of Castile. As if this were not enough, on many occasions she had to face enemies as powerful as her new husband, Alfonso I the Battler of Aragon, who shut her up in the fortress of El Castellar. Urraca escaped, meeting him later with her own armies, and being defeated in the battle of Cadespina. She also showed her capacity for decisiveness, confronting Bishop Gelmírez, whom she ordered imprisoned. María de Molina, for her part, had one of the most turbulent lives with respect to the rights of succession. She managed to defend the rights of her family with diplomacy, intelligence, and courage right up to her death. Her life inspired Tirso de Molina's play *La prudencia en la mujer*.

Leaving aside those marvelous displays of early Spanish-language lyric known as the "jarchas," where the poet has a young women voice feelings of love during her lover's absence, describing the pain of separation, there are also numerous examples of female protagonists in works more solidly based in Spanish. A suitable beginning is found in the first great Medieval epic, the *Poema de Mio Cid* (1150). Here female characters acquire respect and importance within the period context. Since this work is so clearly historical, it leads one to believe that the overall attitude of that era was not very misguided. For example, when Pedro Bermúdez, one of the Cid's men, accuses one of the princes of Carrión of a "lack of honor," he tells him:

I will fight it out here   before King Alfonso
for the daughters of the Cid,   Doña Elvira and Doña Sol,
because you abandoned them   I now defame you.
They are women   and you are men;
in every way   they are worth more than you (*Poem of el Cid* 285).

This is not the only instance in the poem where the importance of women is stressed. A few verses before the end, by way of a moral, the minstrel tells us, speaking in reference to the Cid's daughters, "May whoever injures a good woman   and abandons her afterwards / Suffer as great harm as this and worse, besides" (*Poem of el Cid* 311).

It is interesting to observe how only a few centuries later, in 1619, the most prolific Spanish author of all time, Lope de Vega, published his play *Fuente Ovejuna*, with a female character who could very well have been inspired in a heroine of the chronicles of the encounter. It is well known that Lope was a great reader of all kinds of books, from which he very often derived the source of the plots of his plays (Lope 13). And historical readings most often inspired Lope's genius: "Books of a historical nature were an important area where he found inspiration to go on writing the *comedias* which were impatiently awaited by actors and public" (Lope 13).

In any case, the character of Laurencia in *Fuente Ovejuna* possesses all the power and drama of an Eufemia, the female protagonist of Villagrá's *Historia de la Nueva México* or of a Mencía de Nidos, the female protagonist of Ercilla's *La araucana*. She is a leader capable of encouraging with word and deed the courage needed from those around her. These Spanish women from both sides of the Atlantic were true examples of what became known as the "manly woman" in Spanish drama (McKendric 43). It was extraordinary circumstances such as the need to go to unknown lands sometimes, or a propensity and natural inclination for adventure other times, that made these women depart from the general norm of women of their time and status.

> The interest, sometimes scandalous, they aroused might have made them the source of the literary phenomenon. It would certainly have indicated to dramatists and theatre managers that such characters would have very great audience appeal (McKendrick 43).

These "women-at-arms" characters could not go unnoticed in the theater of the period, especially in those cases where the female protagonists were magnificent examples, full of dramatic possibilities. The debate over the position of woman as a "moral entity," the existence of these new liberated women, and the ideas of Erasmus on the matter all influenced the Golden Age theater, which was distinctly popular in character, to echo that reality, although not all the theatrical possibilities that the topic merited were exploited (McKendric 44).

Lope's genius got the most out of the character of Laurencia in the most moving scene of *Fuente Ovejuna*, which is the brilliant Spanish playwright's most popular work of those staged in recent times (Lope

10). Laurencia is brutally raped by the Comendador Fernán Gómez, and she comes before the council of men to potest their lack of courage before the tyrant.

I was taken
    Under your eyes to Fernán Gómez' house
    While you looked on like coward shepherds, letting
    The wolf escape uninjured with the sheep.

    They set their daggers to my breasts! The vileness
    And filth of what they said to me! The threats
    They made to tear me limb from limb! The foul
    And bestial tricks by which they tried to have me!
    Do you not see my hair torn out? These cuts
    And bruises and the bleeding flesh that shows
    Through my torn rags? You call yourselves true men?
    Are you my parents and relations, you
    Whose entrails do not burst with grief to see me
    Reduced to this despair? You're all tame sheep!
    Fuente Ovejuna means the fount where sheep drink—
    And now I see the reason! Cowards, give
    Me weapons! You are stones and bronze and marble
    And tigers—tigers? no! for tigers follow
    The stealers of their cubs, and kill the hunters
    Before they can escape back to their ships.
    No, you are craven rabbits, mice, and hares!
    You are not Spaniards but barbarian slaves!
    Yes, you are hens to suffer that your women
    By brutal force should be enjoyed by others.
    Put spindles in your belts. Why wear those swords?
    As God lives now, I shall make sure that women
    Alone redeem our honour from these tyrants,
    And make these traitors bleed! And as for you,
    You chickenhearted nancy-boys and sissies,
    Spinning-wheel gossips and effeminate cowards,
    We will throw stones at you...(Lope, *Life* 115-16).

Laurencia's stance when she insults the men of Fuente Ovejuna, calling them "cowards" and telling them to put on "spindles"[23] instead of swords, is not unknown in the history of the conquest. During the conquest of Mexico (1519-21), one hundred years before the publication of Lope's play, there is a record of two women, Beatriz and Francisca de Ordaz, who said substantially the same thing to soldiers of Narváez's troops, when they were subdued and dominated by those of Cortés. As is well known, Cortés, with a much smaller number of soldiers, managed to take the encampment of Narváez's men by surprise, taking him prisoner and simultaneously earning the cooperation and the respect of his soldiers. The testimony to this event is as follows:

> Some women, one called Francisca de Ordaz and the other Beatriz de Ordaz, sisters or relatives, coming to a window, knowing that Narváez had been taken prisoner and his men had surrendered without resistance, said in a loud voice: knaves, monks, humiliated cowards who should carry spindles rather than swords; you have given good account of yourselves; by this cross we shall give our bodies in front of you to the serving men of those who have defeated you, and so much the worse for the women who came with such men (Cervantes de Salazar 23; bk. 4, ch. 86)!

The resemblance between Laurencia's insults and those of the Ordaz sisters is striking. If Laurencia calls the men of her people "sissies," among other things, the Ordaz sisters swear that they will give their bodies to the servants of Cortés's men, "in the presence" of Narváez's men, to the ridicule and shame of the latter. This threat is noteworthy not only for its moral content, nor because it was made by women, but because of the time when it occurred, a period that was not so morally rigid as we might believe if we based ourselves on the information presented in many documents of the time. On the other hand, given the dramatic possibilities of the event, it would not be ill-advised to think that Lope had based his character Laurencia on one taken from these real events which occurred during the most critical moments of the conquest. The Ordaz sisters, of course, were flesh-and-blood persons. Biographical information exists about them, in which it is stated that they were also sisters of the conquistador Diego de Ordaz, and that they defended Cortés in Mexico City from his enemies: "Francisca was a 'very valiant woman, she did very good deeds,' and married Juan González de León; Beatriz married the professed Jew Hernando Alonso, who was sentenced for his religion (1528). They had both arrived in Mexico with Hernán Cortés's fleet"(Borges 421-22).

Did Lope de Vega have any contact with ladies on the other side of the Atlantic? It would appear he did. He maintained an epistolary relationship with a Peruvian woman poet, known by the pseudonym

'Amarilis,' who with the Atlantic in between, allowed herself liberties and amorous hints that she otherwise would not have done. Addressing Lope, the poet says:

> I wish, then, to begin to tell you
> Of my parents and land and of my station,
> So you will know who loves you and writes you:
> Although now memory torments me,
> Renewing my pain, which though wept over
> Is present and lives in the soul...(Menéndez 82).

Menéndez y Pelayo discusses her and her relationship with the "Phoenix of Geniuses:" "Before 1621, she wrote to Lope de Vega, of whom she was a fervent admirer, an elegant epistle in *silva* meter, which with Lope de Vega's reply in tercets (*Belardo a Amarilis*) was inserted at the end of his *Filomena*" (Menéndez 81).

The Spanish critic also provides biographical data on Amarilis, a figure who has been unjustly shunted aside to a very secondary position in many anthologies and literary histories, where she does not even always appear. Fortunately, Menéndez y Pelayo saw fit to devote needed attention to her to make up for this lack as far as was possible. It is speculated that the lady in question was born in the city of León de Huánuco, also called León de los Caballeros, forty leagues north of Lima, and descended from the conquistadores of that area, who were likewise founders of that city (Menéndez 83-84). Her surname, according to Menéndez y Pelayo, must have been Alvarado, given that the founder of the city in question was Captain Gómez de Alvarado, the brother of Cortés's adelantado and captain, Pedro de Alvarado: "And if we observe that the poetic name *Amarilis* is commonly a disguise for *María*, we shall have the full given name and surname of the discreet young woman of Huánuco: Doña María de Alvarado" (Menéndez 83-84).

The woman poet in question attracts the attention of scholars not only because she corresponded with the most popular writer of her time and the most prolific writer in the Western world, but for the beauty and lyric quality of her verses. Calling her a "phenomenon of literary history," Menéndez y Pelayo points to the fact, extraordinary in his opinion, that any person at the beginning of the seventeenth century, without consideration of sex, far away from the great cultural centers of that time such as Mexico or Lima, could have written poetry of that quality (Menéndez 84):

> There is hardly the least trace of poor taste in her Epistle, nor of mannerism; everything is natural, straightforward, refined, with a kind of simple seriousness and unaffected mastery. The poetess courts Lope de Vega in literary fashion, but with such discretion, with such ingratiating and courtly gentility, with such delicate, feminine tact, that the great poet must have felt flattered with her praise and not offended by the clouds of intrusive incense (Menéndez 84).

Menéndez y Pelayo's praise for the Peruvian poet is unceasing; he unreservedly calls one of her verse epistles dedicated to Lope (Belardo) "the best piece of poetry from early times in Peru" (Menéndez 87). It begins as follows:

> Finally, Belardo, I offer you
> A pure soul vanquished by your valor:
> Accept the gift, for you may prize it;
> And if you give me in faith what I deserve,
> My plea will be favored (Menéndez 87).

We cannot let these highly beautiful verses pass unnoticed and forgotten within Golden Age literature.

MARÍA DE ESTRADA, BEATRIZ BERMÚDEZ DE VELASCO, AND OTHER "FIGHTING" WOMEN IN THE MEXICAN CONQUEST

"It is not good, Sir, for Castilan women to let their husbands go off to war without them, for it is their duty to die where they die, if they must lose their life." (Herrera, decade 1, ch. 1)

The shadow cast over many of the great women of the encounter has kept notice of many of their deeds from surviving the generation they lived in. Most of the time, the stories and exploits in which they played a lead role have not been recorded in the annals of history, unless they were so notable that there was no alternative but to include them.

In his *Historia verdadera de la conquista de la Nueva España*, Bernal Díaz del Castillo mentions some of these women. The event narrated below occurred in the month of August, 1521, at a celebration organized by Hernán Cortés after ha had imprisoned Cuauhtémoc and taken possession of the Aztec capital

By then the tables had been cleared, and the ladies that were there got up to dance with the young gentlemen weighted down with their cotton armor, which seems to me when you looked at it was something to laugh at, and they were the ladies that I will name here, for there were no others in the entire camp, nor in New Spain; first, old María Estrada, who later married Pero Sánchez Farfán, and Francisca de Ordaz, who married a gentleman who was called Juan González de León; the Bermuda lady, who married Olmos de Portillo from Mexico; another lady who was the wife of Captain Portillo, who died on the brigantines, and who because she was a widow was not brought out to the celebration, and a certain Gómez lady, who had been the wife of Benito Vegel; and another lady who was called Bermuda [Section repeated], and another beautiful lady who married one Hernán Marín, whose given name I no longer remember, and who came to live in Guaxaca; and another old lady who was called Isabel Rodríguez, at that time the wife of a certain de Guadalupe, and another somewhat elderly lady who was called Mari Hernández, who had been the wife of Juan de Cáceres, the rich man; and I no longer remember whether there were other women in New Spain [This entire passage was crossed out in the original] (371 n.; ch.156).

Eight women are mentioned—a most significant fact, if as the author says, "there were no others in the camp nor in New Spain." María de

Estrada is discussed on two other occasions. In the first reference to her, she is mentioned together with "our Doña Marina," Cortés's interpreter, as one of the women survivors of the Sorrowful Night, June 30, 1520: "But I have forgotten to write about the content that came upon us to see alive our Doña Marina and Doña Luisa, the daughter of Xicotenga, whom some Tlaxcaltecs helped escape over the bridges, and also a woman called María de Estrada; we had no other woman from Castile in Mexico but her" (Díaz del Castillo 258; ch. 128). According to the information presented, this María de Estrada would have been the only Spanish woman who was with Cortés from the beginning. She is mentioned once more, in chapter 138: "He named as Captain of Tezcuco, so that he would watch and make sure that no Mexican had dealings with [the young ruler of Texcoco], a good soldier called Pero Sánchez Farfán, who was the husband of the worthy and honorable woman María de Estrada." Nevertheless, another "five women from Castile" are mentioned among those women who arrived with the reinforcements that Cortés had obtained when he defeated Pánfilo de Narváez (Díaz del Castillo 260-61; 128). These five women were killed and sacrificed together with 860 Spanish soldiers and 1,200 Tlaxcaltecs in the famous battle of Otumba. Bernal Díaz says, "I say that in a matter of five days more than eight hundred sixty soldiers were killed and sacrificed, with seventy-two whom they killed in a village called Tustepeque, and *five women from Castile*; and those killed in Tustepeque were among Narváez's men, and they killed more than one thousand two hundred Tlaxcaltecs" (260-61; ch. 128).[24]

　　If we are to believe Bernal Díaz, these were the first Spanish women killed in battle. Diego Muñoz Camargo, in his *Historia de Tlaxcala*, gives an account of the extraordinary feats of María Estrada:

> On that reckless, sorrowful night, they killed a page of Hernán Cortés's, named Juan de Salazar, before his eyes, where also a lady named María Estrada displayed valor, doing marvelous, heroic deeds with a sword and buckler in her hands, fighting bravely with so much fury and spirit, that she outdid the effort of any man, no matter how brave and valiant he might be, and she put fear into our own men, and the same woman did likewise on the day of the memorable battle of Otumba, on horseback with a spear in her hands, which was an incredible thing in so virile a spirit, worthy to be sure of eternal fame and immortal remembrance . (Muñoz 219 n.)

María de Estrada was only one more example, like that of other women who would have to undergo the same circumstances. Not many cases are known of women who were involved in this kind of situation, but those that have been preserved are substantial enough. In addition to those mentioned above, other accounts of María de Estrada have come down to us. In one of them, Cervantes de Salazar attributes to her the following words addressed to Cortés when he wanted them to stay and rest at Tlaxcala: "It is not good, Captain, Sir, for Spanish women to let their men go off to war; where they die, we women shall die, and it makes sense for the Indians to understand that we Spaniards are so brave that even our women know how to fight." ((209; lib. 5, cap. 166).

Herrera y Tordesillas takes up the same information, and adds the names of other women, among them that of the mulatto Beatriz de Palacios, whom he mentions first: *"For it was not good for Castilian women to let their husbands go off to war, and where the men died, the women would die. These women were Beatriz de Palacios, María de Estrada, Juana Martín, Isabel de Rodríguez, the wife of Alonso Valiente, and others"* (73; Década 3, bk. 1, ch. 22).[25]

Herrera y Tordesillas provides the following information about Beatriz de Palacios:

> Beatriz de Palacios, a mulatto, was of great help when Cortés was thrown out of Mexico, and in this encirclement she was married to a soldier named Pedro de Escobar; and she served her husband so well and his comrade's men, that when he was tired from fighting during the day and had guard and sentinel duty, she would do it for him very attentively; and leaving her arms she would go out to the countryside to pick greens, and boil them and dress them for her husband and his comrades. She cured the wounded, saddled horses, and did other things like any soldier (Herrera 73; Década 3, bk. 1, ch. 22).

The chronicler Torquemada, describing the events of the Sorrowful Night and how Cortés's page Juan de Salazar was killed in his presence, also mentions María de Estrada, saying that she had as much courage and spirit in battle as if she were "one of the bravest men in the world:"

> And likewise María de Estrada showed herself to be very brave in this difficulty and conflict; with a sword and buckler in her hands she did marvelous deeds and went at the enemy with as much courage and spirit, as if she were one of the bravest men in the world, forgetting

that she was a woman, cloaked with the valor that men of valor and honor have in similar cases. And so many were the marvels and the things that she did that she put a fright and awe in all who saw her ((504; bk. 4, ch. 72).

There is one episode of the conquest of Mexico, narrated by Francisco Cervantes de Salazar, in which another woman, sword in hand, insulted the Spaniards so as to encourage them to stand up to the Aztecs, who were making them retreat. This event occurred in one of the encounters during the capture of the Aztec capital, Tenochtitlán. The name of this woman, "of noble lineage" as the document says, is Beatriz Bermúdez de Velasco. The Mexicans having been surrounded by the Spaniards on the lake and on land, they had no other option, discounting surrender, than to make a desperate assault on their enemies. They did just that, with such bravery and good fortune that, killing and wounding as many as they could, they succeeded in making three batallions of Spaniards and Indian allies "shamefully turn their backs," and head to their camp in retreat. It was at that point, when Beatriz Bermúdez, seeing the sorry prospect that was before her, stepped in:

> Beatriz Bermúdez, who had just arrived from another camp, seeing both Spaniards and friendly Indians in disarray, fleeing, went out to them in the middle of the causeway with an Indian shield and Spanish sword and with a helmet on her head, her body protected with padded Indian armor, and said to them:
> Shame, shame, Spaniards! This is a humiliation! What is this, that you are running away from such vile folk, whom you have defeated so often? Go back and help your comrades who are still fighting, doing what they should be doing; and if not, by God I promise not to let a man of you pass without killing him; for those who come running away from such base people deserve to die at the hands of a weak woman like me (211; bk. 5, ch. 169).

Such was the shame of the Spanish soldiers, and the impact of Doña Beatriz's words, that they turned back toward the enemy "now victorious," with the result that this battle was the "bloodiest and hardest fought that had been seen up to that time." One might ask, in the face of these events, if the well-known *furia* attributed to the Spaniards was not inspired by the women in the first place, who wanted their men to be "capable" of defending their families in case of war.

Cervantes de Salazar finishes his account of this event by saying that on that day, after a long period of time, the Spaniards came out victorious, and were able to rescue their comrades who had remained behind, "from which it will be understood how much a woman as brave as this did and can do with men who prize honor more than life, who tend to be Spaniards among all nations" (212; bk. 5, ch. 169).

It was also in Mexico that a woman, Beatriz Hernández, was the one who decided to move the city of Guadalajara to a more secure site. Due to repeated Indian attacks, the city had had to be moved first from the Nochistlán plain (1531) to the site of Tlacotlán four years later. The Indian attacks were incessant, and a new move was necessary. It seems probable that because of the pressure brought to bear by the governor, Nuño Guzmán, who had chosen the second site, the men meeting in council could not bring themselves to come to a decision. Beatriz Hernández's tirade was needed to make them react and change the site.

> Sirs, it seems that you cannot decide to move the city. Well, I have come to say it on behalf of all: We shall move, and better to do it as soon as possible, even before the time you had in mind. That is, what I mean to say to you is this: We are going to move the city to the Atemaxac Valley, and know ye that if it is not so done, it will go against the service of God and the king.

Crestfallen, the men agreed, and the city was moved to the place where Guadalajara is found today, in the Atemaxac Valley (Tapia 25).

Nevertheless it is another woman who gives most "contentedness" and inspires most admiration in the soldier-chronicler Bernal Díaz: Doña Marina. There can be a number of reasons why Bernal Díaz puts so much care and attention in his descriptions of this woman, but in any case his portrait of her is the best-drawn, in terms of both her physical presence and her character (Johnson 67-68). This emphasis shows the importance that Bernal gave to Cortés's "tongue;" he makes her a fundamental, indispensable tool in the conquest of the Aztec people. Already in the first mention he makes of her in his book he calls her "excellent." It is the moment when the Tabasco chieftains bring several presents to Cortés and his men: "Those presents were nothing compared with the twenty women, among them a most excellent woman who was named Doña Marina, as she was called after she became a Christian" (58; ch. 36).

Chronicler Díaz del Castillo also gives information about the oriign of the name *Matanzas*, given to a river and port in Cuba, where the Indians apparently killed some thirty persons. Mention is made of two women, one of them, "who was beautiful," was saved because she was carried off by the chieftain: "I knew the woman who, after the island of Cuba was won, was taken from the chieftain in whose power she was, and I knew her married on the same island of Cuba, in a city known as Trinidad, with a resident there who was named Pedro Sánchez Farfán" (16; ch. 8).

Bearing in mind that Pedro Sánchez Farfán was the husband of María de Estrada, we may surmise that this is a reference to the same person. The chronicler of the *True History*, once again, provides details about the presence of women on the attempted expeditions to the Pacific Ocean, with Cortés as captain, and about parties given by him as Marquis of the Valley and Viceroy of Mexico. As for the expeditions to the Pacific Ocean, Cortés had already sent Diego Hurtado de Mendoza as captain-general with the purpose of reaching the Moluccas in search of pearls and other riches. The plans did not go as expected, since half of the expeditionaries mutinied and nothing more was heard of Diego Hurtado de Mendoza, his captain-general: "nor of his ship, nor did he ever appear" (541; ch. 200). In view of this event, Bernal presents a written portrait of his captain, Cortés, that is highly significant and very human, in which "married women" also appear, ready to participate in the expedition:

> And when Cortés found out about it, there was great mourning for what had happened, and as he was a man of good heart, who did not rest in the face of such events, he decided to send no more captains, but to go himself in person...And since it became known in New Spain that the Marquis was going in person, they believed that it was for a sure and rich purpose, and a great number of soldiers came to serve him, both horsemen and other harquebusiers and crossbowmen, and among them thirty-four married men who joined him; in all there were three hundred twenty persons, *including the married women* (542; ch. 200).[26]

This expedition failed because several of the ships went aground and could not continue the voyage. Once again, married women were present, in this case thirty of them. It is notable that when Cortés went to the aid of the soldiers he had left on the island of Santa Cruz, he took so much meat with him that many of the survivers, because they had spent so much time without eating "anything of substance," perished due to "diarrhea and so many complaints." Bernal Díaz says, "And the soldiers who had been waiting for him ate so much meat that since they were weak from not eating 'anything of substance' from many days back, they had diarrhea and so many complaints that half of those remaining died" (543; ch. 200).

Bernal Díaz also provides not only the names but a physical description of these women. The festivities held in 1538 as a result of the peace made between Emperor Charles V and François I, the king of France, were notable for their formality and ostentation. Bernal Díaz compares them to those that "were given in Rome by the consuls and captains who had won battles" (544; ch. 201). In fact the Spaniards had no reason to envy the Romans. Neither Hernán Cortés and the Viceroy of Mexico, Antonio de Mendoza, spared expense on all imaginable kinds of delicacies and entertainments, worthy of the most sophisticated European cities. Bernal Díaz tells us, with respect to the women's frills and finery:

> For I wish to tell about the many ladies, wives of conquistadores and other residents of Mexico, who were at the windows of the great square, and about the wealth of crimson they had on, and of silks and damasks and gold and silver and jewelry that were very rich; in other corridors there were very richly dressed ladies, attended to by young men. And then the great sweets that were given to all those ladies, both those at the windows and those in the corridors: they served them marzipan, candied citron icings, almonds and confections…, all served on rich dishes of gold and silver (546; ch. 201).

In the same chapter, Bernal Díaz not only speaks of the extravagance and ostentation of the upper-class ladies, but includes people of all social conditions: "And everything was done up so naturally, that many people of all kinds came with their wives to it" (546; ch. 201). The first dinner was held in Hernán Cortés's palaces: "And the Viceroy dined there with all the gentlemen and conquistadores he had around him, and with all the ladies, wives o the gentlemen and conquistadores and other ladies, and it was all done most formally." (Díaz del Castillo 546; ch. 201).

Bernal is very explicit in listing the entire series of delicacies served at these parties. Consumed at the other dinner, held at the Viceroy's house, were, among other things, goat, doves, quail, duck, partridge, chicken, fish, beef, pork, venison, and every imaginable kind of fruit, cheese, and beverages, from wines to the indispensable, very American "cacao." Nor was there a lack of music to accompany the diners:

> ...a great deal of music and singing at the head of every table, and trumpetry and many types of instruments, harps, *vihuelas*, flutes, *dulzainas*, shawms, especially when the headwaiters served the cups that they brought to the ladies who were eating there, who were many more than went to the Marquis's dinner, and many golden cups, some with carob drink, others with wine, and others with water, others with cacao and with mixed red and white wine; and after this they served very large savory turnovers to other, more distinguished ladies, and in some of them there were two little live rabbits, and others were full of quail and doves and other little birds...(Díaz del Castillo 547; ch. 201).

Such luxury and ostentation is impressive, despite the fact that it was a logical compensation for many years of war and sacrifice. The luxury in which the previous lord of Mexico, Moctezuma, lived, is likewise impressive, not only for the five thousand invitees who ate daily at his palace, from what "was left" from the Royal Plate, but also for the variety and exquisiteness of that plate (Torquemada 231; bk. 2, ch. 89). Cortés also made note of the albinos and monsters that Moctezuma had for his diversion and entertainment: "He had another house where he had many men and women monsters, where there were hunchbacked dwarves and others with other deformities, and each one in his own room, in the manner of monsters" (Cortés 46).

There can be no doubt about the profound impression that the Aztec capital made on the Spanish commander, nor that he knew that sooner or later it would come into his hands. In any case, Cortés was conscious of the need for and importance of the presence of women and their families for the survival and good governance of the new society. These women would change the habits of their men, who had grown used to living like adventurers. Cortés issued a decree ordering all those who had their wives in the Antilles or in Spain to send for them, and he gave them a period of a year and a half. Before the time was up, the order was obeyed by all. Cortés had with this measure established a permanent base for the Spanish presence in the Americas (Acosta 143).

Brother Pedro de Aguado in his *Historia de Venezuela* (1581) discusses another "anonymous" woman who had to make use of the "strength of her arm." Unfortunately, although memory of her deed remained, that was not the case with her name. The event occurred on the island of Trinidad (Venezuela). During a skirmish between Spaniards and Indians, a Spanish woman who did not respond to the advances of an Indian was the motive for him to attack the Spanish encampment with his men. When the Indians attacked, she armed herself with a sword and a pillow as a shield to defend her and stood up to them as if she were a valiant captain:

> When our Spanish woman heard the voices of the Spaniards who were returning victorious to the cry of "Santiago, Santiago," her joy was such that she fell as if dead. Picking herself up, she then told them about her defense and her astonishing deed. "This act of this virile woman was so courageous that it is certainly worthy enough for specific mention to be made of her and her name, which I should like to know, so as to stamp it on this place in letters of gold" (Villafañe 137).

In his *Historia de la ciudad de Puebla de los Angeles*, Colonel Antonio Carrión mentions in passing two cases where women displayed their facility with weapons. The first case was a combat in which women killed their rivals in open country: "Doña Juana and Doña Luisa Morales," Méndez states in *Historia de Potosí*, "killed Don Pedro and Don Graciano González in a pitched battle, riding on horseback with sword and spear" (Villafañe 141). In the second case, a mother and her two armed daughters defended their husband and father putting his enemies to flight and killing one of them: "In 1626, Doña Bartolina Villapalma, with two unmarried daughters, all three armed with spears and bucklers, defended her husband, who was in a critical situation, having been attacked by his enemies. They killed one and put the others to flight" (Villafañe 141).

There were so many demonstrations of heroism and valor by Spanish women during the first years of the encounter that it is difficult to understand the lack of attention given to them and the silence that has surrounded them. Not all these brave women managed to come out of such difficult circumstances successfully; some lost their lives in the attempt.

One event worth mentioning in this regard occurred during the conquest of Florida accomplished by Hernando de Soto. The occasion was the battle of Chicaza, in which the Spaniards had lost many of their men and their horses. In this case we have the name of the woman,

Doña Francisca Hinestrosa, the only Christian woman known to be on
the expedition. Her name is mentioned because the incident was so
tragic; otherwise it would have gone unnoticed like many others.
In that situation,

> they lamented a special case that happened that night, which was that
> among them there was a single Spanish woman, named Francisca de
> Hinestrosa, married to a good soldier called Hernando Bautista, and she
> was about to give birth in those days. Since the enemies' surprise
> attack was so sudden, the husband went off to fight and, when the
> battle was over, when he returned to see what had become of his wife,
> he found her reduced to ashes because she had not been able to escape
> the fire (Garcilaso *La Florida* 419; bk. 3, ch. 37).

In another equally tragic case, the husband was present at the side of
his wife and daughters. The event occured on an expedition led by
Pedro de Alvarado, who left Nicaragua heading for Peru. On the way
to Quito, passing through the snow-capped Andean peaks, many of the
men of the expedition perished—among them, a family of four. When
the father saw how his wife and two daughters were too fatigued to go
on, and found himself incapable of helping them, he sat down with them:
"And so all four froze, and although he could have saved himself, he
preferred to perish there with them...it is lamentable that the first
Spanish woman who went to Peru should have perished so miserably"
(Borges 402).

At all latitudes of Spanish America examples of feminine valor
followed one after the other. Beatriz Bermúdez in Mexico, Inés Suárez
in Chile, Isabel Roncero and her daughter María in Colombia, Catalina
de Miranda in Venezuela, Juana Hernández in Peru, María de Nidos in
New Mexico, and many others who, though anonymous, contributed to
the best of their ability (Delgado 104-105). We shall discuss some of
them in more detail later on. Among those whose actions are known,
and there are not many, one cannot ignore María de Nidos, who, when
Francisco de Villagrá was defeated by the Araucanians and decided to
leave the city of Concepción, went into the middle of the public square
and said, "General, Sir, if your grace wishes to retreat for personal gain,
go straight away; but at least allow us women to defend our houses and
do not force us to seek asylum in other people's houses" (Delgado 104-
05). A similar case occurred in New Mexico during Juan de Oñate's
expedition, when the wife of royal ensign Peñalosa was able to halt the

retreat of the defeated Spanish troops, as we shall see later (Delgado 194-05).

These are only two cases; no doubt the majority of those that occurred remained anonymous. One should not lose sight of the enormous expanse of territory and the relatively short time within which these incidents occurred. It is hugely difficult to track down the events in the place where they occurred. Women showed that it was often they who took the initiative and inspired the courage and spirit that was needed for the men to give their lives fighting for their families.

The acts of María de Estrada and the other women are unusual, and they deserve to stand out in history and in the memory of those who participated in such critical moments of the contact between these peoples. These women not only showed that they could rise to the occasion, but they stood out among the most extraordinary examples of bravery seen in humankind. Let us hope that some day they will occupy the position they deserve, rather than to be forgotten like so many others.

THREE EPICS OF THE ENCOUNTER OF AMERICA

In three of the best-known literary epics of the Spanish encounter of America, Alonso de Ercilla y Zúñiga's *La araucana*, Captain Gaspar Pérez de Villagrá's *Historia de la Nueva México*, and Juan de Castellanos's *Elegías*, marvelous examples of women's courage and daring in the struggle with the enemy are to be found. These works, following the Renaissance Classical tradition, are saturated with Greco-Latin mythological nomenclature, but in the case of both *La araucana* and *Historia de la Nueva México*, historical accuracy is present throughout. The first edition of *La araucana*, which appeared in 1569, narrates the events involved in the fighting between Spaniards and Araucanians for control of the territory known today as Chile. The work is characterized by its faithful reflection of the historical occurrences. The *Historia de la Nueva México*, by Captain Gaspar Pérez de Villagrá, born in Puebla de los Angeles (Mexico), was published in 1610, a decade before the landing of the English Pilgrims and fourteen years before the appearance of Captain John Smith's *General Historie of Virginia, New England, and the Summer Isles* (Pérez de Villagrá *History* 17).

Villagrá participated in the conquest and colonization of New Mexico, carried out by Juan de Oñate in 1598. Appearing in this work is the first Hispanic heroine of what is today the United States. She is Doña Eufemia, Don Francisco de Sosa y Peñalosa's wife, who organized a stubborn resistance on the roofs of the houses of the town of San Juan, a place where forts had been built for defense against the Indians. The encounter of New Mexico had episodes worthy of the best epics. In winter, a handful of Spaniards had to attack the village of Acoma, located on a mesa to which access was most difficult—leaving their wives and a few men to defend the fort town. The town had four entrances, where all available forces were deployed. The Indians approached from all directions, threatening the defenders with death and insulting them. But Doña Eufemia was not to be intimidated:

> [All] took up their posts and then noticed
> That all the tops of the houses
> Were garrisoned and occupied. And then
> The General shouted an order that
> Some Captains go out and observe
> What folk those were, and what intention

They had, at that moment, upon that post.
And then valorous Doña Eufemia
Put the camp at ease, with ladies
That were then in the camp, saying
That if the General ordered them all down,
They would defend all of the town,
But, if not, he should then leave them alone,
If they wished to keep safe all that
Which they now occupied and held.
At this the General, with much pleasure,
Congratulating himself that he had
In women a courage of such esteem,
Ordered that Doña Eufemia command
All of that summit, and thus all,
As the brave Amazons obeyed
Great Martesia, thus, as one,
Discharging flying balls into the air,
With gallant spirit they did promenade
The roofs and lofty terraces,...
The adversaries, seeing the caution,
The warning, preparation, in all things
Did turn their backs and not reveal themselves...(Pérez de Villagra,
Historia de la Nueva Mexico 242-43).

Ercilla's heroine, Mencía de Nidos, differs from Villagrá's in that she herself is the one who urges the others to remain in the village of Concepción, from which they are all fleeing. Mencía de Nidos does not have the support and cooperation of her companions, who are all escaping in desperation, fearing an Araucanian attack. Only one old man rebukes the Spaniards for their attempt to retreat:

...he said to them: Base, craven folk,
dishonor to Spain's honor and spirit,
what is this, where go you, who leads you astray (Ercilla 129)?

Mencía de Nidos prefers to risk her life for something which she has worked for and which belongs to her. She is not about to leave houses, cattle and other animals in the hands of the Indians, and she is prepared to risk her life, wielding a sword if necessary:

Mencía de los Nidos, a noble,
Discreet, brave, and valorous lady

Was the one who gained so much fame
At a time when it was denied to the men:
Being sick and weak in her bed,
She heard the great commotion, and valiantly
Seizing a sword and shield,
She followed the residents out as best she could.

Now they were walking up the mountain,
Turning their aggrievèd faces back
To the houses and lands they were leaving,
Hearing the chickens squawk in great number:
The cats mewing with horrible voice,
Dogs howling in great sadness,
Procne with distressèd Philomela
Displayed deep sorrow in their songs.

But Doña Mencía felt greater grief,
and giving clear sign and show of it,
blocked the way with naked sword,
and half up the slope, amid them stopped.
Her head turned toward the city, she did say:
"Oh valiant nation, whom the land and fame
You've won has cost so dear,
By rigor and blade of sword!"

"Oh, how often were you called
Impatient, arrogant, and rash,
In doubtful circumstances bold,
Heedless of the measures required:
And we saw you bring, tamed by the yoke,
so great a number and a host of adversaries,
and take on and achieve such great endeavors,
that you seemed to be immortal!"

"Turn a kind eye back to your village,
Raised by you from its foundations;
Look at the lush and fertile fields
That ready for you have their tribute;
The rich mines and those copious
Earth rivers of gold, and the cattle
Which now wanders lost from peak to peak
Searching for its shepherd now unknown" (Ercilla 130-31).

It would be a slight not to mention the Indian women in Villagrá's work. Just like the Spanish women, they showed themselves capable of sacrificing their lives for a just cause. In this case, Villagrá narrates a collective suicide of four Indian sisters and their mother, who decided to throw themselves on the fire when they discovered the corpse of their brother and son. This was the noble Zutancalpo, who drove the women of his family to desperation with his death. This passage, full of emotion and tragedy, begins with the lament and the sad end of the mother. It is one of the most moving passages in the work.

"It remained only that this last trial,
This final sorrow, should have come to me
In my old age, poor, sad, and afflicted."
And shedding a great rain of tears,
Through bitter sorrow and through fiery love
Being deeply moved by her tragic distress,
She gave a hundred thousand grieving sighs
From out the depths of her anguish-wrung breast.
And as the madness of desperation
Is the most cruel executioner
Of him who suffers from such an evil,
So, desperate and utterly heedless,
She cast herself backward into the flames.
And after her the four grieving sisters
Did also choose to be consumed there,
Together with their dead, beloved brother.
Thus they, with him, did hurl themselves
In, next their mother, who burned there.
And like to the most monstrous snakes
Or poisonous, deadly vipers,
Who with each other intertwine
In clinging knots and twist about,
So these poor wretches were entwined
Among those ashes and embers
Which, crumbling and soft, seething
Fiercely, did burst out in a thousand spots,
And they, struggling up on the glowing coals,
With shoulders, hands, and feet, jointly
Attempted to get out. But all in vain,
For as we see sink neath the waves
Those who are overcome upon the deep,
Who, uselessly, with arms and legs

> But shorten the sad thread of life,
> And in a time unfortunate, short, brief,
> Their souls, immortal yet oppressed,
> Escape from their mortal prisons,
> So these did make untimely end.
> Yet giving in that last farewell
> Their last embraces mid the coals,
> And thus, leaving their fatherland beloved,
> They gave a long farewell to its ashes...(Pérez de Villagrá, *Historia* 277-78).

Although it is true that the mention made of these women is due to historical reasons, and has a strong epic-literary tone, there were also other women, most of them anonymous, present in the most difficult moments of the encounter. Many are not mentioned even by name, but there they were, by the side of the conquistadores, in weary moments and at festivities, setting a tone of dignity and nobiity in the difficult times of encounter (Romero 1294). Life took on a different meaning: tournaments, parties, and dances were organized in the women's honor. Trade began to provide all types of merchandise and products which, although they were not essential, were aimed at putting some color into female clothing and finery. Women provided joy and diversion amid the daily round of work: "All at once a tragedy involving jealousy would color the landscape red. They would provide gentle embraces, consolation in difficult times, irreplaceable help in the home, stimulus for action and progress" (Romero 1294).

A writer "sui generis" who must be included among the most important members of the group who wrote works of an epic nature in his time is Juan de Castellanos (1522-1607). He wrote one of the most unusual books of the colonial period: *Elegias de varones ilustres de Indias* (1589), in which many women are mentioned along with the men, or *varones*, some of them in a more sensual manner than one would expect from the pen of a priest. The *Elegías* consists of some 150,000 hendecasyllabic verses. It is the longest poetic work written in the Spanish language and one of the longest in any language (Gómez 51). The amount of information supplied by this work is simply fabulous, almost all of it taken from oral sources and also from Gonzalo Jiménez de Quesada's *Compendio historial*. Castellanos possessed an exceptional memory, which helped him document everything he saw and heard. As a historical source for everything relating to the first years of the Spanish colony, he is compared to Fernández de Oviedo and Father Las Casas: "Everything points to the fact that he wrote the work first in prose and then transcribed it in verse, following the advice of some friends, who perhaps convinced him that he could emulate Ercilla" (Gómez 51).

The information contained in the interminable verses of this prolific Sevillian poet very often contains highly valuable data for our understanding today of the early events of the encounter, in verses such as the following:

> And the first who brought forth flour
> And first made refined bread
> Was Eloísa Gutiérrez, a noble lady,
> Wife of Captain Juan de Montalvo (Romero 1: 1300).

Castellanos does not fail to mention those women who had to fight at their husbands' side and who even had to dress "in men's apparel." As we can see, this did not only happen in the dramas of the Golden Age:

> Which women, their persons well armed
> In usurped battledress,
> Were gripped with such fury, that they felt
> Like other, second Amazons,
> And in the attitude they struck
> Were all Minervas or Bellonas,
> And the fiercest risk of risks
> Banished feminine fear (Romero 1: 1302).

Not every allusion is full of praise; dark patches also appear, as in all histories. In the following example, the poet gives news of the punishment meted out to an Indian woman by her mistress, Ana de la Peña, the wife of the Portuguese Antonio de Pereira. The reason was jealousy, since the Indian woman in question, "Francisca," was "beautiful," which was probably enough to make her suspect in the eyes of her mistress Ana de la Peña.

> As luck would have it, though she had not sinned,
> The mistress of this suspect Indian woman
> Wounded her lovely members with lashes
> And did crop all her hair (Romero 1: 1302).

The Indian woman, Francisca, decided to take revenge, together with her husband; and they went to seek aid from her relatives, the "Tupe" Indians. After seducing the chieftain, she incited him to rebel against the Spaniards, who were living confidently in the village of Valledupar. Here began the tragedy. The Indians attacked, burned, destroyed. As a result of this tragic incident, this most valuable list of names appears.

> The slaughter began. *There was no house without tears, / Pain, dread, terror, mortal fear.* Those clubbed to death included the beautiful Guiomar de Urrea and he sister Doña Beatriz, Ana de Aníbal, Isabel de Briones, Baría Becerra, virile Elvira Franca, Ana Ruiz, and Ana Fernández. They broke in their foreheads, they cut off their ears, and they stripped them bare. Catalina Rodríguez, married that very day, was killed in her bed (Romero 1304).

No more than fifty were killed, because the "Zamoran with the injured hand," Antonio Flores, seized a horse and galloped headlong into the mass of Indians, whom he managed to disperse. Upon returning to the town he contemplated the tragedy:

> Some women naked, others half-clothed
> And all marked with their blood;
> Their inmost vitals pierced
> By the terrible blows and wounds;
> Heads split in pieces,
> Ears and noses severed;
> Others with bodies turned to ashes
> By fire in their own nests (Romero 1: 1304).

Later the Spaniards managed to regroup, defeat the Indians, and punish those responsible. All this disaster for "a suspicion."

Juan de Castellanos also describes another woman, who although "very lovely" did not have the reputation that some would have wished. On the other hand, many gave thanks to Heaven for the "generosity" of this beautiful woman. Her name was Doña Inés de Atienza, and she was the lover of Governor Pedro de Ursúa, as well as Juan Alonso de la Bandera, Cristóbal Hernández, Lorenzo de Salduendo, and others—love affairs that ended up costing her her life. It was no less than the tyrant Lope de Aguirre who ordered her killed.

Lovely Doña Inés was the lady
Who would rightly have been called fair
Had she respected the reputation
That every maiden should respect (Romero 2: 1432).

It would not be within human nature to look only for the extraordinary, singular aspects of these women. In some cases, totally negative lines appear criticizing them. For better or for worse, there they were, participating the expeditions of exploration or encounter. In *Milicia indiana*, a certain Vargas Machuca, a veteran of the vicissitudes of the Americas, recommends to his leader that he not take women along, unless the intention is to settle. He gives several reasons, the first being the difficulty and the "unbearable" hardships incurred with women on the road, due to the uncomfortable country and the disease they transmit to the soldiers. The same author says that the soldier had to be convinced not to take them along: "persuading the men on account of the risk that they are known to run, of their weakness, of their inability to keep up with the work: besides this, they cause disturbances and death, as has been seen many times (*Milicia indiana*, vol. 1, 118)" (Romero 2: 1433).

Much more frequent are the accounts praising the virtues of these women; the above quotation is unusual within the general context. It would be interesting to know something more about the personality of those who made the type of statement offered by Vargas Machuca, who speaks so freely of the women's "weakness" and the "nuisance" they cause.

Another interesting point with respect to the prolific poet Juan de Castellanos is the fact that he possessed 26 slaves "to attend and serve him" (Cortés Alonso 958). This detail is "interesting" because, thanks to him, we are able to form a better idea of what the treatment of domestic male and female slaves was like in this historic period: "A man of his time, as Brother Bartolomé de las Casas himself was with respect to them, he possessed them with no scruple (Cortés Alonso 959)." In her article on domestic slaves in America, Vicenta Cortés Alonso speaks openly on the subject of slavery and particularly of Juan de Castellanos's slaves. It is interesting to note the poet's benevolent, familiar manner with his slaves, as he is characterized in this article.

In Juan de Castellanos's era, slavery was recognized, and was an institution practised and respected by all those who could afford it.

Apparently Castellanos was "humane" in his treatment of his slaves.[27] The poet freed some of them, following the recommendations of the Church, and he helped others and treated them favorably to the extent of his capabilities. He is called a "prudent and kind-hearted master" (Cortés Alonso 978).

Before sitting in cold judgment on so sad and real a subject as that of the lack of freedom for human beings, we would do well to note how some who practised such abominable customs as slavery treated their slaves in a more humane way than many others did and do their servants in more modern periods.

Thanks to Villagrá, Ercilla, and Castellanos, authors of these three encounter epics, *La conquista de la Nueva México*, *La araucana*, and the *Elegías*, it is possible to confirm the historical importance some women had in the events that took place during the most critical moments of the encounter.

FEMALE HISTORICAL FIGURES ON THE VERGE OF FICTION

As we have seen, it was in many and varied incidents that women played the lead in acts of heroism and superhuman sacrifices in the encounter and exploration of new territories. One of the greatest of these was the transoceanic voyage itself: inclement weather, pirates, shipwrecks, hunger, revolts, and the other events of the interminable days of sailing through all kinds of seas and winds. The travel accounts seem largely to be in agreement that the two most dangerous sites for navigation were Cape Horn at the extreme south of the South American continent and the Cape of Good Hope at the extreme south of Africa. The sudden shift of winds and currents has made these two places the sites of the greatest sailing disasters.

The Portuguese Bernardo Gomes de Brito's *Historia trágico-marítima* includes a selection of the most notable disasters that occurred during the expansion of the Portuguese empire into the Orient. One of them involves the "Wreck of the great San Juan galleon" in the vicinity of Natal (today South Africa) in 1552, under the command of Manuel de Soussa y Sepúlveda, who was accompanied by his wife, children, and eighty crewmen. The behavior of his wife, Leonor, until her death, made this sad and noteworthy event one of the best examples of the martyrdom of a woman who held fast to her principles, to the last consequences. Needless to say, to judge this type of event it is necessary to understand the scrupulously religious mentality of the period. Once shipwrecked, the Portuguese were captured by the "Kaffirs," who took them prisoner:

> And Doña Leonor was so weak now, so sad and disconsolate to see how her husband was and to see that they were separated from the other people and to hold it impossible that they would be able to rejoin them, that to think of it is something that breaks one's heart! Walking along in that way, the Kaffirs once again came upon him and his wife and the few who were in their company, and they stripped them bare right there, without leaving anything on them. Seeing themselves both in this fashion with two very young children before them, they gave thanks to Our Lord (Gomes 38-39).

In these circumstances Doña Leonor represents, together with her husband, the ideal prototype of the woman of that period, a martyr, who was able to put her Christian ideals before the threat of death, which was

ever more certain. Don Manuel de Soussa likewise upheld his honor as
a Christian gentleman, feeding and defending, as best he could, the
members of his family. Their strong religious sense and blind faith in
God gave courage to these people in the face of the danger to them that
the local inhabitants of these lands represented: the "Kaffirs," natives
who when all is said and done were defending what belonged to them.

> Here they say that Doña Leonor did not allow herself to be stripped,
> and she defended herself with fisticuffs and blows because she so much
> wanted the Kaffirs to kill her rather than to see herself naked before the
> people; and there is no doubt that her life would have ended then and
> there if Manuel de Soussa had not begged her to let herself be stripped
> and reminded her that they had been born naked, and since God was
> content with that, she should be too. One of the great hardships they
> felt was to see the two small children, their offspring, before them,
> crying and asking for something to eat, and they could not help them.
> And when Doña Leonor saw herself naked, she threw herself on the
> ground and covered herself all over with her hair, which was very
> long, and made a hollow in the sand, where she put herself up to the
> waist and did not come out of there again...To see such a noble
> woman, the daughter and wife of such honorable gentlefolk, so
> mistreated, and with so little civility! When the men who were still in
> their company saw Manuel de Soussa and his wife naked, they moved
> away from them a bit, out of the shame they felt seeing their captain
> and Doña Leonor that way (Gomes 38-39).

The narrator of this incident knows how to put a dramatic note into
everything that happened. Although the characters are in principle real,
they attain an aura of divinity, behaving more like supernatural beings
than like flesh-and-blood persons. It is the gruesomeness of the tragedy
that invites readers to sit down and read passages that arouse their
interest and curiosity, for, since they are real, it is much easier to
identify with the characters. Nowadays there are television programs
that have a parallel dimension. Presented in them are the greatest
imaginable disasters of modern life and the struggle of individuals to
overcome the difficulty, although the outcome is sometimes tragic.
Persons also appear who are capable of sacrificing their lives generously
for their loved ones. The difference between one type of story and the
other lies in the quality of the narration. A good storyteller can get
every last drop out of a tragedy; a mediocre one, however, will leave

unwritten a host of dramatic and novelistic possibilities that are much appreciated by the public at large, in this case the Portuguese public.

Returning to the above story, we should observe the narrator's mastery in holding the reader's attention with the most chilling incidents, while at the same time presenting the greatest possible nobility in beings who are at the gates of death.

> Although his head was injured, Manuel de Soussa did not lose sight of the need his wife and children had to eat. And, still lame from a wound that the Kaffirs had inflicted on one of his legs, and thus wounded, he went to the woods to look for fruit to give them to eat; when he came back, he found Doña Leonor very weak, from both hunger and crying; because since the Kaffirs had stripped her, she had never come out of there nor stopped crying; and he found one of the children dead, and with his own hand he buried it in the sand. On the next day, Manuel de Soussa went back to the woods to find some fruit, and when he returned he found Doña Leonor dead and the other child, and next to her five slave women were crying with enormous shouts (Gomes 38-39).

Despite its moving dramatism, perfectly apt for a literary or theatrical work, this passage serves as an example of what the tragedies of sea navigation between lands as far removed as Portugal and India or Spain and the Philippines could often be like. This kind of tragic situation occurred for different reasons.

During the sixteenth century (1506-1600) 6,799 ships crossed the Atlantic, in other words an average of 71.6 ships per year. Of this total, 106 ships, or 1.56%, were shipwrecked for different reasons: 70 sank, 9 fell to pirates, 4 to storms, and 21 were lost for reasons yet unknown (Martínez 152-53). The number of losses is not high for that period, if one considers the precarious stability of the ships of the time. This same number would be high nowadays. The greatest danger to navigation during the sixteenth and seventeenth centuries was the ocean itself. José Luis Martínez informs us of the percentage of losses of ships that occurered in the sixteenth century between Spain and the Indies: "If to those 70 sinkings we add 4 attributed specifically to storms, it develops that 70% of the risks of navigation must be attributed to the violence of the sea, but in fact to the fragility of the ships or to errors of navigation" (152-53).

One of the most spine-tingling events in the history of the encounter in which a woman took part was connected with the story of Lope de Aguirre, which tells of his crimes and his madness. Captain Aguirre was part of the tragic expedition of Pedro de Ursúa, who with the permission of the Viceroy of Peru, Andrés Hurtado de Mendoza, went off in search of the mythical lands of El Dorado, along the Amazon River. The tragic story of the death of Lope de Aguirre's daughter, Elvira Aguirre, at her father's hands, has come down to us through different sources. This is one of the most grotesque, macabre historical episodes in the whole repertory of the encounter. Paradoxically it is one of those that has interested readers the most.

Seeing that he only had a few soldiers left for his defense, Lope de Aguirre entered the fort with the intention of killing his daughter, "'so that something I love so much will not end up as a mattress for villains.' When he announced his purpose, his daughter hugged him and said don't kill me, father, because the devil has deceived you. The tyrant stabbed her three times shouting the words 'My daughter!' (O' Sullivan -Beare 186)".

This infamous occurrence is also mentioned in Lucas Fernández's *Historia general del Nuevo Reino de Granada*. It should be noted how each writer puts special emphasis on the thing that he considers most "unheard of" within the repugnant context of the action committed:

> And the devil having put the thought into him of bringing the process of his cruelties to a close with the most unheard-of cruelty that could fit into the stupidity of a beast that would kill his own daughter when he did not have the courage to die fighting, he went to her and aimed his harquebus at her, saying that she should put her trust in God because he intended to kill her, and when his daughter asked why, he answered so that she would not be affronted by being called the daughter of a traitor. Then the Torralba woman, holding on to the harquebus, sought with pleas to dissuade him from that intention; but he, who was inflexible in his decisions, leaving the harquebus in her hands, pulled out his dagger and stabbed his daughter to death (271-72; bk. 12, ch. 7).

This information is corroborated by the "account" that the rebel soldier Francisco Vázquez submitted to the court in Madrid in the sixteenth century. At the most dramatic point of his report, Vázquez says that when the tyrant was practically alone, "the devil, desperate, instead of repenting for his sins committed another, greater cruelty than those that went before, with which he put the seal on all the others: he stabbed the only daughter he had, whom he seemed to love more than himself (Vázquez 163)."

Such an unprecedent event did not go unnoticed by the sharp sensibility of the famous Spanish writer Ramón del Valle Inclán, who in his well-known novel *Tirano Banderas*, based on the life of an imaginary dictator of a supposed Hispanic American country, presumably Mexico, repeats with some variants the same tragic scene of the death of the daughter at the hands of her father.

> Daughter of mine, you have not managed to be married and a great lady, as this sinner thought who right now is forced to take the life he gave you twenty years ago! It is not fair for you to stay in the world to be enjoyed by the enemies of your father, and for them to disgrace you calling you the daughter of that bastard Banderas!
> Hearing this, the serving women who had the butt of his weapon in hand beseeched him utterly terrified:
> Tyrant Banderas hit them in the face:
> You bitches! If I spare your life, it is because you must shroud me like an angel.
> He took a dagger out of his shirt, held his daughter by the hair to keep her there, and closed his eyes. A rebel report says that he tore her open with fifteen stab wounds (Valle Inclán 361).

In his work *La aventura equinoccial de Lope de Aguirre*, another excellent Spanish novelist, Ramón J. Sender, portrays with precision and mastery the last minutes of Lope de Aguirre's unfortunate daughter:

> In Doña Elvira's room were the Torralba woman with her visionary eyes, huddled in a corner, and the girl in the middle of the room trembling like a little bird. Lope de Aguirre still had his dagger in hand, and was intent on the noises from outside.
> "Entrust yourself to God, my daughter, because I have come to kill you."
> "Father, have you lost your mind?"
> "Look on that crucifix there and entrust yourself to God, because you have to die, daughter of mine."
> He was holding a harquebus in his left hand and the dagger in his right.
> With loud shouts the Torralba woman threw herself upon him and

managed to take the harquebus away from him, but not the dagger. Lope pounced on his daughter, took her by the hair, and began to stab her while the girl said, in broken phrases and pleas, "Stop now, Father, the devil has deceived you."
And thus Elvira died before she was fifteen years old (Sender 400-01).

Chronicler Juan de Castellanos, a contemporary of these events, also recounts the tragic occurrence, putting these words into Elvira's mouth:

The girl answered him, "Father of mine,
I thought you'd give me better news,
What evil, what outrage, what blunder
Have I committed that I must die?"
Better for God to do it, and I trust in him
That I shall not die in this fashion:
This payment you give me, this husband
For all that I have done to serve you.

"Christian folk they are whom I stay with
And whom I shall give no cause for discord;
To show such force before a weak woman
Is not ill will, but derangement:
Woe is me, for I am unable
To find mercy in my father!
No more, Sir, hold your right hand."

He answered, "Nothing avails you, daughter,
Pass ye where mortals pass,
Let the sinful folk be stopped,
And evils end with their evils,
My day is come, let your hour come:
I do not wish for disloyal men to call you
Daughter of the traitor, or traitress."
And to top off his evil deeds
He stabbed her in her breasts (Romero 2: 1443-44). I, 687

It is not surprising that certain passages of the history of the encounter and colonization moved indirectly into the area of literature. In this case, the harshest individualism of a soldier in the service of Spain, who seeks to impose himself by controlling his men and the lands he may conquer, is compared with a dictator who, with no less individualism, seeks to remain as the sole leader of his country, and when he is trapped is capable of killing his own daughter. That daughter, Elvira, is portrayed from different angles, even at different ages, by the different authors. She is precisely the opposite pole from her father: sweetness, goodness, modesty, resignation. A halo of sainthood could even be put on her for her martyr's death. These differences and similarities, which fluctuate between the history and the fiction of these beings who were so extraordinary and yet so real, have not failed to create current interest in the literature of our time.

A passage that is of great interest because it possesses all the features necessary for writing a novel is the one appearing in Ruy Díaz de Guzmán's *La Argentina*. In this work published in 1612, narrating the events that took place in the River Plate provinces in 1526, the story is told of a married woman, Lucía de Miranda, who participated in Cabot's expedition in that year. This woman aroused the desire of the local chieftain, who in order to possess her burned the fort of Corpus Christi, so as to be able to carry her off and live with her. Díaz de Guzmán mentions the following incident in which a woman is the protagonist.[28] "But Lucía did not abandon her husband, and she saw him secretly. A jealous concubine of the chieftain discovered what was going on and told the chieftain about it. He imprisoned Lucía and her husband and burned them alive" (Díaz de Guzmán 25-26).

This event is important not only because it is an example of the classic love triangle in an exotic setting, nor because it makes reference to the sacrifice of a woman for the sake of being with her husband, or because several women are mentioned, but rather because of the literary skill with which the author of the chronicle commits the event to paper. In *La Argentina* this type of occurrence is what makes a work like this not only a documentary chronicle of the encounter, but also a work of great literary value, in which fiction is rounded out by historical evidence. In this case, a white woman is forced to have "relations" with an Indian. Lucía de Miranda ends up swelling the ranks of those women who underwent the most horrible deaths in the encounter.

In itself, the topic of the abduction of white women by Indians is not new, although it has many variants. What is in fact important is that not many cases are recorded in the Spanish encounter. María Teresa Villafañe tells a story that could just as well provide a filmscript. It is the kidnapping of one of the nuns of St. Elizabeth of Hungary, Francisca Ramírez, who in 1598 was living within the fortress of Santiago de Chile. This nun's work was to take care of the sick and wounded and to attend to the needs of the population. Apparently the Araucanian chieftain Huentemagú, captivated by the beauty of her blue eyes and her blond hair, seeing that he could not win her love, decided to carry her off. So great was the psychological influence exercised by the nun Francisca Ramírez on this Indian, that he ended up being baptized with all his family. Fearing that in his absence or in case of his death some other Indian would violate the nun's chastity, Huentemagú decided to take her back to the fort and ask to be her servant, to live at her side in a purely spiritual union (Villafañe 139).

In the same work by Ruy Díaz de Guzmán there is another novelistic incident, in which another woman plays the lead role. It is the case of "La Maldonada." This woman was fed by a female puma for several days because she had helped the puma bear her two cubs: "Díaz de Guzmán tells how [Francisco Ruiz Galán] once sentenced a woman, known as La Maldonada, to be tied to a tree so the animals would eat her. La Maldonada saw a female puma come near, who instead of devouring her protected her from the other animals" (27). The narration itself carries all the force of a "wondrous" event. In fact, the event itself is not so extraordinary as it is depicted. It boils down to the capture by a Spanish captain who had gone out to reconnoiter the surrounding towns, of a Spanish woman who had abandoned the Spanish camp out of "hunger," and had ended up in the hands of the Indians. The punishment meted out, which was brutal and disproportionate, had an unexpected, nearly divine outcome.

> As soon as Francisco Ruiz Galán saw her, he ordered that she be thrown to the beasts, so that they would tear her apart and eat her; and, carrying out his order, they took hold of the poor woman, tied her very tightly to a tree, and left her about a league outside the village, where that night a great number of beasts came out to devour the prey, and among them came the female puma whom this woman had helped with giving birth, and being familiar with her, it defended her from the others that were there and wished to tear her apart (Díaz de Guzmán 128; 13).

This occurrence demonstrates the excessive authority that one individual, in this case Francisco Ruiz Galán, could come to possess, at a great distance from Spain, so as to make such brutal, unjust decisions about one of the women in his camp. Understandably, the circumstances recounted have Greco-Latin and even Biblical roots, in legendary stories such as that of the founders of Rome, Romulus and Remus, suckled by a female wolf, stories of martyrs in the Roman colosseum, and all manner of miracles brought about by divine intervention. The first that comes to mind is that of the prophet Daniel, who was thrown to the lions' den but was respected by them, a sign that "God" was on his side. Early in the morning the king went to the lions' den and asked Daniel:

> "O Daniel, servant of the living God, has your God, whom you serve continually, been able to deliver you from the lions?" Then Daniel said to the king, "O king, live for ever! My God sent his angel and shut the lions' mouths, and they have not hurt me, because I was found blameless before him; and also before you, O king, I have done no wrong." Then the king was exceedingly glad, and commanded that Daniel be taken up out of the den. So Daniel was taken up out of the den, and no kind of hurt was found upon him, because he had trusted in his God. (Daniel 6.21-25)

The parallelism between this Biblical passage and the incident that occurred to the Christian woman, La Maldonada, in Ruy Díaz de Guzmán's work has historico-dramatic resonances that create greater interest in the work for those readers for whom it was intended.

In his edition of *La Argentina*, the historian Enrique de Gandía at no time dismisses the historical veracity of two of the three most novelistic episodes. Although it is true that at some point of the history all that mythological underpinning of Amazons, miracles, monsters, apparitions, and such shows up, it is noteworthy that a modern researcher should display that commonplace need to believe in the fantastic, to unleash the imagination in the face of the most surprising and unusual events, and not to show clearly the creative possibilities of the writer of a work. Enrique de Gandía says in one of his notes, referring to the incident of La Maldonada, "We believe that the story of La Maldonada may be true, because Francisco Ruiz Galán had the habit of punishing the conquistadores by tying them to a tree so that they would be eaten by animals. Antonio de la Trinidad, for example, accused him of this crime" (Díaz de Guzmán 48; ch.7).

It is frankly difficult to separate fiction from historical evidence with respect to the acts committed toward some of the women when the information is loaded with exaggerations that verge on the novelistic—especially if this information comes to us from sources traditionally considered reliable. From ancient times, writers such as

Homer or Lucian of Samosata have been aware of this duality. Herodotus himself, considered by many to be the "father of history," is credited with more than a few fantastic digressions. Nor does the Bible escape this feature; on the contrary, it is one of the best examples of it.

The encounter of the Americas was the ideal scenario for giving free rein to the imagination. There are many Spanish and Portuguese sixteenth-century chronicles with these characteristics; nevertheless the one by Spanish explorer Alvar Núñez Cabeza de Vaca stands out among them, not only because it includes more fictional elements, but because it combines historical documentation with the novelistic. The Portuguese João Mendes Pinto in his work *Peregrinacão*, also speaks of miracles and describes monsters with a dragon's shape (18-19; ch. 14).

Many works of theater were inspired by this type of event. Paradoxically, most of them were staged outside of Spain:

> This whole question of the vacuum of the Americas in Spanish drama from the political and historical points of view lies in the hidden and deep psychological characteristics of the Spaniard: his sense of pride, his desire for recognition, and his expectation of wealth—factors which the American encounter did not offer him at the time with any certainty (Sánchez 17).

There is a need to investigate what the real motives were that caused the most historically important events of the Spanish nation, such as those that occurred during the sixteenth century in the Americas, to pass almost unnoticed in Golden Age drama (1501-1681).

ISABEL BARRETO

One of the most significant voyages in terms of miles covered was that made by Alvaro de Mendaña's expedition, his second voyage to the mythical Solomon Islands. He set sail on June 10, 1595. "The total number of crew members was three hundred seventy-eight men and some ninety-eight persons among women and children" (Fernández de Quirós 27). This expedition is noteworthy not only because of the number of women that went along, but also because one of them was Alvaro de Mendaña's wife, Doña Isabel Barreto, who was to become governor and leader of the expedition upon her husband's death. This voyage also covered the greatest distance reached by any Spanish ship in the sixteenth century, an even longer distance than was traveled by the ships that made the annual voyage from Acapulco to the Philippines. To cross the entire Pacific Ocean was an enterprise worthy of the boldest, most intrepid spirits, especially since the location of the mythical Solomon Islands was not known with total accuracy. As for the crew of the expedition, Roberto Ferrando says, "The most notable fact that we noted was the mass marriage of fiteen couples on the eve of the arrival at the Marquesas, when the signs of landfall were unmistakable" (Fernández de Quirós 27). The impression that the Polynesian natives had of Castilian women seems also to have caused some commentary: "They looked at the ship and the people and at the women, who upon seeing them had gone out to the gallery, and they looked at the women with affection and laughed a great deal when they saw them" (Fernández de Quirós 73; ch.6). In any case the description that the Spaniards made of the Polynesian women was more descriptive: "And all who saw them said they found them pretty of leg, hands, beautiful eyes, face, waist and figure, and that some of them were more beautiful than Lima ladies, and the women of that place are very much so" (Fernández de Quiros 82; ch. 9). There is no doubt that the native women were beautiful, and that they made an impression on the Spanish sailors and soldiers, especially after such long months of sailing. On one occasion mention is made of a native woman who came up to Isabel Barreto, who out of curiosity tried to cut off a bit of her hair: "A very beautiful Indian woman sat down next to Doña Isabel to fan her; the Indian woman had such blond hair that Doña Isabel tried to have a bit of it cut off, and seeing that she drew back, they stopped doing it so as not to make her angry" (Fernández de Quirós 78; ch.8).

This voyage might have gone unnoticed if only its material results had been taken into account, or the historical or testimonial quality of the account written by the Portuguese—Portugal was under the Spanish Crown from 1580 to 1640—Pedro Fernández de Quirós. Thanks to him, the chief navigator of that expedition, accurate notice was given not only about the Australian continent and the surroundings, named "Austrialia of the Holy Spirit" in honor of Phillip III, king of the Austrias, but also of the greatest responsiblity ever exercised by a woman at sea. Isabel Barreto, the widow of Governor Alvaro de Mendaña, had to take charge of the expedition in one of the most tragic and distressing situations in which not only a woman but any human being has been involved.

Doña Isabel Barreto, like her husband Alvaro de Mendaña, who had influenced her since they had been betrothed, dreamed and supposed that to the south of the Solomon Islands was the legendary country of Ophir, from which the gold and precious stones had been taken to build Solomon's temple. These must have been the rumors that circulated in the salons of the Viceroy of Peru and his wife: García Hurtado de Mendoza and Teresa de Castro, when the adelantado arrived at the by then very active social center of Lima (Villafañe 134). Isabel de Barreto did not hesitate to include members of her hamily in the expedition that she herself was going to participate in: "Because of her marriage to Don Alvaro and the marriage contracts, she and her brothers Lorenzo, Diego, and Luis formed part of the expedition, and also another woman, Doña Mariana de Castro, priests and maritime folk" (Villafañe 134).

Thanks to the bravery, the character, and the perseverance of this woman, despite the high number of losses they sustained "with fifty persons less, who died after the departure from Santa Cruz," the expedition managed to arrive safely. In Professor Roberto Ferrando's documented analysis of this account, *Descubrimiento de las regiones australes*, one senses, however, a negative perception of this singular figure.

> We now have Doña Isabel Barreto as governor of the Santa Cruz colony, adelantada of the Western Islands, marchioness, etc. In her we have the first woman who would bear those titles, execpt, of course, marchioness. Virile in character, authoritarian, indomitable, she was to impose her despotic will on all those who were under her command, above all on the dangerous voyage to Manila.[29]

It was true that Isabel Barreto could boast of the titles mentioned, although as we have seen, she was not the first woman governor, since in 1541, Beatriz de la Cueva, wife of Cortés's captain Pedro de

Alvarado, became governor of Guatemala as did Isabel de Bobadilla in Cuba, among others. As to the qualifiers "virile, authoritarian, indomitable," I do not think for a moment that they should be seen as negative qualities, but rather as indispensable for leading a crew and a voyage of that type. The ability to lead sailors and soldiers who were continuously plotting all kinds of conspiracies, who would stab one another, as in fact they did, over differences of opinion, was not any easy job for anybody. Isabel Barreto displayed exceptional aptitude for command and the necessary toughness to get obedience from crude, adventuring men who were on many occasions desperate and inclined to the must unexpected acts. Although these same men were capable of commiting the most lofty acts of heroism, they were also capable of cutting off the head of their superiors if they thought it necessary. Before governor Alvaro de Mendaña died and left his position and authority to his wife, there were signs of unrest and the beginnings of mutiny among some of the soldiers. Some were beginning to question the adelantado's opinions, saying that the land was very poor and unprofitable and the the place they had settled was not appropriate. It seemed that nothing could satisfy them:

> What had seemed very good to them yesterday, now seemed bad to them; they were led by their whims, and forgot the obligations that bound those who served under their King's flag. In short, a paper appeared with certain signatures, and what it said was that they were asking the adelantado to take them away from that place and give them a better one or take them to the islands that he had spoken so highly of (Fernández de Quirós 104; ch. 16).

The most interesting aspect of this information is that it comes from Pedro Fernández de Quirós himself, the chronicler and chief navigator of the expedition, who for his part had a number of verbal disputes with the "adelantada." Despite this, he chose to commit to paper those moments when Doña Isabel showed forbearance, on several occasions commuting the death penalty for several of her subordinates. Doña Isabel hated the "company commander" because he was the instigator of the revolts that were being plotted, and of many of the deaths inflicted on the natives, with the result that they revolted and attacked the Spanish encampment, and this fact was used as an excuse to leave the village that they were beginning to build. In the following lines Quirós shows us Doña Isabel's determined character, when the "company commander" arrived on the adelantado's ship: "His wife Doña Isabel prodded him, saying to her husband (as she told it), 'Sir, kill him, or have him killed. What more do you want, for he has fallen into your hands? And if not, I shall kill him with this machete.' The adelantado was cautious, and did not do it" (117; ch. 19). Although Doña Isabel's threat did not get beyond words, there is no doubt that she was a "fighting" lady. On another occasion, Quirós says that he, the chief navigator, was the target of the wrath of some soldiers, "and it was well known that they were coming to kill the chief navigator, and there were those who swore in the trial that they had been saying, 'Let's go kill that man who is the reason that we are in this land'; and others swore that the threats went so far as to say 'that they would drink out of his skull.' Things did not look good; God knows what their intentions were" (116; ch.18).

Once Governor Alvaro de Mendaña had died—of natural causes—and now traveling to the Philippines, Quirós complains that it was not he who was making the most important decisions. It was the female governor, lady and master of the Pacific, and she let everyone know it. Quirós complains about this: "I know not what I can do so that this lady will come to her senses. She must think that I was born with the obligation to serve her and suffer her" (161; ch. 35). Nearing the Philippines, "the governor ordered a proclamation to be issued that on pain of death no one was to go on land without her permission" (Fernández de Quirós 162; ch. 35). It seems that a married soldier disobeyed the order and went to a village in search of food, and for that reason the lady governor ordered him to be made prisoner and tried. The soldier's wife, crying and protesting, asked for justice and pardon for her husband, for which purpose the chief navigator, Quirós, went to talk with the governor. She answered him that the soldier had to pay for his disobedience:

> And the chief navigator replied saying that the children of God are disheartened with the penalty of eternal damnation, and those of the Holy Mother Church with the penalty of excommunication, and those of the King with the penalty of a traitor, loss of life, honor and belongings, and that then the sword would not be bloodied. The chief navigator implored her not to threaten others so much, and that he would vouch for them and take charge of them. At that the prisoner was freed (Fernández de Quirós 162-63; ch. 35).

Doña Isabel knew very well that if she did not put some "fear" into the sailors and soldiers, it would be hard for her to hope to arrive in port alive. No matter how Machiavellian this way of behaving may seem, I do not think there was any other possible way, considering the crisis situation that they were going through: "They were so bored by now, that they put no value on life; and there was one man who asked the chief navigator why he was tiring himself and tiring them: it was better to die once rather than many times; that they should shut their eyes and let the ship go to the bottom" (Fernández de Quirós 147; ch. 30). A very special spirit was needed so as not to break down in such circumstances. Despite the criticism of which she was the target, most of it related to the misuse of water and provisions from the storeroom, Isabel Barreto did not fail to sympathize with and suffer the anxieties of all the rest. According to Quirós's text, in which criticisms predominate, moments of humanity appear in this person who felt the need to ask Heaven for strength to get through all those calamities. "The lady governor in her retreat [a small room on the boat for privacy] appeared to be making her peace with death. Prayers in memory of Christ's agony in the garden, her eyes turned Heavenwards, saying short prayers, as distressed and tearful as any of us" (Fernández de Quirós 157; ch. 34). After all was said and done, she was a woman of "flesh and bone" like everyone else, but brave enough to defy the devil in the presence of death itself to the extent she felt befit her by right and by her authority. And the truth was that on that voyage to Manila thorugh seas never before navigated, death showed up every day.

> The ration given out was a half pound of flour, from which without sifting some pancakes were made, mixed with salt water and grilled on coals; half a pint of water full of rotting cockroaches, which made it very loathsome and fetid. There was not much peace, beset by so much sickness and discontent. What could be seen were the sores, which were very big on feet and legs; sadness, moaning, hunger, sicknesses and dead men with the cries of those who touched them; for there was hardly a day when one or two were not thrown into the sea, and some days three or four. And such it was that in order to take the dead from between-decks there was no little difficulty (Fernández de Quirós 145; ch. 29).

In such situations, a woman who was capable of maintaining a firm spirit deserves credit. Isabel Barreto enters the history of exploration and encounter as a woman capable of enduring with courage and resignation the most difficult physical and spiritual ordeals imaginable for a person. On their arrival at the port of Cavite in the Philippines, they were greeted with a "salvo" from "all the artillery and harquebusery toward the royal standard that was flying" (Fernández de Quirós 168-69; ch. 37).

After her interminable voyage, Isabel Barreto was married for the second time to "a young gentleman named Don Fernando de Castro, a cousin of Governor Mariñas" (Fernández de Quirós 180; ch. 40). The new couple made another voyage to New Spain and from there to Peru, where they set up on an encomienda inherited from her previous husband. Little more is known of their lives, which are lost among speculation and legend (Acosta 135).

> In a fragile woman's body we find the temperament of a Cortés, a Pizarro, with the title of adelantada, governor, and admiral, who did justice to her responsibilities, despite the hostile pen of Quirós, who on narrating his history leaves us with an astonishing portrait of the woman who managed to dominate those men of lax discipline, originating in factions and from demoralization on those anxious voyages (Acosta 153).

That woman's body could not have been all that fragile, to withstand what she withstood and to cross the ocean yet again, this time in the company of her new husband.

INÉS SUÁREZ

There are very few documented examples of women such as Isabel Barreto, who not only were capable of following their husbands and lovers to the end, but managed, in adverse circumstances, to become captains and leaders of entire armies when conditions required. Not many are known who, even at the price of earning the enmity of many, were able to play such a leading role as Doña Isabel did. This kind of woman did not stop at maintaining a passive stance in events but managed, when necessary, to make decisions as crucial as that of personally carrying out the most extreme sentence that can be given to a human being: death.

It would be naive to criticize out of hand the actions of these women without first knowing the conditions that drove them to act. Outstanding among this group of persons was Inés Suárez. She did not go unnoticed, like many other women, because she was the lover and companion of the conquistador and governor of Chile, Pedro de Valdivia, one of the "greats" of the encounter of the Americas. Nevertheless, not much has been written by historians on the first women who arrived in Peru and Chile, although it is known that by the middle of the sixteenth century many Spanish women and women of other European nationalities had arrived. From that time on, every ship that arrived at Pacific ports brought women who were coming to join their husbands, fathers, or brothers, or who were simply coming, as was the case of many, to seek adventure (Acosta 153). These first women colonizers not only arrived by ship in Peru and Chile, but some took the chance of making the exhausting land trip across the kingdoms of Nueva Granada and Quito, arriving at Cuzco and going on from there to Lima (Acosta 153).

Valdivia, the conquistador of Chile, had been married in Spain to Marina Ortiz de Gaete, who lived in Salamanca until 1554 (Valdivia left for the Indies in 1535), when she was informed that her husband had become governor of the province of Chile. Doña Marina, who had been receiving a punctual and generous pension and all kinds of amenities over the last twenty years, finally decided to join her spouse. Without waiting for his approval and thinking only of being at her husband's side, she sailed in a fleet heading for Panama, so as to cross the isthmus and from there go down to Chile by ship. She imagined that now, together with her husband she could enjoy the fruits of his conquests. When Doña Marina arrived in Panama, she found out that Valdivia had been sacrificed by the Araucanian Indians. Despite everything, she decided to continue her voyage as far as Lima and thereby claim her husband's possessions. Although she wrote a petition to the king, explaining her sad situation, it is not known whether she ever received anything: "Her heart filled with grief, but she resolved to continue her trip to Peru...From there she went on to Chile to claim her husband's wealth; but she obtained nothing. Valdivia's possessions had been sold by his creditors so as to collect what he owed them" (Acosta 152-53).

According to the facts and the evidence that has come down to us, it could be said that the true love of the conquistador of Chile was Inés Suárez. Doña Inés, from the Extremaduran city of Plasencia, had been born about 1507. She set sail for the Americas in 1537, and we do not know if she was a widow by then, since she had been married in the city of Málaga (O'Sullivan-Beare 222). In principle, Doña Inés went as Valdivia's servant, to take charge of his house. She was, in addition, the only woman who accompanied Valdivia's troops in the conquest of Chile. She had the personality and the courage to pass publicly as the governor's lover—not a negligible gesture, considering the weight of Catholic morals at that time. But the most important thing of all is that through information provided by "a hundred witnesses," the general consensus is that she was a "good," Christian woman, in the broadest sense of the word.[30] She was always ready to give aid and comfort to the sick wounded and to give what she had. She managed to earn the good will of almost all those who knew her. It is no wonder that Valdivia held her in higher regard than even his own wife.

Inés Suárez was a woman of exceptional qualities. Not only was she beautiful, kindly, and loyal to her people, but she also possessed a large dose of ingenuity which at one of the most critical moments saved the Spanish encampment. It is not strange that Don Pedro, who did not take up with just any woman, should have accepted her in the sight of all as his real wife (O'Sullivan-Beare 225).

Inés Suárez had to test her bravery in the most critical circumstances. On September 11, 1541, the Spanish troops were being defeated by the Indians after an extremely arduous battle; there was almost no hope for the Christian troops. Inés Suárez's participation and her courage at that moment were decisive in saving the day. The Indians were already declaring victory when...

> she threw a coat of mail over her shoulders and thus went out to the
> fort and stood in front of all the soldiers, encouraging them with words
> so carefully thought out that they were more those of a brave captain
> used to being at arms than of a woman familiar with pincushions. And

at the same time she told them that if anyone felt exhausted from his wounds he should come to her to be cured by her hand; at which some came over, and she herself cured them as best she could, almost amid the very hooves of the horses; and when she finished curing them, she persuaded and encouraged them to go back into battle to give assistance to the others, who were in it and were nearly collapsing (O'Sullivan-Beare 20).

Despite all her efforts and those of her compatriots, the battle was lost. Only seven chieftains remained prisoner in the hands of the Spaniards and it was Inés Suárez no less who proposed that their heads be cut off and thrown to the enemy. In fact, not only were their heads cut off as Doña Inés had suggested, but apparently it was she who did it. They say that she went up to those who were guarding the chieftains, Francisco Rubio and Hernando de la Torres, and told them to kill them before it was too late and they were freed by their men. As if this were not enough, once the chieftains were dead, she went back to encouraging the Christians who were fighting and to aiding the wounded: "And Hernando de la Torre said to her, more seized with fear than full of enthusiasm to cut off heads: 'Madam, how is it that I am supposed to kill them?' She answered, 'Like this,' and unsheathing her sword she killed them all with such virile spirit as if she were a Roland or a Ruy Díaz" (O'Sullivan Beare 231).

It would make no sense to judge this incident without taking into account the critical situation in which the population of Santiago found itself. It was Inés Suárez's "tremendous" decision that saved what remained of the Spanish troops and made the Indians retreat in terror, seeing the dreadful death their leaders had suffered. Inés Suárez was the one who devised and carried out this truly surprising deed. How many people would have been able to undertake this mass decapitation, fearing on the other hand the terrible reprisals that it could bring on? Once again it was a woman who took action and put an end to an untenable situation. With an unmatched spirit, Inés Suárez showed that she was a lioness in war and a woman full of love, strength, and care for those around her.

Envy, always present in ambitious and egotistical spirits whenever things go well for their neighbors, made its appearance. The enemies of the conquistador of Chile found in Inés Suárez an excuse to accuse him of carrying on an extramarital affair and serving as a bad example for his fellow citizens. Attorney La Gasca ordered Valdivia to separate from the person he loved most to comply with the social and "religious" ordinances of the moment. Valdivia married Doña Inés off to the man who was later the governor of Chile, Rodrigo Quiroga.

In recognition of her outstanding performance in the war against the Araucanians, Inés Suárez received an encomienda in her name. She showed on the other hand, that in spite of the fact that she had been Pedro de Valdivia's lover in a "notorious" way, her achievements transcended the moral and social circumstances of the moment. On January 20, 1544, in the reading of the royal warrant granting the encomienda to Inés Suárez, the reasons why this woman excelled in both difficult moments and in everyday life are clearly stated.

> You, Doña Inés Suárez, came with me to these provinces to serve His Majesty in them, undergoing many hardships and fatigues, because of both the length of the journey and the encounters we had with Indians, and the hunger and other wants that came upon us before this city [Santiago] was settled, which for the men were very hard to take, and all the more so for so delicate a woman as you, and besides this, in the uprising in this land and the arrival of the Indians in this city which they threatened to take over, your effort and perseverance was a reason that they did not take it over, because all the Christians who in the city had to do so much to fight the enemy that they did not remember the chieftains who had been taken prisoner, which was the main reason why the Indians had come, to free them, and you, drawing strength out of your weak powers, had the chieftains killed, laying your own hands on them, and this was the reason that the greater share of the Indians went off and stopped fighting, seeing their lords dead (Villafañe 130).

Inés Suárez must not have had such "weak powers," nor must she have been so "delicate" as she is described. For some sad time more, unable to be at the side of the woman he loved most, Pedro de Valdivia continued fighting for the interests of the Crown. Valdivia lost his life fighting against the Araucanian Indians.

This kind of heroic act turns these figures into almost mythological beings, belonging more to the world of epic literature than to history itself. To find similar deeds, we have to go back to the most ancient accounts documented by humankind. What better parallel to this story than that of Judith in the Bible, the Jewish woman who because of her beauty and seductive powers was able to put an end to the Assyrian threat to the people of Israel? "And they marveled at her beauty and admired the Israelites, judging them by her, and every one said to his neighbor, 'Who can despise this people, who have women like this among them?'" (Judith 13.6-8)

When she arrived in the Jewish camp, with the head of the Assyrian leader, the magistrate of the city, Uzziah, stressing the importance of her action, blessing her and giving her thanks said to her, "O daughter, you are blessed by the Most High God above all women on earth; and blessed be the Lord God, who created the heavens and the earth, who has guided you to strike the head of the leader of our enemies. Your hope will never depart from the hearts of men, as they remember the power of God." (Judith 13.18-19)

Unlike what we read in the Bible, "Your hope will never depart from the hearts of men," Inés Suárez, like so many other women has remained almost forgotten. To recover those stellar moments of the female epic of the encounter, there is a need for those pens to immortalize her deeds and "surprise us" with events which unless they were documented by several sources, would easily become confused with the deeds of other, legendary figures.

MARÍA DE VERA AND CATALINA XUÁREZ MARCAIDA: WOMEN SETTLERS

It was María de Vera who put the shroud on Catalina Xuárez Marcaida, Hernán Cortés's first wife, and was also the first woman called in by him after his wife had died. There are solid reasons to believe that María de Vera was the sister of the famous explorer of the southwestern United States, Alvar Núñez Cabeza de Vaca. As for María de Vera's genealogy and her relationship to the author of the *Naufragios*, they coincide not only in their paternal surname "Vera," but also in their age and the fact that Hernán Cortés had some acquaintance with the Duke of Medina Sidonia, for whom Alvar Núñez worked for several years: "He provides a precious detail for anyone who knows the civil law of those times; if in 1512, the guardianship of four siblings—Alvar Núñez, Juan de Vera, Francisco de Vera, and María de Vera—was given over to their uncle Pedro de Vera Hinojosa, that is unmistakable evidence that she, the youngest of all of them, was already at least twelve years old" (Barris 46).

The reason why the siblings of the explorer from Jerez went unnoticed is that they used their paternal surname "Vera," which created the impression that they were people from different families. If María de Vera's date of birth is previous to 1500, she could very well have been the "housekeeper" of a woman as prominent as Hernán Cortés's wife, Catalina Xuárez Marcaida, was at that time. It should be remembered that her possible brother, Alvar Núñez Cabeza de Vaca, was also the "chamberlain" of the Duke of Medina Sidonia.

> 12/11/1522. Thursday. The Duke granted to Alvar Núñez Cabeza, his chamberlain, the authority to substitute in his place and in name of his lordship another power, which before this he had granted to said Alvar Núñez, so that in the name of the Duke, he might appear before His Majesty's bookkeepers who have charge of the books of the grand master's offices and orders, and request and take with him any draft for the maravedís that are owed him, which are set down in said books of the order of Santiago, which are 12,000 maravedís per year.[31]

In any case, whether María de Vera, who shrouded Catalina Xuárez Marcaida, was or was not the sister of the explorer of Florida is today conjectural. Hipólito Sancho de Sopranis, who has undertaken several genealogical studies of Cabeza de Vaca's family, says of María de Vera, "Doña María de Vera, who at one point in the partition, alluding to her

young age, he calls the girl, made a brilliant marriage with Ruy Díaz de
Guzmán, the son of Alonso de Riquel and Doña Brianda de
Guzmán...Blessed with a longevity that greatly exceeded her brothers',
she was still alive on December 4, 1577" (Sancho de Sopranis 78-79).

The Argentine historian, Enrique de Gandía, mentions in his edition
of Ruy Díaz de Guzmán's *La Argentina* that a sister of Alvar Núñez
Cabeza de Vaca married the grandfather of the author of that work.
Nancy O'Sullivan, basing herself on the historian Alfonso Toro,
summarizes the first moments after the death of Catalina Xuárez
Marcaida:

> And amid the natural confusion, several women appeared, all of them
> servants in Cortés's house, and all the more interesting because he had
> carnal relations with almost all of them, as we shall state. When
> Cortés's wife died, his servant Alonso de Villanueva went to call *María
> de Vera*, who was the first woman to see the dead woman. A witness
> in the impeachment trial, Juan de Burgos, testified to these matters. He
> being at home, said Alonso de Villanueva went "to call María de Vera,
> this witness's housekeeper, for Don Fernando had called for her, and
> this may have been at twelve midnight, and said María de Vera went
> to the house of said Don Fernando with said Villanueva, and one-and-a-
> half to two hours later said María de Vera returned to the house of this
> witness and said to this witness, 'I have just laid out Catalina Xuárez,
> the wife of Captain Fernando Cortés.' And this witness said to her,
> 'What? Is Catalina Xuárez dead?' 'Yes, for I have left her shrouded,
> and this traitor Fernando Cortés killed her; because when I was putting
> the shroud on her, I saw signs on her throat showing that he had
> strangled her with cords, which seemed very clear;' and Diego de
> Soria's wife and María Destrada, and the wife of the late Xaramillo
> [Doña Marina?], who were there, showed said María de Vera the signs
> of the cords that said Catalina Xuárez had on her throat, where it
> appeared that she had been strangled, and said María de Vera pretended
> not to see..."(O'Sullivan-Beare 73).

It should be noted that one of the witnesses was María de Estrada.
In fact on March 10, 1529, María de Vera, "thirty-five years old," was
questioned (Toro 73). If Doña Catalina's death occured in October or
November, 1522, María would at that time have been twenty-six years
old. Thus the year of her birth would be 1494, and she would be four
years younger than her brother Alvar Núñez Cabeza de Vaca. This fact
by itself would not be significant; it is however, when we learn that

Hernán Cortés had sexual relations with all or almost all the women who worked for him: "for he had an infinite number of women within his house, from the land, and others from Castile, and according to general rumor and his reputation among his attendants and servants, it was said that he had had access to all the women in his household" (O'Sullivan-Beare 88).

One of the most interesting points in that whole trial was María de Vera's reluctance to testify against Cortés, although all the proof went against him. One wonders whether this attitude was brought on by simple fear or if, on the contrary, it was love that drove her to defend her master. At no time did María de Vera publically accuse Hernán Cortés of the death of Catalina Xuárez; on the contrary, she defended him whenever the opportunity presented itself. "And it should be noted that María de Vera, who provided Juan de Burgos with so many details about the way she had found Marcaida's body and what happened in Don Hernando's house when she arrived, was not equally forthcoming when she was called to testify, perhaps out of fear of Cortés, and she even went so far as to say that Doña Catalina had been previously sick, but then had gotten well" (Toro 84).

In the questioning of María de Vera, the witness gave to understand that the death of Catalina Xuárez had been expected, and that there was no reason for surprise at her sudden death, given Doña Catalina's weak, sickly nature. In the trial conducted for this purpose, María de Vera answered the fourth question as follows: "She had seen Doña Catalina ten days before, and she had heard, a good two weeks before said Catalina died, that she was sick; but after this she found out and heard that said Doña Catalina had gone out to mass" (Toro 73).

Another of the eyewitnesses, Ana Rodríguez, said that Violante Rodríguez, upon asking María de Vera a question, had a sense that the latter was refusing to go against the interests of the conquistador of Mexico.

> Seeing that spectacle, Ana Rodríguez asked Don Hernando, "What were those red marks that said Doña Catalina had on her throat," and he answered, "that he had taken hold of her there to revive her when she fainted." This made the Rodríguez woman suspect that Cortés had strangled his wife, and Violante Rodríguez had the same suspicion, and she told María de Vera "that poor Doña Catalina had died like the wife of Count Alarcos [strangled]"; at which María exclaimed, "Be quiet,

for the love of God, don't let Don Hernando know it!" This phrase shows us how fearful she was (Toro 85).

María de Vera is not the only one who defended Hernán Cortés. Francisco Fernández del Castillo, in his book *Catalina Xuárez Marcayda*, also rejects the possibility that Cortés had strangled his wife. And the reasons he gives are not negligible. The first and most basic is that Cortés possessed all the means he could have wanted to get rid of his wife: poisons, Indians who would have participated in an ambush, and many resources available to one of the most respected and astute men in New Spain, "rather than to resort to the brutal procedure of strangling her while alone in the marriage bed so that he would be identified as the assassin. That is so infantile that it can only be believed if one is blinded by passion" (Fernández del Castillo 39).

Cesáreo Fernández Duro, for his part, concludes that Doña Catalina's sudden death may well have been due to a genetically inherited illness, since it would appear that her sisters died in similar ways.

> Slanderous tongues spread malicious rumors that motivated a trial to determine the causes of death; but the fact is that the other sisters had died previously of the same sudden affliction. Of one of them, Leonor, married to Andrés de Barrios, a gentleman of the Arcos lineage, Viceroy Antonio de Mendoza said of her "that she should have lived to be the governess of princes, in view of the valor she had" (Fernández Duro 15).

More recently, in another study on the conquistador of Mexico, Fredo Arias de la Canal points out that the cause of the death of Catalina Xuárez was due to the attack of an "aggressive somnambulist," in this case her husband, Hernán Cortés. Arias de la Canal says that an aggressive somnambulist is a person who defends himself pseudo-aggressively while asleep. Arias explains that in one of these attacks, Cortés was defending himself from his maternal image: Catalina Xuárez, his wife:

> For that reason, when he awoke he said to the young women, "I think that my wife is dead," since he himself was not sure of what he had done....That Cortés had frequent bouts of somnambulism can be deduced from the statement of María Hernández de Quevedo: "Because said Catalina had much conversation and friendship with this witness; because they knew each other from Cuba, and said Catalina

would tell this witness many times about the bad times she spent with said Don Fernando Cortés, and how he often threw her out of bed at night, and treated her badly in other ways."[32]

Thus the true intention of María de Vera, supposed sister of Alvar Núñez, in the defense she made of her master Hernán Cortés, is open to question. Cortés himself had the opportunity some years later to hear the fantastic stories of Alvar Núñez Cabeza de Vaca and the other three survivors of the failed Pánfilo de Narváez expedition through the territories located to the north of New Spain—Quivira and Cibola—and the supposed riches of those territories.

Something is known about Cortés's second wife, Doña Juana de Zúñiga, who also went over to Mexico, where she stayed until his death in 1547. Later, the Marchioness of the Valley would return to Spain with her children. "After richly celebrating his marriage to Doña Juana de Zúñiga, Cortés returned to Mexico, taking along his wife and her mother, accompanied by a large company of matrons, maidens, servants and protégés" (Acosta 144). There were thus many women who went to the Americas who are known because they had a direct or indirect relationship with Hernán Cortés.

LEONOR PONCE DE LEÓN

It would be unfair to deal with the Caribbean islands and not mention Leonor Ponce de León. She was important not only because she was the wife of Juan Ponce de León, the great explorer who entered history as the dreamer who sought to find the "fountain of eternal youth" in Florida, but because of something more important: she was a great woman. Doña Leonor is remembered in history as a person who with her example managed to attract the attention of other ladies who over time would become part of the social and family foundation that would be created in Puerto Rico. "In our first family, the female influence was providential and fortunate for our country, according to material archeological evidence" (Tío 23). Through the research he carried out at Doña Leonor's residence in Caparra, Aurelio Tío offers a portrait of that woman "located in the jungle and surrounded by hostile Indians:"

> Excavated were Sevillian blue tiles, fine china tableware, and perfume bottles that indicate, even in a jungle country, Doña Leonor Ponce de León put her household together with the beauty and artistry that her position and situation allowed, with neither pomp nor ostentation, but rather with the sobriety that since that time our country has developed out of imperious necessity in the material order, in accordance with its geographical limitations and scarcity of natural resources (Tío 23).

It is not only moral or spiritual factors that do credit to this woman. Leonor Ponce de León can also claim some historical distinction, since she was the first Spanish woman to reside in Puerto Rico, once Juan Ponce de León obtained authorization to bring over his entire family on May 2, 1509. "As ladies-in-waiting for his wife, he was permitted to bring along the wives of two veteran expeditionaries who were already in Puerto Rico, Pedro Campano and Diego Gómez, on a ship owned by Ponce de León, Grand Master Alonso de San Martín" (Tío 21-22).

The same writer adds some further virtues to this important woman, during the first years of Spanish presence on the island, which leads us to believe that the ladies who accompanied her were not without virtues of their own: "We have ample evidence that the first woman settler of Puerto Rico, Doña Leonor Ponce de León, exercised an extraordinary and lasting influence on the morals and the culture of our people with her exemplary conduct" (Tío 22). In fact it is surprising how after so many years of North American influence, the Puerto Rican people have managed to maintain their own identity, often standing out in both arts and letters.

Like it or not, Spanish women were there, where the situation required. Oftentimes, going beyond the norms of the period, they followed their husbands and lovers to the very jaws of death. In America, in the Mediterranean, in the "Invincible" Armada, or even in the Battle of Lepanto itself. This is how Cesáreo Fernández Duro ended his address on "women in the conquest," read before the Royal Academy of History in 1902:

> In the armada called *Invincible*, the express purpose of which was to invade England, since the prohibition of the embarkation of women was rigorously observed, the women chartered ships on their own and followed the fleet, prepared to participate equally in the benefits of success and in the hardships that fate might have in store. And what benefits the galleys of the Holy League sought! And nevertheless skirts were seen at Lepanto as in other enterprises (Fernández Duro 27).

If women were present at the two most critical naval encounters in Spanish history, what reason is there to think that they were not involved in other, lesser campaigns?

WOMAN-AT-ARMS: WITHOUT GEOGRAPHICAL LIMITS

Germán Arciniegas describes the first women who arrive in Colombia with Jerónimo de Lebrón, the governor of Santa Marta. Once these regions had been discovered by the explorer Jiménez de Quesada, they made ready to go up the largest river in Colombia. Once again, the women were clearly present at a highly critical moment. Traveling on the six brigantines that Lebrón had fitted to go up the Magdalena River were one hundred forty soldiers, one hundred eighty horses, and six women. "Only thirty capable persons remained in Santa Marta. Even Isabel Romero, who was about to become a mother, asked for a place on the brigantines" (Arciniegas 110-111).

We have already seen how Francisco de Orellana's wife accompanied her husband on the Amazon River; Lebrón's women followers were to do so on the most important river of Colombia, the Magdalena, which had been discovered by Rodrigo de Bástidas in 1501. The difficulty of the voyage, its violence and dangers, leave no doubt as to the type of energy that these six women had who went on those ships up the Magdalena and through the jungles in the direction of Vélez. They witnessed the attack of five hundred canoes with feathered Indians, who were halted with cannon bursts; and they were also present at the "punishment" that Jerónimo de Lebrón inflicted on the fierce Carib Indians. One of them was even abducted by the Temalameque Indians .[33] "The half dozen who left Santa Marta could only be rounded out due to the initiative of Isabel Romero" (Arciniegas 111). It is worth taking the time to ponder the moral force of these women.

There is notice of another singular woman, María de Carvajal, who arrived in Colombia together with her husband, the conquistador Jorge Robledo, discoverer of the provinces of the Cauca and Antioquía (Colombia): "This lady belonged to the family of the Marquesses of Jodar. It is believed that it was through the influence of her relatives and due to her own efforts that Robledo managed to have the King name him Marshal and Governor of the lands that he would conquer" (Acosta 151).

There is also a human and physical description of this lady which gives an idea of the attraction that she must have exerted because of both her noble birth and her personality.

Doña María was beautiful, eloquent, most active, and during the voyage that she made to the Indies with Inspector Miguel Díez de Armendaris, she managed to ingratiate herself with him to the extent that this magistrate took up the defense of Robledo against [Sebastián de] Belalcázar in the quarrels that those conquistadores had, quarrels that ended tragically with Robledo's death as the victim of Belalcázar's ambition (Acosta 151).

Nevertheless, it is also asserted that Doña María was quite boastful and conceited, and that her relationships with her servants were rather despotic: "She often put on airs, she was high-handed with her subordinates, and she demanded to be called nothing less than Señora Marshal" (Acosta 1510).

As luck would have it, Doña María suddenly found herself "widowed and abandoned." Aptly enough, as Soledad Acosta de Samper says, widows in the first years of the encounter, because of the high mortality rate of the colonizers due mainly to the climate or to wars, had little problem remarrying, and on occasion did so up to four times: "But in that period a Spanish woman in America—even if she were old and ugly—was a very desirable commodity in the colonies, and as soon as their husbands would die they would find a replacement" (Acosta 151). This was the case of the beautiful and difficult María de Carvajal, as of many other women who would do the same to promote the development of the overseas society. The young and attractive María de Carvajal "followed the example of her compatriots and shortly gave her hand in marriage for the second time to the Treasurer of the Royal Exchequer of Santa Fe (in Bogotá), where she had gone for more information as soon as she had learned of Robledo's death" (Acosta 151).

THE NUN-ENSIGN AND ST. ROSE OF LIMA: POLAR OPPOSITES

Fable is often mistaken for reality, as often occurs with events that happened several centuries ago. This is the case of the "nun-ensign" who, disguised as a man, went over to the Americas, where her reputation, somewhat legendary, is still alive. This woman was an adventuress of the highest order, a "Doña Juana" who conquered American geography and forbidden loves wherever she went. Feared for her strength, courage, and dexterity with steel arms, she commanded Spanish troops on several occasions, having defeated many men in duels. She was so glib that she managed to convince the Pope himself in Rome to allow her to dress as a soldier. "Catalina de Erauso's destiny led her from the Spanish convent where she was doing the novitiate to the hardly explored territories of the Americas, the only place where her restless and even violent nature found freedom amid solitude and unspeakable dangers" (Iglehart 9-11).

This heroic woman, although she was a flesh-and-blood person, was an inspiration to writers of her time, who included her in theatrical works in order to take advantage of the enormous dramatic possibilities of such an unusual personage (McKendric 213). If, as we have seen above, there were numerous situations when women tested their valor, in her case, all the established molds were broken. The sole fact that this figure existed in Spain in the seventeenth century made it possible for the audience of her time to accept the existence of such an unusual character: "She is that extraordinary trans-sexual figure Catalina de Erauso, heroine of Pérez de Montalbán's (?) *La monja alférez* and one of the few real examples—and an extreme one at that—of the seventeenth-century *mujer varonil*" (McKendric 213).

But even more interesting that the dramatic possibilities that have been taken from this figure, were her own autobiographical writings. They were written around the years 1625 or 1626, shortly before she embarked for the second, definitive time to America (Erauso 5). This female personage had no reason to envy the most dapper young gentlemen of her era, not only because she was able to slay her male opponents when the occasion required—including her own brother, involuntarily—but also because she had the same sexual preferences that they did. Catalina de Erauso says in her autobiography, "A few days later, he let me know that he would look favorably on my marrying his daughter, whom he had there with him; she was very dark and ugly as

a devil, very contrary to my taste, which always went to good faces"
(Erauso 35).

Not even her brother, Miguel de Erauso, was spared from this tough
woman's force; one night in a dispute he was killed by stab wounds from
his own sister. It can be seen, therefore, that it was not only male
explorers who had "adventures" and "conquests" in the lands of
America, but their little sisters could have equally intense and exciting
adventures, even though such complete accounts of these were not
written.

If we had to contrast this singular figure with another no less
distinguished but of a diametrically opposed nature, we would have to
mention "St. Rose of Lima," who for the kindliness and sweetness of her
character as well as for her femininity, became the "patron saint of
America."

St. Rose of Lima was the daughter of María de la Oliva and the
Spanish sergeant, Gaspar de Flores. This child was born amid the
turbulence of early colonial life, the exploitation of mining in search of
precious metals, and the preparations for new explorations. She added
a note of warmheartedness that would provide comfort and hope in the
coarseness and warlike atmosphere of those years (Villafañe 141).

St. Rose of Lima was a Peruvian Dominican religious, born in Lima
(1586-1617), who according to Catholic tradition received "God's call"
through a miraculous voice: "Rose of my heart, be my bride." And so
this mystical love, like her whole story, known to all but never
sufficiently repeated, led her to be enthroned as "St. Rose of Lima"
(Villafañe 142). Pope Clement X declared her "the universal and
principal patron of all and any provinces, kingdoms, islands and
mainland regions of all America and the Philippines" (Villafane 1420).

> And this is the miracle of America, the Hispanic lineage of which gave
> such beloved fruits which flourish in new generations of women,
> preparing to occupy their place in the social, historical, and cultural
> evolution of those legendary lands of the Indies, where the heart of
> yesterday's and today's woman is also fertile ground for generous
> sentiments, virtues, abnegations, and sacrifices (Villafañe 141-42).

Anyone who has been in Hispanic America has experienced the
fervor and sincere devotion that many Indians have for the "saints." It
would be unjust to state, simply because one does not share the Catholic
ideology, that they do not have an authentic, valid spiritual life. When

everyday life has little to offer, one always looks to the "great beyond" with hope.

PART FOUR: WOMEN IN INTELLECTUAL LIFE

WOMEN IN SIXTEENTH-CENTURY SPANISH AND HISPANIC AMERICAN SOCIETY

Although it is true that traditionally women have not occupied the privileged place of men in Spanish society, it is also true that many families flourished thanks to the courage and dedication of women who sacrificed themselves to bring their children up. Throughout its history, Spain has had a great number of wars, which have created a high male mortality rate at times. Very often it has been the widows who have had to take their husbands' place so as not to slip into poverty. Chivalry, a quality so linked to honor, has made Spanish men respect and defend women up until the present time, as a characteristic of their temperament. Then too, in some cases it is women who remind men—forcefully—of the role they should play as men. This behavior has been prevalent for centuries, and it appears to be an effect of the most important cultures that occupied the peninsula, whether the Roman or the Islamic. In Law 2 of the *Siete partidas* of Alfonso X the Wise it is stated, "How the King must love, honor, and protect his wife." Three reasons are given by the Wise King: first, since the couple is a unit, the more the wife is honored, the more the husband will be honored. Second, when a woman sees that she is honored by her husband, she will have "more reason to wish for his good and his honor;" and third, he says that when the wife is honored, the children she has will also be more honored and more noble (129).

These words of Alfonso X served the general population, "all those of his land," as an example for behavior: "Thus the king who loves, honors, and protects his wife in this manner will be loved, honored, and protected by her, and will give good example to all those of his land; but to do all these things well and completely, it is necessary to have a group of men and women who fear God and know how to protect the honor of him and her" (128).

The sources of the *Partidas* are to be found in the ancient "fueros" or regional law codes, in the writings of St. Augustine and St. Gregory, and of course in various passages from the Bible. Antonio Sánchez Romeralo and Fernando Ibarra stress the importance that these laws had in the new terrritories discovered in the Americas, Africa, and Asia. They were the legal code most in force until surprisingly recent times, even in areas of the United States: "for example, in Louisiana, in a 1924 court sentence; some laws dealing with 'community property' in the United states, which were in force in some states and today have spread to all of them, are derived from the *Partidas*" (38).

If we put this way of thinking into the context of the encounter, we can find very significant examples. The Franciscan Brother Juan de Torquemada, first among the Franciscan chroniclers who managed to publish his main work, not only mentions women, but speaks of the almost sacred duty to respect and protect them. The Chichimec Indians, at one point called "Huachichiles," attacked a Spanish village, killing all the people in it and also carrying off with them three Spanish women. Shortly thereafter, the Spaniards found the corpse of one of these women "full of arrows." The enormous indignation and rage over this incident—not the attack on the encampment, but the death of this defenseless woman—is reflected as follows by the Franciscan chronicler:

> It must have been because she was old (they say she was over seventy years old) that they killed her, and like barbarians, they did not take into account that she was a woman and for that reason worthy of esteem and respect, for naturally it is because of women that we live and we are, for they bring us up and give us milk, when in the first, young years of our life we do not have the knowledge to take care of ourselves, nor the shrewdness nor the cunning to feed ourselves; but as people who lacked this discourse and reason, they killed her and left her in those mountains, as full of arrows as a sea urchin is full of spines. Our people were greatly sorrowed by it, and having buried her, because she was a Christian, they went on ahead; and I believe that in order to go with much haste and greater spirit to catch up with their enemies, they were guided by their anger and rage at having seen such a spectacle; it being a vile, cowardly thing to lay hands on a woman, unless she has great blame; and that each one was vowing in his heart to avenge the outrage as injust, done to a weak woman, without resistance (640-41; bk.5, ch. 23).

In another of his commentaries, on some internal disputes among Mexican peoples, Juan de Torquemada says: "...especially the women, whose tongue is fiercer and crueler when passion and anger govern and direct it" (177; bk. 2, ch. 58). In a certainway this shows that the overall view of women is not simply that she is a naturally defenseless being, but rather that she is different, worthy of respect not only because of her weakness but also for her ability to do harm.

Through the Catholic tradition the mother is identified with the Virgin Mary and baby Jesus. This Marian identification has been with the Spaniards from their earliest days, and it went over to Hispanic America and took root in such a way that today one can say that the cult of the Virgin there in many cases prevails over any other type of identification, whether it be of a political, religious, or even a sports nature.

It is necessary to see what the deepest roots of the treatment accorded to women and the concept of woman have been in Spain, and what the effect of certain key works has been, so as to understand this specific way of being and thinking. Without proposing to undertake a sociological or anthropological study of the treatment that agrarian peoples have given to the members of their societies, it is worth recalling that until very recently, in the case of Spain, agriculture together with religion has been the axis around which most social manifestations have revolved: music, dance, ceremonies, literature, superstitions, etc. As a traditionally agricultural and maritime country with a relatively small urban population, especially in Castile, Spain based its models mainly on Greco-Latin teachings and the Bible. More specifically, during the Middle Ages, the dominant Scholastic thought managed to masterfully syncretize Aristotle's thought with the "Holy Scriptures." This syncretism would likewise be used later to adapt Christian thought to the Amerindian religions. Aristotle and the Bible would therefore be two fundamental references for the interpretation of female nature and its concept. The greatest intellectuals and theologians of the period—Sahagún, Las Casas, Sepúlveda, Durán, Montesinos, etc.—mention the "philosopher" everywhere, and his word would always be taken into account. The Catholic Church would therefore be the vehicle employed to carry out indoctrination in the newly discovered lands, in the same way that it had been done for centuries on the Iberian peninsula.

Aristotle, in his *Politics*, a work translated to Latin in the thirteenth century by St. Thomas of Aquinas, mentions woman together with slaves, and the idea the "non-Greeks" had of her.

> 1252a34 Nature, then has distinguished between female and slave: she recognizes different functions and lavishly provides different tools, not an all purpose tool like the Delphic knife; for every instrument will be made best if it serves not many purposes but one. But non-Greeks assign to female and slave exactly the same status (57; bk.1, ch.2).

For its part the Bible repeatedly mentions woman and the behavior that she should observe in society, her obligations and rights vis-á-vis her husband and her other duties of a social nature which have as a common basis the family, as the center of Judeo-Christian society. The overall tone with respect to women varies according to the different books of the Bible. As a rule, a sense of dependence on the husband emerges, and in some cases absolute contempt for women is expressed, mainly in the Old Testament. An example is found in this passage from Esther:

> Thou hast knowledge of all things; and thou knowest that I hate the splendor of the wicked and abhor the bed of the uncircumcised and of any alien. Thou knowest my necessity—that I abhor the sign of my proud position, which is upon my head on the days when I appear in public. *I abhor it like a menstruous rag* (Esther 14.15-16).

Appearing in Deuteronomy is another singular example of the role of women in situations as common as a fight between two men. Although in this case the woman in question is capable of seizing the genitals of her husband's enemy in the confrontation, the punishment sought for the women, no matter how painful her action was, is disproportionate and inhuman:

> When men fight with one another, and the wife of the one draws near to rescue her husband from the hand of him who is beating him, and puts out her hand and seizes him by the private parts, then you shall cut off her hand; your eye shall have no pity (25, 11-13).

In Proverbs, an even more telling case is cited of the ability of the "lascivious" woman to attract, through all kinds of amorous insinuations, the attention of a "poor" husband who is naive and defenseless before such open provocation. It should be noted above all how the woman is presented as a serpent that bewitches a defenseless victim, "simple" and "without sense" with her provocations and her guile:

and I have seen among the simple,
    I have perceived among the youths,
        a young man without sense,
passing along the street near her corner,
        taking the road to her house
in the twilight, in the evening,
        at the time of night and darkness.

And lo, a woman meets him,
        dressed as a harlot, wily of heart.

She is loud and wayward,
   her feet do not stay at home;
now in the street, now in the market,
   and at every corner she lies in wait.
She seizes him and kisses him,
   and with impudent face she says to him:
"I had to offer sacrifices,
   and today I have paid my vows;
so now I have come out to meet you,
   to seek you eagerly, and I have found you.
I have decked my couch with coverings,
   colored spreads of Egyptian linen;
I have perfumed my bed with myrrh,
   aloes, and cinnamon.
Come, let us take our fill of love till morning,
   let us delight ourselves with love.
For my husband is not at home;
   he has gone on a long journey;
he took a bag of money with him;
   at full moon he will come home."

With much seductive speech she persuades him;
   with her smooth talk she compels him.
All at once he follows her,
   as an ox goes to the slaughter,
or as a stag is caught fast
   till an arrow pierces its entrails;
as a bird rushes into a snare;
   he does not know that it will cost him his life.
   (Proverbs, 7.7-23)

   The poor bird falls into the snare, hypnotized by the serpent. From
Genesis to Malachi, from the beginning to the end of the Old Testament,
and even in the New Testament, one can observe to a greater or lesser
extent a misogyny characteristic of a patriarchal society. It would be
tedious to quote all those biblical passages that confirm this, but one of
the most representative is the following, which comes from the New
Testament:
"For a man ought not to cover his head, since he is the image and glory
of God; but woman is the glory of man. For man was not made from
woman, but woman from man. Neither was man created for woman, but
woman for man" (Corinthians, 11.7-9).

The following fragment refers to the "dissolute woman:"

to preserve you from the evil woman,
    from the smooth tongue of the adventuress,
Do not desire her beauty in your heart,
    and do not let her capture you with her eyelashes;
for a harlot may be hired for a loaf of bread,
    but an adulteress stalks a man's very life.
Can a man carry fire in his bosom
    and his clothes not be burned? (Proverbs, 6.24-27)

It is not difficult to imagine the repercussions of the above reasoning if it is literally interpreted, above all for a people predominantly illiterate or not very educated.

This way of thinking about women has been transmitted through the Catholic Church up to the present time. It is in the technological society we live in, as oppposed to the agrarian, that distances and differences between the sexes have begun to be reduced. Of course it would be absurd to undertake a literal analysis of the "Holy Scripturees." Nevertheless they have influenced and continue to influence Western society to a greater extent than is generally believed, sometimes unconsciously. At any rate, leaving aside the theological comparison between Yahweh, the Old Testament God, and Jesus Christ in the New Testament, there is on the whole a notable shift in emphasis with respect to women from the Old to the New. Yahweh says to Saul: "Do not spare them, but kill both man and woman, infant and suckling, ox and sheep, camel and ass" (1 Samuel, 15.3). This way of thinking does not mesh with "Love thy neighbor" in the New Testament, where vengeance and hatred turn into love and resignation.

In the Spanish Middle Ages some laws regarding women existed which give insight into their rights and limitations, in case of abuse by men. An example of these rights are the Jaca "fueros," granted in 1077 by King Sancho Ramírez. These rights, in the opinion of Antonio Ubieto Arteta, "extended to many Spanish towns." The following clauses are worthy of note:
k) If anyone transgresses with a woman with her consent when she is not married, he shall not pay a fine; but if he uses violence, he shall take her as his wife or provide her with a husband.

l) The offended woman must seek justice in the first two days after her dishonor, presenting witnesses. If the first three days go by with no complaint, she shall have no more right (Ubieto 135-36).

It is no doubt important, from the sociological point of view, to observe the development of women in Spanish society. This can provide much better understanding of the later development of their participation in the period when they lived and their subsequent position in the Americas. In this regard, one should always take into account the more or less narrow range of action imposed by the Catholic Church to a greater or lesser extent in different periods. For that reason we should look more deeply into everything relating to the activity of women in overseas territories and above all evaluate their actions, not as marginal, sporadic occurrences, but as the basis and underpinning of a society that is still with us. The best testimony are the voices of these women—those voices that have been preserved. Fernández Duro says that it was the mothers of sixteenth-century Spaniards who made possible such a formidable display of energy on all the seas and continents of our planet:

> What greatness, what boldness, Spain showed in the sixteenth century! The world had never seen such energy, activity, and fortune. There were no obstacles for Spaniards on the rivers, in the mountains, nor in the deserts. A few of them came together, created squadrons, conquered empires, and, founding cities, they devised a way to unite seas and climates. One could say that they came from a line of giants or demigods. They were...they were sons of such mothers (Fernández Duro 26).

Inca Garcilaso de la Vega (1536-1616), the Peruvian chronicler who was the son of a Spanish captain and an Inca princess, echoes the opinion of some young ladies who went over to the Americas hoping to find the man of their dreams, in this case the conquistador, and were surprised to see how wounds, inclement weather, and illnesses had left their mark on the faces of these men, who were not as they had imagined. This was the comment of one of the marriageable maidens whom Pedro de Alvarado took to Guatemala:

> Do they say that we are to marry these conquistadores?" said one woman; another said "Are we to marry these broken-down old men? Let her who wishes get married; I certainly do not intend to marry any of them. This is a hoax, it looks as if they have escaped from hell, the

way they are maimed. Some are crippled, others lack limbs, others are missing an ear, others an eye, others have half a face, and the best off has it once, twice, three times (Borges 408).

Many of these first women became widows several times, specifically because their husbands died in the various campaigns of the early years.

It was the descendants of the women who came with the conquistadores who definitively put down their roots in a new society that would attain the same splendor and refinement as that of Spain. The transplant had been successful. The violence of the "encounter" in the first years had produced a new society that had inherited the foundations of Spanish culture and which had in addition all the appeal and richness of the highly varied pre-Columbian cultures.

> The first generation is that of the Creole woman, the daughter of a woman settler; the woman who educated her own and others' children tempered the barbarous customs of the period of wars. The truth is that despite all the ups and downs, women made the home possible, and it was there that transculturation was forged; thanks to their presence, society became less vulgar and reached a level of notable refinement. Peace was a long time coming; periods of truce favored settlement in towns and cities. There ballads and Medieval verse flourished, along with Gothic architecture, the Canary Islands balcony and the Andalusian patio (Borges 436).

Whether in Mexico City or Lima, the Creole woman took pleasure in all those sophistications that were enjoyed by the women of Seville or the Court. They all had servants. In the middle of the sixteenth century, navigation between Mexico and the Philippines began, and this added to the finery of Creole women as well as Spanish women, with articles that are today very Spanish, but were originally quite exotic, such as the Manila shawl or the fan. Brother Reginal de Lizárraga writes on the women of Peru:

> that one hardly knows how husbands can stand it. The vanity of these women is excessive and we do not know where it will stop...; I do not believe that in what has been discovered of the world there is a city this size or four times larger that runs to such vanity as does our city...Very rightly this vanity could be moderated by the viceroys. But I do not know why it is not moderated; and yet I do know why neither

husbands have the spirit to moderate it nor governors either (Lizarraga 38; bk. 1, ch. 51).

The Creole woman participated in all the goings-on in her society. She was present at all those social events and frequently in commercial dealings, without failing to oversee home life. Just as in Spain, she took charge of marrying off her sons and daughters, some of whom were destined to uphold the family tradition and enrich it, and others of whom ended up swelling the ranks of the Church.

WOMEN IN SPANISH INTELLECTUAL LIFE DURING THE SIXTEENTH AND SEVENTEENTH CENTURIES

In the same way that an attempt has been made to exclude women from the first pages of the encounter with the Americas, the intellectual contribution of many talented women has also been ignored. Many, despite the remote location of their settlements, managed to produce some of the finest examples of the lyric poetry of their time.[34] Given the social stratification of the epoch, a large number of these women carried out their work in convents. Others, however, combined their married lives with cultural labors. Convent life was to some extent an advantage for achieving the necessary freedom without the presence of a husband and children to absorb the time, concentration and dedication required by artistic activity. Even so, things did not always go smoothly in the convent. The best-known case is that of Sister Juana Inés de la Cruz, who had problems with high-ranking clergymen, and the envy of those close to her and strangers because among other things, she was superior in intelligence and culture to the greater share of her contemporaries.

Many convents were well stocked with books, often donated by those families that had a member within the convent or simply by persons sympathetic to the different religious orders. In the peace of the cloister, some of these women managed to acquire a formidable intellectual development. But despite the quality of the material that exists on such extraordinary women, there has been a tendency to keep them out of sight. As the Spanish thinker Benito Feijóo (1676-1764) said of the disputes between men and women: "The truth is that neither the women nor we ourselves can be judges in this suit, because we are parties; and thus the sentence would have to be entrusted to the angels, who, since they have no sex, are impartial" (46).

The Argentine writer Vicente G. Quesada complained at the beginning of this century about the very scant information offered by the French Larousse encyclopedia about colonial life in Mexico, when it said the following on the subject: "The only books that were known were the almanac, Father Ripalda's catechism, the *Christian Year*, the lives of the saints, and others of that type" (Quesada 125). Refuting this, Quesada wrote:

> Finally, I shall recall the very notable modern publication, *La bibliografía mejicana del siglo XVI*, which is most learned, and constitute the most conclusive evidence to disprove the superficiality of

the Larousse *Dictionnaire*, which asserts what it does not know...The famous Mexican writer Francisco Pimentel has published his learned work, *Historia crítica de la literatura y las ciencias en México, desde la conquista hasta nuestros días*; it is a work made up of four parts, divided thus: novelists, orators, historians, and scientific writers. From this brief account one can see that it is inexcusably rash to purport to give notice of the intellectual movement in the Viceroyalty of Mexico without knowing the works of Pimentel and of García Icazbalceta, or the original or corrected edition of Beristain (126).

Professor Boxer, who was aware of this fact and was the author of several books on the colonization of Hispanic America, states that it is worthwhile to compare the social position of Spanish women in contradistinction to Anglo-Saxon women, for despite what is commonly believed the legal position of Spanish women was stronger than that of their Anglo-Saxon counterparts: "It is commonly assumed that the latter had every advantage over the former, but I think this assumption may be largely or even entirely erroneous. From the works of José María Ots Capdequí, Professor Brading and others, we know that the legal position of women, and above all widows, in the Spanish-American world was in some ways stronger than that of their Anglo-Saxon counterparts" (Boxer 52).

In the most important urban centers of Mexico and Peru one could clearly see the direct participation of women in the most diverse social and cultural activities. This participation even went to the extreme of literally insulting the competent authorities when they deemed it necessary. "These women who cried must have been the same ones who thought that the main cause of those deaths were the provisions of the New Laws, because they had no qualms about insulting Viceroy Blasco Núñez Vela, whom 'the Spanish women shouted at and cursed as if he bore upon himself the wrath of God'" (Borges 418).

The same happened in Spain. In the cultural area, María de Zayas y Sotomayor, a great novelist and defender of the qualities of her sex, stood out among the writers of the first half of the seventeenth century. Her narrative and dramatic work enjoyed great popularity in Spain and Hispanic America. "There has hardly been a novelist more beloved of Spanish readers than Doña María de Zayas, as can be seen in the many reeditions made of her works" (E. Fernández de Navarrete xcvii). She counted among her admirers the indefatigable and brilliant Lope de Vega, who praised her in his work *El laurel de Apolo*. "Doña María did not lose any opportunity to take the side of women against the tyranny of men, assuming that like despots, they wish to keep them ignorant so as to keep them under control" (E. Fernández de Navarrete xcvi).

But it need not be exclusively a woman who defends the qualities and rights of her sex. Several examples can be cited from the beginning of Spanish literature in which woman is defended and even understood by male writers of the age. The brilliant Archpriest of Hita wrote these verses in the fourteenth century:

> Now all you ladies, lend your ears to hear my lesson strong,
> And listen to the words I speak: Beware the cavalier!
> Take care no fate befalls you like the one the lion brought
> The poor jackass who ended up without his heart and ears.[35]

In sixteenth-century Spain one cannot underestimate the influence of the most famous intellectual of his time, Erasmus of Rotterdam. With an uncommon mental acuity, Erasmus addresses the most mundane topics as well as the most profound. His writing, always on the verge of heresy, were a clear expression of his ideological independence. He too gave an opinion of women, and of the impact that a good education would have on the fulfillment of daily tasks:

> With regard to female education, Erasmus is unequivocal. In *Abbatis et eruditae*, he categorically states that education and *learning* are as desirable in a woman as in a man. And although there is naturally no suggestion that the education and learning should be directed towards a career, there are no carping restrictions as to what the education should consist of or where the learning should end (McKendric 9).

It was one woman in particular who attracted the attention of the Dutch scholar: Catherine of Aragon, the daughter of Isabel, the Catholic Queen. This lady's virtues must have been extraordinary for such renowned freethinkers as Erasmus to call her a "miracle of female learning."

> At the centre of the movement was a Spanish woman: Catherine of Aragon, first wife of Henry VIII of England. Her mother, Isabel la Católica, had made sure that Catherine and her sisters received an advanced and enlightened education under two eminent Italian humanists, Antonio and Alessandro Geraldini, and Catherine herself

was considered by Erasmus and Sir Thomas More to be a miracle of female learning. At her request, Juan Luis Vives between 1524 and 1528 wrote his *De institutione feminae christianae* for her daughter Mary, and he dedicated it to Catherine (McKendric 6).

But despite the influence Erasmus had or did not have over Spanish thinkers in the sixteenth century, Brother Luis de León is also worthy of mention for his independent cast and for being a defender of individual freedom. Although he was a representative of the Catholic Church, it is well known that he had to suffer the consequences, including rejection by the Church, when he expounded his ideas, writings, and biblical translations. Brother Luis, in his work *La perfecta casada*, makes clear his idea of woman and her function in the society he lived in. For Brother Luis, woman was not an idealized image such as that of "courtly love" or of the neo-Platonic writers, but a flesh-and-blood being who had rights and responsibilities in her society just as men did (McKendric 10).

It would be exaggerated to assert that Brother Luis de León puts women over men in the social context. Nevertheless, if we take into account the limitations that his profession and his times placed on him, we can see that he attempts to make it clear that (married) women deserve all possible respect and help from their husbands. From the usual biblical point of view, Brother Luis says of woman:

> Because, although it is true that nature and her station place an obligation on the married woman, as we have said, to take care of her house and to gladden her husband and free him of care, from which obligation no bad condition of his releases her, that is no reason for people to think that husbands have the liberty to be lions to their wives and make them slaves; rather, as in everything else, man is the head; thus all this loving and honorable treatment must start with the husband. Because he must understand that she is his companion, or to put it in a better way, part of his body (Fray Luis de León 21; ch. 3).

The Catholic Queen Isabel has already been mentioned as the driving force behind the whole overseas enterprise, but it was also through her that certain studies and knowledge became fashionable for different women of her time—the fifteenth and sixteenth centuries. Beatriz Galindo, commonly known as "La Latina," was the one who taught Queen Isabel Latin. In his work *La leyenda negra*, Julián Juderías says, "Women joined men in this thirst for learning, and we see Doña Beatriz

Galindo, the Queen's Latin teacher; Doña Lucía de Medrano, who taught Classics at Salamanca; Doña Francisca de Lebrija, who held a chair of rhetoric at the University of Alcalá" (Juderías 74).

Eustaquio Fernández de Navarrete tells us that when the famous Antonio de Nebrija, who with the encouragement of the Catholic Queen published the first European grammar in a Romance language, was old and sick, his daughter Antonia substituted for him in his classes of philosophy and rhetoric at the University of Alcalá (xcvi).

There is no reason to think that the more privileged classes of women who went over to the Americas did not enjoy the same benefits and freedoms as their counterparts in Spain. As for the less privileged classes, the Spanish monarchy took pains, from the first, to teach all its subjects, men and women, including the natives of conquered territories, to read and write:

> The education of the American Indians was a sincere concern of the kings of Spain almost from the discovery of the New World. Among the Catholic Monarchs' first instructions to their governors in the Antilles islands were those given to Nicolás de Ovando in 1503, ordering him to build a school in every village next to the church, "where all the children there may be in each of the villages shall come together twice a day so that the chaplain may *teach them to read and write*" (Vega 9-10).

In Cristóbal de Villalón's Renaissance work *El Crotalón*, there appear some very graphic images of women of the time and of the "excess of freedom" which, as the author states through one of his characters, they enjoyed. From the anthropological and social point of view, the following lines offer a good picture of the physical appearance of the women of Villalón's time, and their attitude, seen from the partial vantage point of the character in the work:

> Yet do not think, Demophon, that the vanity and perdition of these loose women will go up to God without punishment; for I make bold to tell you that it is very sure that punishment will not be lacking. For God will see the dissolution, brazenness, shamelessness, and lack of devotion that there is in the women of this time; seeing that both virgins and married women, widows and single women, all as a rule live very loosely and very dissolutely in their gaze, their walk, and their swaying about, very curiously, and they go through the street with a curious step in their walk, their head uncovered and their hair with

large, dishonest partings; their neck very high and stretched out, winking their eye at all the men they meet, swaying their bodies lasciviously (Villalón, 860-61; vol.2, canto 20).

Although this passage may seem humorous in our time, it was less so in the period when it was written, since the view of woman as an integral part of the father's or the husband's estate made it so that her behavior could potentially threaten the "honor" of her possessor. In spite of this, it is clear that women had some degree of freedom that was not limited to the halls of a convent or to an existence completely removed from the hubbub of worldly life. In the following passage, a continuation of the preceding one, one can observe the set of accessories and adornments that women of the time used in their dress and on their bodies. The complexity and sophistication of the attire described is noteworthy.

For this common dishonesty of theirs it is certain that the time will come when God shall give them a great punishment; all their hair shall be shorn, making them all bald; and the time will come when God shall take away all their jewels, rings, bracelets, earrings, necklaces, bangles, and hairclips. He shall take away their hair parters, curlers, cosmetic jars, bottles, and coloring trays, and all types of make-up, perfumes, tanned gloves, creams and hand oils, and other fragrances. Pins, needles, brooches. He shall take away their very thin dresses, and the mantles, skirts, long dresses, front-slit skirts, tunics, and mantillas; and in place of that curled and teased hair of theirs he shall give them a mop of hair and baldness, and instead of those hairbands and jewels that hang about their forehead, he shall give them a headache, and rather than very enameled and worked gold braiding he shall give them ropes of very rough esparto for them to put on and tighten around them; and instead of that very strange and sumptuous garb of their body he shall give them silica; and in this way God shall make them weep over their lasciviousness and disorder, and do severe penitence for their lust and dishonesty. Then no one will love them because of their stench and misery; when seven women shall give themselves to a man and he shall flee from all of them, despising them and hating them as a great evil (Villalón 860-61; vol. 2, canto 20).

This is an excellent list of female adornments, few of the Spanish words for which—*briales*, *saboyanas*, *nazarenas*, *rebociños*—are recognizable today. The author of these lines must have experienced great frustration with women; they cannot have paid much attention to him. Misogyny, which was evident in the earlier quotation, reflects some naïveté in this case. The model of woman presented above must have been quite attractive and sophisticated, having a great variety of adornments, many of them of Oriental origin, and perfumes that rival those used by modern women. It would be unfair and exaggerated to say that the overseas discoveries were due to pressure brought to bear by women on their lovers so that they would bring them "more swiftly" all that endless store of exotic refinements that existed in the Orient. But it is true that women were great consumers of perfumes, make-up, silk, jewels, and other sumptuary items, and were very conscious of what we understand today as "fashion." Martín Fernández de Navarrete in his indispensable work on the first overseas voyages, *Colección de viajes y descubrimientos*, mentions in passing the situation of some women during the fifteenth century. It was in that very period when the Portuguese and the Castilians entered into conflict over the control of some possessions on the shores of Africa.

> And the luxury increased to such an extent that even the wives of workmen and artisans were in their dress taken for women of high birth and station, using as they did clothing of rich silken fabrics, of gold, of wool, with sable and fur linings, and with trimming of gold, silver and pearls, spending on which, because it was the ruin of families, the Courts of Palenzuela sought to correct, to no avail (M. Fernández de Navarrete 75: 21).

The same author stresses the importance for Castilian commerce of having a good navy that would protect ships from pirates and other dangers. In the inventories preserved from the Duke of Béjar and Alvaro de Zúñiga, one can see these gentlemen's luxurious taste for Oriental pearls, precious stones, fabrics, and other items of great value. We also know about the jewels that Rodrigo Ponce de León, Marquis of Cádiz, gave Doña Beatriz Pacheco (M. Fernández de Navarrete 75: 22). It was clear that from that time on navigation would be the swiftest and most important means of trading with those countries of the Orient that before could only be reached by land routes.

Simultaneously, one can observe a certain development of women in their milieu, which amounted to an exchange of information at all levels, naturally including the cultural level. It was not uncommon for them to have books of plays at hand, and it was even assumed that they wrote plays (Bell 95). In fact, the suspicion that ladies went so far as to write plays was well founded. There is no reason to doubt it. For example, Ana Caro Mallén de Soto, one of the most famous lady playwrights of Seville in the seventeenth century, the author of *El conde de Partinuplés*, used the theme of love, in its most diverse physical and spiritual varieties, as the core of almost all her works (Perry 57). This fact also indicates that the audience favored so popular a theme. Here is another example:

> The drama of this period did not present love and marriage as a simple partnership, however, and many dramatists contrasted "profane" with "honest" love. Feliciana Enríquez de Guzmán, who wrote *Tragicomedia: Los jardines y campos sabeos* in Seville in the early seventeenth century, presented the hero Clarisel as the victim of "perverted" and fickle Belidiana in part 1, so blinded by her beauty that he feels himself "in shackles and in chains" (Perry 57).

But it was not only plays that Spanish ladies of the period wrote; others went so far as to write scientific treatises. At the end of the sixteenth century, Oliva Sabuco de Nantes Barrera wrote a medical paper on human nature, warning that lust could be harmful to the body. She based this on the presumption that lust caused the brain to emit a liquid that went to the stomach, cooling it off and weakening it, and in this way interrupting vital functions (Perry 58).

It is known that there were many women students in the era of Isabel the Catholic and that she encouraged them in these endeavors. This initiative on Isabel's part bore fruit in subsequent decades. Besides the well-known novelists María de Zayas y Sotomayor and Mariana de Carvajal, there was a whole series of female writers in all genres who flourished on both sides of the Atlantic. They are notable not only because of their number but above all because of the quality of their works. Some of them, like Luisa de Padilla, Countess of Aranda, whom Serrano y Sanz calls "the most notable of the women who flourished in Spain in the seventeenth century," are perfect examples of this kind of woman. One has also to consider the number of women who wrote with male pseudonyms.

The information existing on different facets of female life is not abundant. Despite this, through a new interpretation of the texts, both Medieval ones and the chronicles of the first years of discovery and encounter, we can form a clearer idea of the true situation of women.

Given the widespread interest now in everything relating to women, some relatively recent studies have helped us to consider new perspectives. Modern scholarship is calling into question traditional stereotypes of female passivity and the signficance of females, and also the traditional misogyny attributed to the Middle Ages. It is ever more clear that the life of women varied considerably according to period, social position, or geographic situation, so to make categorical judgments of the "situation of women" can lead to serious mistakes (Dillard 9). In order to understand the Spanish woman who went over to the Americas it is fundamental to take into account the enormous differences of all types that existed in Castilian and American society.

In a recent study on the education of women in viceregal America, there appear some significant examples of Spanish women who devoted a great part of their lives to teaching. Doña Catalina de Bustamante stood out among these Spanish women educators who went to the Indies. José de Jesús Vega and María Luisa Cárdenas de Vega say in their work *América virreinal: La educación de la mujer* that a few years after the encounter of the Americas, this woman devoted herself to working on behalf of the Indians, although unfortunately her name and her teaching accomplishments have been ignored by modern historians (Vega 12-13).

Catalina de Bustamente is mentioned several times in the Vegas' study. And there are several old sources that recognize the presence of this distinguished "lady, much honored and giving good example" of whom Zumárraga spoke. A report was sent to Charles V on Catalina de Bustamante's activities in New Spain, signed by four of the best-known missionaries in Mexico.

> The report says that the Franciscans of Texcoco had just built a new monastery and given over the old one *to an honored, honest, most virtuous lady called Catalina de Bustamante so that there she might teach the daughters of the gentlemen of the area...who with God's grace and alms that don Hernando [Cortés] gave them for their sustenance [had in that house-home] up to three hundred women, rather more than less* (Vega 14).

These "house-homes" were not run necessarily by nuns, but by what were called "beatas" or devout women, who were not subject to ecclesiastic authority, although they devoted themselves to an "honest business." These "house-homes" were called "beaterios," and, being the first schools for women in New Spain, were different from convents

(Vega 20-21). It was thanks to the example of women like Bustamante who devoted their lives to the education of Indian women that other women continued in her footsteps: "Motolinía says clearly 'from this first retreat' [in Texcoco, run by Catalina] 'other honest and very virtuous ladies came out who taught the littler ones'" (Vega 23).

But Catalina de Bustamante, although she was a singular woman and the initiator of the education of women in Mexico, was not an isolated case; instead, she fits into a pattern to which many of the pioneer women in New Spain adapted themselves, creating institutions for female education. In 1530, some years later, one of the great patrons of female instruction in America appeared: Empress Isabel of Portugal (Vega 24).

Thus from the beginning of the encounter, there were several teaching institutions run by women, in which instruction was not given by nuns. One of the most outstanding institutions in the educational system was the Colegio de Niñas or Girls' School, set up in Mexico City at the beginning of the sixteenth century with female teachers who were not nuns. These lay women, commonly known as "friends," were the successors of the old beatas. The permanent location of the school was set in 1548, and it served as a school on that same site until 1862, when the building was converted into a warehouse (Vega 60).

It should not be forgotten that women did not have more privileges simply because they led a secular life. It was rather the other way around. Lay women did not inspire the same respect as nuns, who in addition had constant contact with people of both sexes who were not of the church (Arenal 297). Within convent walls, many of the social barriers that limited women in that period disappeared.

THE FEMALE PRESENCE AND THE MONARCHY

The Spanish monarchs were aware that without the female presence it would be difficult to consolidate an encounter on all levels. Most of the viceroys and high officials brought their wives with them; and in the major cities of Hispanic America, such as Mexico City, Guatemala, Lima, or Potosí, there were women with a good education (grammar, Latin, poetry, history, music). The was the origin of an elegant and to some extent sophisticated society in which women took part in more important matters than did their counterparts in the Portuguese colonies. "There were brilliant viceregal courts at Mexico City and Lima, far exceeding anything that could be found in Portuguese or English America during the seventeenth century" (Boxer 39).

The statistics that we possess today not only demonstrate that women arrived in the Americas in sizeable numbers, but also participated actively, being present in some cases on the front lines. It is difficult to recreate the state of mind of those women, who lived in such remote times. One has to search in the documents of the period to recover from the past all those treasures of history, so often misrepresented and manipulated to serve the purposes of the present. It is in the old manuscripts that one finds testimony of their presence, so full of pain, tragedies, and of course love affairs. The arrival of these women was a breath of hope and illusion for those men who were already in overseas lands and saw what they most desired coming from their homeland: lovers, mothers, sisters. It was a breath of life and poetry that softened the customs of those rude, romantic pioneers: "because to be involved in such enterprises, they had to have something of the romantic in them, something that is so characteristic of the Spaniard; and they would abandon, in such tender arms their rough manners, which they had acquired in harsh experience in jungles and mountains" (Villafañe 125).

Today we know that official policy in sixteenth- and seventeenth-century Spain favored the emigration of women to the Americas. To affirm the contrary not only is false, but it implies total unfamiliarity with the first two centuries of Spanish colonization. The presence of these Spanish women was a fact: "The ordinances on the subject clearly show that there was special interest in settling women and that an attempt was made to defend their position as women married to conquistadores and colonizers" (Villafañe 126). The monarchs understood that it was practically impossible for the men to live without women, and given this, it could be expected that abuses would be committed against Indian women which would affect the social morality and the good government of the colony. Besides, without definitive settlement with homes and families, it would be difficult to achieve a permanent presence in the new colonies (O'Sullivan-Beare 45).

Beginning with the Catholic Monarchs, the interest in establishing nuclear groups based on the Christian family was clear. The *capitulaciones* or agreements made in this regard between the conquistadores and the Crown were numerous. The one between Rodrigo de Bástidas and Charles V can serve as a good example. The date was November 6, 1524 in Valladolid. Bástidas's intention was to establish a permanent colony at the mouth of the Magdalena River in territory that is today part of Colombia. This is how the document signed by the Emperor begins:

> The King: Since in your name, Rodrigo de Bástidas, resident of the city of Santo Domingo, on Hispaniola island, I was told that in the service of the Catholic Queen my Wife and in our service you volunteer to settle and would settle within the next two years the province and port of Santa Marta which is in Castilla de Oro called the Mainland, and that you would settle it within the next two years, building in it a town in which there will be no less than fifty residents, fifteen of whom shall be married and shall have their wives with them, and that you shall have done it within two years, and from now on as many Spanish Christians and Indians as possible...(Restrepo 1: 30).

There are many occasions when the monarchy's support of feminine emigration is clearly shown; it would be difficult to enumerate all the instances. The truth is that the legislation in force favored the emigration and relocation, especially if they were married, with a whole series of incentives:[36] the fare to take the family on the voyage, tax exemption for articles they took with them, priority in appointments to offices, destinations, and hiring for those who went over with their wives, including in addition to residents of Castile and León, subjects of the Crown from other areas, including the Genovese and Portuguese if they were accompanied by their spouses (Fernández Duro 15-16).

Penalties were even imposed against those married men who did not take their wives with them to the Indies within one year. In a warrant issued to the Viceroy of New Spain, Charles V recommended that he "attempt to persuade those single men to marry who are of age and in conditions to do so," by promising them that when they married they would be favored in the allotment of Indians. On the island of San Juan de Puerto Rico, official appointments and public offices were to be held by married men in the first instance. The same was true in Mexico of the post of corregidor (Konetzke "emigración" 140-41). Philip II, like his predecessors and successors, was to restate and justify the benefits which would be reaped by those who had their wives there: "those who have served in the discoveries of the Indies and also those who aid in settling them who have their wives there shall be favored in any development," always ordering that they be qualified for those positions, and that after the conquistadores, married colonists be considered for the position of corregidor (Konetzke, "emigración" 141).

Ordinances in favor of marriage are clear, whether they show open preference, as in the above-mentioned cases, or, on the other hand, coercive methods were used so that this policy would be carried out. Sebastián Ramírez de Fuenleal, the Bishop of Santo Domingo and President of the Audiencia of Mexico, proposed that those encomenderos who were not married and had not taken part in the conquest have the Indians granted to them taken away, with the stipulation that they would be returned if within a period of one year they had been married (Konetzke, "emigración" 142-43).

The most interesting point in all of these official directives dealing with female emigation to the Americas is very simply that freedom be given to women to decide if, married or unmarried, they wished to go over to the new continent, not as an imposition but as a principle: "The spirit of the ordinances with regard to ensuring the marital life of married persons meant that a woman whose husband invited her to come over to the Indies could refuse" (Villafañe 127). One has to consider the "real" options, in addition to the legal and economic ones, that were left to the woman if this happened.

If from the outset we understand that these women had freedom of choice before entering into the interminable hardships and adventures that overseas voyages involved, we can see their achievements and efforts in sharper relief. Many times these women would cross the ocean once or repeatedly with no other motive than to defend the rights and interests of those close to them. The most impressive aspect of all this is that they did what they did on their own initiative, risking their lives so that justice would be done when necessary, and so that those on the other side of the ocean would not lack what they needed. The authorities, aware of the legal loopholes that existed in the new colonies, hastened to put laws into effect that would benefit those who were less favored by circumstances. The marriage institution, the significance of which is basic to the legal and social life of women, had to be legislated with a series of new ordinances, clauses, modifications, and clarifications for America. Existing legislation had Spanish law as its basis, but in America these changes were necessary for political and social reasons (Villafañe 126).

In order to summarize what had been provided in terms of legislation involving women who had family or interests in the Indies, it is worth mentioning that a series of ordinances existed that protected women from being abandoned by their husbands. A heading from the law code of 1680 (book 4, title 3) clearly shows the concern of the authorities over this matter: "Of married men in Spain and the Indies who are absent from their wives and spouses" (Villafañe 126-27).

The list of ordinances became interminable. In the reigns of Ferdinand the Catholic King, Charles V, Philip II, Philip III, or even Charles II, there is a constant insistence on the theme. The reason for this insistence is quite obvious, since with an ocean in between, there must have been many men who took advantage of the situation and lived a double married life in the absence of the strict control and watchfulness of their wives who were in Spain. Law 27, book 9, title 26 states: "We proclaim that all married and engaged men in these kingdoms are prohibited from embarking for and going over to the Indies 'unless they take their wives with them,' even if they are viceroys, judges, governors, or are to serve us in any office or post in War, Justice, or the Treasury, because it is our will that all those mentioned take their wives with them" (Villafañe 127).

It was the clergy who were in charge of informing the competent courts about those married men who remained in the Indies without their wives. Ferdinand the Catholic issued a number of ordinances in this regard.[37] In 1514, King Ferdinand gave this order in a provision for the island of Hispaniola: "I give license and permission for any person born in these kingdoms to freely marry women who are native to said island without incurring any penalty for it" (Villafañe 129).

Nor should one forget those women who decided to go over to the "new lands" single. These women also played an important part in the development of the new colonies. Spanish spokesmen of the time, such as the administrators of the Indies and all the chroniclers, did not ignore the social importance of these women in the policy of settlement: "It is true that the newly settled towns in the Indies cannot be considered fixed or stable or permanent until Spanish women enter into them, and the encomenderos and conquistadores marry, for many good and healthy causes and reasons there are for this end" (Villafañe 126-27).

If the intention was to have a constant presence in America, the single women who went there would always be one more incentive for the male colonist or conquistador to stay in the same place. A family could be started, if desired, with no need to think about returning to the mother country, either to enjoy wealth that had been acquired or to "search for" a wife. Problems arose when there was an excess of single women, which to some extent altered the existing social structure, since there were not many options for those women beyond marriage or the convent.

> Since experience had shown that an excessive number of women had a pernicious influence on customs and morals, the king was urged not to authorize so many women to emigrate to Peru. The city of La Plata, founded in 1538, issued a report in 1577 stating the urgent necessity of founding a convent, since in the territory of the Audiencias de Los Charcas there was a great number of young women who, unable to marry, were in great danger of becoming lost women (qtd. in Konetzque, "emigración" 149).

It is sad to see how the figures for these women were handled, as if it were a matter of cattle or sumptuary goods. On the other hand, irregularities also existed—Spanish women settlers who lived together with men who were already married in Spain. Normally, this occurred when the conquistador's stay went on longer than it should in places where there were few Spanish women. Many times these unions produced children, and this made the situation even more difficult for the women who were in Spain waiting for a husband who no longer had any intention to return. The documents from the legal inquiries tend to cite these cases, since it was necessary to punish extramarital affairs and safeguard the good family behavior that there was such a desire to uphold. "One example is found on the island of Cuba, where in 1532, the following women were living with married men: Olalla Hernández Santillana, Aranda 'the woman from Córdoba,' Catalina de León,

Catalina Sánchez, Francisca Hernández, Mayor de Azebedo, Juana de Valeros, and 'a woman who was in Ayala's house'" (Borges 416).

The cases cited were not isolated ones, much less in Cuba, the nerve center of all movement back and forth between Spain and the Americas. These eight accusations should not be considered extraordinary, especially in the most cosmopolitan site in the Indies in that period, where fleets arrived at all times. Apparently, similar cases existed in the River Plate, Peru, and New Spain (Ratcliffe 347). The legal freedom for these women to live as they wished was limited by a morality that granted social acceptance to these women only if they entered into marriage or the convent. Men, in the same circumstances, were judged by a much more permissive "morality."

WOMEN AND THE CLERGY

Another factor to be considered, when analyzing the presence of women in the Americas, involves the most important institution that arrived from Europe: the Catholic Church. Without criticizing so complex an institution, which was responsible for a good share of happenings in the Americas, it is worthwhile to analyze some notable aspects. Many of the Church's members were fine examples of courage and intelligence, when it came to dealing with the very diverse and thorny matters that the Christians overseas came up against during this period. One should also point out the Medieval way in which the apostolate was carried out and potential Christians were understood and dealt with. Taking into account the privileges and prerogatives that some of the high Church officials had, it would not be out of line to assume that a considerable percentage of the population of "doubtful" origins may very well have come from the Church itself.

The high idealism of the Church in the eleventh and twelfth centuries must have had a great impact on the society of that time. Many were the victims and many the families divided by an "invisible" father. Many of the children or "nephews" of these priests took up similar positions, as if this were any other guild profession passed on from generation to generation—a common occurrence in Medieval Europe—including the privileges that these positions brought. Still by the end of the thirteenth century, the rights of sons and grandsons of priests were protected by law in Spain, and had not been swept away by the Gregorian reforms (Ratcliffe 347). It would be worthwhile to make an examination of conscience to see how much things have changed in the last five hundred years, or if the modern Church has even backed down in the matter of tolerance of sexual relations for Church representatives. From the time of the Riojan poet Gonzalo de Berceo, there is a record in Spanish letters of these love affairs between Church representatives and certain ladies in their areas. In his best-known work, *Los milagros de Nuestra Señora*, Berceo writes with a naive, simple realism humorous and heartwarming accounts of those men of flesh and blood who were pardoned through the intercession of the Virgin Mary. Juan Ruiz made his *Book of Good Love* the most representative work in this regard. It would be tedious to go into the situation of the Church over different periods of the Middle Ages, not only in Spain but in all of Europe. In twelfth-century Muslim Spain, particularly in Seville, the behavior of the (Mozarab) representatives of the Christian Church in Islamic territory was harshly criticized by the Sevillian Ibn Abdun. This precious document shows the strict control of and lack of confidence in women, who were forbidden to enter into the "abominable" Christian churches:

> because the [Christian] clerics are libertines, fornicators, and sodomites. Thus free women should be forbidden to go into the church except on days of ceremony or feast days, because they eat, drink and fornicate there with the clerics, and there is not one of the latter who do not have two or more of these women with whom they go to bed. They have acquired this habit because the illicit has been declared licit and vice-versa. It would be to advantage, therefore, to order the clerics to marry, as occurs in the Orient, and for them to do so if they wish (Lévi-Provençal 150).

Although there was peaceful coexistence during a great part of the Middle Ages between the three monotheistic creeds of Spain (Christians, Muslims, and Jews), this did not imply, contrary to popular opinion, that there was no disdain or ill feeling among these religious groups. Abdun says, pointing out the risk run by a woman who entered the house of a celibate Christian cleric:

> It should not be tolerated that a woman, whether she is old or not, be in the house of a cleric so long as he refuses to marry. They should also be required to be circumcised, as al-Mutadid required of them, for if, as they say, they follow the example of Jesus (God bless and save them!), Jesus was circumcised, and as a matter of fact they, who have abandoned this practice, have a feast day, which they solemnly celebrate, on the day of his circumcision (Lévi-Provençal 150-151).

The Colombian historian Germán Arciniegas quotes a passage illustrating what has just been mentioned but relocated to the colonial scene, saying that even in small towns like Santa Fe with little more than one monastery, a hermitage, the weakness of the flesh caught up friars, soldiers, and viceroys equally: "The good Solís, who died in the odor of sanctity, with his head resting on a pair of bricks, and in a Franciscan habit, at night crossed over the patio of his bishop's palace to go kiss La Marichuela" (118-19).

Arciniegas also cites an event that showed up in the newspaper in Lima in 1667, which must not have been unusual in colonial times. *The Carmelite Friar.*

> A great heretic; being a priest, he said mass, he was a most lustful and
> dishonest dog, who telling of his wrongdoings said that in a certain city
> he had carnally known more than three hundred sixty women and had
> committed many sacrileges in a nuns' convent. They brought him
> prisoner from Buenos Aires through Chile (119).

The disputes in the modern Church over the relations that churchmen
should have with the female sex seem not to have been resolved yet.
There continues to be fear and discomfort with the idea that women
should share not only in the power of the Church hierarchy but also in
the private lives of the members of the institution.

In New Spain, the first bishop of Mexico, Juan de Zumárraga, seeing
in woman a being that inspired irresistible temptation, totally forbade
their presence in his house, even for cleaning and straightening it up.
The Franciscan Juan de Torquemada refers to this behavior as one of this
popular bishop's virtues:

> This most blessed prelate was very fond of virtue and of the virtuous,
> and a most bitter censor of vices and the vicious, and such an enemy
> of idleness that he would not allow anyone in his house to be idle; he
> was very fond of cleanliness, in the interest of which he never
> permitted any woman to enter his house, even if were necessary for its
> service, nor did he permit that any woman go up to the upper part of
> it, or its bedchambers; instead, he had it all closed off like a
> monastery, because he knew...that opportunity can bring down the
> strongest, stoutest hearts (450; bk. 20, ch. 31).

It was not only members of the Catholic Church who favored the
struggle against temptation, literally following that most cruel adage:
"Entre santa y santo pared de cal y canto" (Between male saint and
female saint, a thick wall). In those accounts that we have of social life
in early colonial times, we can see that there was not much difference
between the orders issued in the mother country and those enforced in
New Spain. The social life both of ladies and of some members of the
colonial Church, was more "relaxed" than the rules allowed. Thanks to
information provided by Manuel Romero de Terreros, we have the
names of the first vicereines:

> The wives of the first five Viceroys, Antonio de Mendoza; Luis de
> Velasco; Gastón de Peralta; Martín Enríquez de Almanza; and Lorenzo
> Suárez de Mendoza, the Count of La Coruña, were respectively:

Caterina de Vargas; Ana de Castilla y Mendoza, the daughter of Diego de Castilla, the Lord of Gor and equerry to Charles V; Leonor de Vieo; María Manrique, the daughter of the Marquis of Aguilar; and Catalina de la Cerda, the daughter of the second Duke of Medinaceli (Romero 2).

Precise information exists about the seventh vicereine of New Spain (1586), Doña Blanca de Velasco, the Marchioness of Villamanrique. In this case it is interesting to observe what has been said above about the lack of tolerance existing at that time, which would be hard to understand without some sporadic accounts of colonial life in New Spain. In the following account, written by anonymous authors, of the visit made by Brother Alonso Ponce, General Commissioner of the Seraphic Order to the provinces of New Spain, mention is made of the strenuous measures taken by this clergyman against the members of his order, which in his opinion was very lax, and also of his dealings with the vicereine:

He also garnered the enmity of the governor and the Vicereine, Doña Blanca de Velasco, the daughter of the fourth Count of Nieva, a lady of seemingly loose conduct and more than domineering character...

> At about this same time [September, 1586] the Viceroy and the Vicereine went to rest and take recreation in the city of Xochimilco. He stayed with all his household in our monastery in one of its dormitories, and he remained there seven or eight days, during which the Indians gave great celebrations for them, although they cost them dear, because at one of them two or three of them died from a shot that was fired and went off, and they wounded the principal Indian of that city very badly (Romero 3-4).

Despite the rigid ecclesiastic and civil control over New Spain, there were lapses when even churchmen and women—human beings, after all—were able to have some good times and enjoyment. Going on from the passage just quoted, the author comments in a tone of complaint on the "excessive" freedom among friars who were expected to practise extreme poverty, not to speak of chastity. In the first place, a detailed description appears of the type and amount of all kinds of food, sweets, and wine that were consumed liberally and generously during those festivities. But what most infuriated the author was that women were allowed into the monastery:

And although all of this is evil before God and before men, what seemed worst of all, and what everyone had to gossip about, was the excessive freedom, breach, and dissolution that there was when very purposefully women entered and stayed, not only the vicereine and her women, but many others, within that monastery and went among the cells as if it were a secular thing, and as if there were no apostolic brief prohibiting these entries under grave penalties and censures, and as if, by admitting them, the friars were not included in the brief, and it were not so declared and ordered by our general statutes of Toledo (Romero 4-5).

The concern over the "temptations of the flesh" outside of matrimony was always on the mind of Spanish clergymen, as well as those of other nationalities and religions, who in vain attempted to eradicate something so intrinsic to the human being, as to any other animal species.   This concern was even more pronounced in the Americas, where many tribal societies did not look upon women as an integral part of their private property. The reason for this is obviously sociological, and it has existed from the beginning of time in more "primitive" civilizations: "Thou shalt not covet thy neighbor's wife." Breaking this rule would be tantamount to destabilizing Judeo-Christian society at its foundation, which is based on the family. The penalties applied to these transgressions were sufficiently harsh as to socially marginalize—in the best of cases—those who practised them. Since women were by nature in charge of carrying on the continuity of the species, they were limited in their sexual freedom because of the danger of becoming pregnant each time that so basic a rule was ignored. Fortunately, things have changed for women. Nevertheless, there is no need to mention here the amount of sexual abuse of which modern society is victim.

THE FIRST FEMALE WRITERS IN THE AMERICAS

In what follows mention will be made of some of the female writers who had a direct or indirect relationship with the Americas in the sixteenth and seventeenth centuries. Many of them chose convent life—in some cases as a refuge from husbands—as the only outlet in a social structure in which they had few options. In a period when the religious factor carried almost as much weight as the economic factor, but above all, in order to devote themselves to spiritual life, which was hard to attain in other circumstances. Mariló Vigil notes that the nuns who were nuns out of their own free will had, in addition to religious concerns, intellectual ones too, as was the case of the mystical writer St. Teresa of Jesus (1515-82), who besides having one of the most interesting lives in the period, managed to make time to write some of the most beautiful examples of lyric poetry and especially prose, in the Spanish language. Each one of these women who were devoted to the literary and spiritual life of their times deserves much more space than can be alloted to them in these few lines. Nonetheless, by mentioning them briefly one hopes to arouse sufficient interest so that their lives and works do not remain submerged in the depths of oblivion.

In order for these women of the Church to be able to satisfy their thirst for knowledge it was necessary to break all those barriers posed by limits or restrictions on doing research, consulting or speaking with any religious of any order or any secular priest, whether he be a bishop or a cleric. The intellectual stances of the different religious orders were often very different, as is well known. The theological premises of the Dominicans were not the same as those of the Franciscans, nor were those of the Carmelites the same as those of the Augustinians or Jesuits. It was therefore necessary to have access to these sources of information so as to be able to identify the differences and draw one's own conclusions (Vigil 237-38). The Spanish writer Julio Caro Baroja points out the encyclopedic character of Catholicism, into which very different currents and positions have been integrated, which through dialogue gave some leeway to a believer having more intellectual curiosity so that he or she could compare and evaluate the different options before him or her (Vigil 237-38).

Several of these intellectual women were nothing more or less than the daughters of conquistadores, who although they had been born on American soil, continued to express themselves in the language of their fathers, with no less power than their women contemporaries in Spain.

It is true that there were many female writers in the Americas during the eighteenth century, some of them even devoted to the study of mathematics, like the Mexican Doña Francisca Gonzaga y Castillo. Since this study is limited to the sixteenth and seventeenth centuries, only examples from those two centuries will be included.

Josefa de Alarcón, a Peruvian woman, published in 1648, some *liras* dedicated to the funeral of Prince Baltasar Carlos:

> I see in a small chapel
> The tribunal of the gravest Majesty
> In witness of what it owes
> To Carlos which does not fit in two worlds.[38]

Sister Jerónima de la Asunción was a very interesting case of a woman who had the opportunity to travel to Mexico and later to the Philippines to carry out the missions entrusted to her by her order. Born in Toledo in 1555, she was destined to go all over the world offering her services to all those who needed them, and distinguishing herself for her fervent charity: "Seeing that the galley slaves were treated with excessive harshness, above all when they were taken from one town to another, she tried to lessen the hardships of those unfortunate ones, and succeeded in part" (Serrano y Sanz 268: 65).

Sister Jerónima set sail for Mexico and from there went on to Manila on the famous "Manila Galleon," which sailed annually from the Mexican port of Acapulco. The voyage over the Pacific Ocean lasted approximately six months, and the very act of embarking on such fragile ships required great bravery and determination. Sister Jerónima wrote her *Vida* (biography), in which she tells of the foundation of the Santa Clara convent in Manila, with all the tribulations—she was excommunicated at one point—and satisfactions provided by a life devoted to a just cause. She also wrote a philosophical and theological work entitled *Carta de marear en el mar del mundo*, an allegorical title that give some sense of the enormous distance traveled over the "sea of the spirit" by Sister Jerónima. These are some of its verses of a religious nature:

> I am yours, I was born for you;
> What do you order be done with me?
> Inaccessible grandeur,
> Eternal Wisdom

And goodness of my soul,
God, a being, power, and Highness,
Look upon the great poverty
Of this woman who offers herself here.
What do you order be done with me (Serrano y Sanz 268: 66)?

We have another example in Mexico of a woman completely devoted to God and to the study and composition of works of a theological nature. Doña Ana María del Costado de Cristo was born in the city of Tlaxcala about 1650. She entered the order of St. Francis to devote herself to the work of that order and to writing. It is said that twenty volumes could be filled with Doña Ana María's works (Serrano y Sanz 268: 282). Her works include biographies of Jesus, St. Francis of Assisi, of the "illustrious virgin St. Claire," and of John Duns Scotus.

Not all nuns had lives so dedicated to study and prayer. As can be expected, among such a great number of women, there were all kinds. It would be a mistake to think that all convents were full of "candid doves." A nun in the sixteenth and seventeenth century had much more power than an ordinary woman, since they acted as a group and residence in the places where they lived was permitted only to women. This situation made them much stronger at all levels than a woman alone, protected only by her family. "During the sixteenth and seventeenth centuries, nuns struggled to avoid the cloister and to break free of the control that the friars of the male sections of their congregations exercised over them" (Vigil 230).

Only one year later than Ana María del Costado de Cristo, in 1651, the peerless Sister Juana Inés de la Cruz was born 12 leagues from Mexico City, the daughter of Pedro Manuel de Asbaje, a native of Vergara (Vizcaya) and Isabel Ramírez de Santillana, the daughter of Spaniards (Serrano y Sanz 268: 289). Because she was without a doubt the most important poet of her time and probably the best known in the Hispanic world, we shall not go into depth about her. It is simply worth pointing out that Sister Juana, although she lived in a society where the freedom granted women was not excessive, had the character and determination to leave us the most beautiful love poems, which, although they were framed in a religious ambiance, as could be expected from her status, managed to stand out as the most beautiful of her literary manifestations that are preserved today. Such were her intelligence, sensitivity, and culture that the thick convent walls were not enough to contain the genius of so extraordinary a woman. Let us recall her well-known verses in defense of women:

> Foolish men, who accuse
> Women with no reason
> And do not see you are the cause
> Of the very thing you blame them for.[39]

Nor should one fail to mention other women writers of New Spain who, although they were not so prolific and important as Juana Inés de la Cruz, left evidence of some events which have sociological or testimonial interest. This is the case of Doña María Estrada Medinilla, who had the same first and last names as the woman who accompanied Cortés's troops on their first entry into Mexico. Born in Mexico, she published all her work in the middle of the sixteenth century, concentrating mainly on the arrival of the Marquis of Villena, Viceroy and Captain-General of New Spain, who arrived in Mexico City in 1640. This work was written in *octavas reales* and deals with the bullfights and jousting tournaments with which the viceroy was greeted. It was printed in Mexico in 1641 (Serrano y Sanz 269: 402).

Much more important for our purposes is Doña Isabel de Guevara, who in 1556 wrote her letter describing the help provided by women in the discovery and exploration of the River Plate. There can be no doubt that this letter is one of the most important documents we have that deals with the female contribution to the process of the encounter of America. Its importance is due to several factors. First, it is one of the first accounts, if not the first, to openly explain the indispensable cooperation of women in the discovery and exploration of American lands: "For if it had not been for [the women], they would all have met their end." Secondly, the information contained in these lines presents to some extent the manner of thinking of a Spanish woman in such circumstances. It is extraordinary evidence that gives us first-hand an idea of what the constant courage and sacrifice of many of these women meant. Even at the risk of losing their lives, they did not hesitate to fight by the side of the men for what they considered a "common cause". Because of the historical importance of Isabel de Guevara's letter, I shall quote it complete:

Letter from Doña Isabel de Guevara to the governing princess Doña Juana, explaining the work done in the discovery and conquest of the

River Plate by women to help men, and requesting a repartimiento for her husband. Asunción, July 2, 1556.

Most high and mighty lady:

To this province of the River Plate, with the first governor of it, Don Pedro de Mendoza, certain of us women came, among whom my fortune chose that I should be one; and since the fleet had arrived at the port of Buenos Aires with fifteen hundred men, and they lacked provisions, the hunger was so great that after three months, a thousand of them died; this hunger was so great that not even that of Jerusalem could equal it, nor could it be compared with any other. The men went about so weak that all the work fell on the poor women, consisting of washing their clothes, healing them, giving them to eat what little they had, cleaning them, keeping watch, inspecting the fires, loading the crossbows, when at times the Indians would come to make war, even firing the cannons, and rousing the soldiers, those who were up to it, calling to arms over the field with shouts, commanding and putting the soldiers in order; because at that time, since we women subsisted on little food, we had not become so weak as the men. Your Highness will understand that the women's diligence was such that, had it not been for them, all would have met their end; and if it were not for the honor of the men, I would write many more things in truth and would give them as witnesses. This account I think will be written to Your Highness more extensively, and so I shall leave off. Once this very dangerous whirlwind had passed, the few who remained alive decided to go upriver, weak as they were and at the onset of winter, in two brigantines; and the exhausted women healed them and looked after them and prepared food for them, bringing wood on their backs from outside the ship, and encouraged them with manly words, saying that they should not let themselves die, that they would soon come into a land with food, and carrying them on their backs in the brigantines, with as much love as if they were their own sons. And as we had arrived at a group of Indians who were called tinbúes, lords of much fish, we again served them by seeking different ways to cook it, so that the fish would not go down badly, since they were eating it without bread and they were very weak.

Then they decided to go up the Paraná [River], in search of provisions, and on that voyage the unfortunate women underwent so many hardships, that it was a miracle that God chose to let them live, seeing that the lives of the men were in their hands; because they took all the work of the ship so much to heart, that she who did less than another woman felt ashamed, serving as they did to work the sail, and steer the ship, and take soundings from the bow, and take over the oar from the soldier who could not row, and to draw water from the ship, and encouraging the soldiers so they would not despair, saying that work was for men: the truth is that the women were not compelled to do these things, nor did they do them out of obligation nor were they forced to do, but only out of charity. Thus they arrived in this city of Asunción, which although it is now very bounteous with provisions, back then it was in great need of them, and it was necessary for women to go back to their labors, clearing ground with their own hands, clearing and hoeing and sowing and harvesting the crops, with the help of no one, until the soldiers were cured of their weakness and began to oversee the land and acquire Indian men and women to serve them, until the land reached the state that it is in now.

I have wished to write and remind Your Highness, to inform you of the ingratitude shown to me in this land, because by now the greater part of those who are in it, both the old and the more recent people, have received their distribution [of Indians], but without remembering me and my work; and they left me out, without giving me any Indian or any type of service. I should very much like to be free to present myself before Your Highness with the service that I have rendered to Your Majesty and the injustice that is being done to me now; but that is not within my power, because I am married to a gentleman from Seville, whose name is Pedro de Esquivel, who to serve Your Majesty has been the cause that my hardships have been so forgotten and have started up again, because three times I take him from the jaws of death, as Your Highness must be aware. Thus I beseech you to order that my perpetual repartimiento be granted to me in appreciation of my services. May our Lord lengthen your Royal life and condition for very long years. From this city of Asunción on July 2, 1556.

The servant of Your Highness who kisses your Royal hands

Doña Isabel Guevara

Envelope: To the most high and mighty lady Princess Juana, Governor of the kingdoms of Spain, etc. - In her Council of the Indies (Isabel de Guevara 619-21).

Ironically, the letter was supposed to arrive in the hands of the unfortunate heir to the throne of Castile and daughter of the Catholic Monarchs, "Juana the Mad," who had died the year before. Isabel de Guevara's words are prophetic, not only because her personal achievements were forgotten, but because the very history of women in the Americas has been effaced, and their presence there denied. At least Isabel Guevara had access to a pen. How many could there have been who did not even know how to write?

Another woman of the period was Leonor de Iciz, who lived during the second half of the sixteenth century. She is of interest above all for the sonnets she wrote in praise of Ercilla, the soldier who participated in the conquest of Chile who was immortalized through his epic *La araucana* (Serrano y Sanz 269: 534). Doña Bernarda Liñán did the same, writing a sonnet to the memory of Captain Gaspar Pérez de Villagrá, who participated in the conquest of New Mexico (Serrano y Sanz 270: 14). The writings of these women deal with two of the most dramatic epics of the encounter.

Moving to Peru in the seventeenth century, we find another founder of convents, Sister Bernardina de Jesús, who was compared with St. Teresa for the similarity of her "Letters" with those of the Avila saint. She was a founder of the Tacunga convent in Quito, which was later destroyed in an earthquake. Serrano y Sanz says of her biography, which is somewhat legendary, that she was a Discalced Carmelite from Lima and the sister of María Benavides y Esquivel, the grandmother of the writer Pedro de Peralta Barnuevo (Serrano y Sanz 269: 553). It is said that this saintly woman fed herself for thirty years on "sweets and orange peels; a detail that is as curious as it is unbelievable. When she died, the nuns took care to set out a lily branch, because she had been married, and those flowers appeared miraculously over the body" (Serrano y Sanz 269: 553).

Another Lima woman of the first quarter of the seventeenth century who had the reputation of a saint was Doña Luisa de Melgarejo. This lady was not a religious by vocation but the wife of the doctor Juan de Soto. The only difference is that Doña Luisa apparently had "visions and revelations," which must have made more than one member of the tribunal of the "Holy Office" (Inquisition) nervous. They considered her writings "guilty." The role of "saint" therefore became that of a "possessed woman" or "demonic woman." The Lima inquisitor, Gaitán, wrote a report in which through public opinion and other findings, it was said that Luisa Melgarejo, a "saintly woman" knew when the souls of the dead came out of Purgatory. On November 14, 1623, the decision was made to take possession of all her notebooks in which she had written down the experiences of all her "trances, suspensions, ecstasies, and revelations." These notebooks, when confiscated, showed a series of alterations, erasures, additons, amendments, and even variations in the handwriting, for which reason, after they were examined they were considered guilty.[40]

Luisa Melgarejo must have had a fine imagination, enough, apparently, to convince some members of the Church that "there was something" in her writings. These things were occurring in Lima, one of the most important cultural centers of social and political life in Hispanic America. At the beginning of the seventeenth century, according to the census taken in 1614 by the Marquis of Monteclaros, Lima was a city of 25,000 inhabitants, of whom 11,000 were Spaniards. The number of male and female religious amounted to 1,720 (Pittaluga 77).

On the island of Santo Domingo during the sixteenth century, it is known that a poet with a famous last name in the events of the Americas, Elvira de Mendoza, was born or at least resided. A manuscript of hers, "Cantares míos que estáis rebelados," is preserved in the Spanish Royal Academy of History. Eugenio de Salazar praises her as poet in a "Sonnet to the Illustrious Poet and Lady Doña Elvira de Mendoza, a resident of the city of Santo Domingo" (Serrano y Sanz 270: 53).

Born in Burgos about 1590, Doña Luisa de Padilla merits a special place within the group of women writers of her period. For her fluent, correct style, the novelty of her ideas and her rich erudition, she receives the following commentary from Manuel Serrano y Sanz: "There are few figures in our female literary history who can compare with this eminent prose writer, perhaps the most notable of all those women essayists who flourished in Spain during the seventeenth century" (Serrano y Sanz 270: 95-96). This commentary and comparison should be widened to include also "male literary history."

Doña Luisa was a defender of the work that the Inquisition was doing for the "cleansing" of women, "soldiers of the demon," which was going on in some Spanish provinces in her time. Many of the women who combined magic with curative powers were condemned, not only by men of the Inquisition, but also by women of all social classes, as is the case of Luisa de Padilla, Countess of Aranda. In her work *Elogios de la verdad e invectiva contra la mentira*, she warned against those who practised arts that went against the Christian religion. Black magic, according to Padilla, was the cause of death of nearly as many persons as other, natural causes. Up to six thousand witches had been discovered in Vizcaya and Guipúzcua, and a woman from a small town had confessed to killing eight hundred persons with her "magic" (Perry 31). The "evil eye" and curses, according to this author, were the reasons why the breasts of lactating mothers dried up, married couples separated, and pregnant women had miscarriages (Perry 31).

If one considers that Doña Luisa was related to the highest aristocracy of her time, or, in other words, to some of the people who in a certain way led the destinies of Spain in that period—the Dukes of Lerma, the Duke of Uceda, the Marquis of Cuéllar, the Count of Santa Gadea, the Marquis of Belmont, to mention a few—one can better understand her identificaiton with an institution which in theory sought to safeguard the "eternal" values of a Spain that was destined to be the champion of Catholicism during the sixteenth and seventeenth centuries. Doña Luisa's father was Martín de Padilla y Manrique, an extraordinary military man who demonstrated his valor against Moorish, English, and Dutch enemies; Berber pirates; and the Genoese renegade Muley Faxad. He was a veteran of the Battle of Lepanto, in which he captured four galley ships; and with his squadron he accompanied Queen Margarita of Austria when she came from Genoa in 1598. "On July 24, 1587, he had obtained the title of Count of Santa Gadea and in 1596, theat of Captain-General of the Ocean Sea Fleet" (Serrano y Sanz 270: 95-96).

On the other hand, it is also known that Doña Luisa participated directly, from an early age, in the practice of some intellectual activities, such as history and archeology, at the same time that she was devoting her time to Christian virtues, such as charity and aid to the needy (Serrano y Sanz 270-97). It is much easier to understand this great woman's ideological position if, in addition to the factors mentioned above, account is taken of other factors of a biographical nature concerning her education and marriage.

Another writer was the Mexican María Casilda Pozo, a native of Temestla, Mexico. Born in the month of April, 1682, she left her biography written in sixteen notebooks. The original manuscript is found the library of the San Gregorio school in Mexico City. Her confessor was the Jesuit Domingo Quiroga, who was the one who urged her to write her work (Serrano y Sanz 270: 137). At the beginning of the seventeenth century, forming part of a group of Spanish religious women who went to Manila via Mexico, Sister Juana de San Antonio appears. She stood out for her personal qualities, but her work is also interesting because it offers testimonial information about the way the Chinese and Japanese dressed (Serrano y Sanz 27: 225).

Another nun who died "in the odor of sanctity," an Ecuadorean, was Gertrudis de San Ildefonso, born in 1652, who professed her vocation in the Santa Cruz convent of Quito, leaving a written account of her life at the order of her confessor, Father Martín de la Cruz, who then wrote a biography "in three thick volumes." Gertrudis de San Ildefonso died in 1709 (Serrano y Sanz 270: 300).

Sister María Ana Agueda de San Ignacio was born on March 3, 1695, in the diocese of Puebla de los Angeles, on a farm in the district of Santiago Tecalí (Serrano y Sanz 270: 300). This Mexican nun wrote several works during her life in the convent, where she held the post of prioress for many years. Among her works, all of a devout nature, extolling "divine love," she wrote a curious, "voluminous" treatise on the *Leche virginal de la Soberana Madre de Dios*, on which Father Juan de Villa Sánchez made the following commentary: "in which, speaking first in a natural sense of the benefits that we owe to Our Lady, she goes on to discourse in a mystical and allegorical sense, understanding doctrine to be in the [Virgin Mary's] milk" (Serrano y Sanz 270: 301). Also Mexican was Sister Petronila de San José, who served as abbess of the Royal Monastery of Jesús María in Mexico City. She wrote the *Vidas de varias religiosas ejemplares*, a work of some importance, since apparently "Don Carlos de Sigüenza y Góngora made use of this work in writing his *Parayso occidental* (Mexico, 1684), as he himself states in his introduction, saying that it is Sister Petronila 'to whom, if there is something good in this history, everything is owed'" (Serrano y Sanz 270: 354). Less well known was her compatriot Sister Luisa de Santa Catalina, a native of Xacona, "a town located in the vicinity of Zamora (Mexico)," who was baptized in 1682. She wrote the *Cartas espirituales a su confesor el P. Juan López de Aguado*.[41]

All these writings, most of them unknown to the general public, are important because they give us a different perspective. They show us the highly refined sensibility of many women who remained and continue to remain "in the shadows" of the rich period of Spanish literature that was the Golden Age. That age also, in its literary and artistic dimension, belonged to women.

PART FIVE: SPANISH, INDIAN AND
MESTIZAS WOMEN IN THE NEW SPAIN
SOCIETY

STORIES OF SOME OF THE FIRST WOMEN WHO WENT TO THE AMERICAS

The following is a presentation of some women who went over to New Spain in the first quarter of the sixteenth century and who left information about themselves. A biographical index of these women was included by Francisco de Icaza in his *Diccionario de conquistadores*, and a number of its entries appear below.[42]   Icaza's work, taken from different petitions and briefs, gives a general idea of the problems and needs of the first women who arrived in these territories.

The woman settler became a widow in a few years. To widowhood were added new troubles. Not to mention similar losses of her children in the struggle, she had to face other problems created by her new station. One of them would be a second marriage, more or less imposed upon her; another was the lack of property, and as a consequence, family economic instability, which particularly affected her daughters, who were left with no security (Borges 411).

The information presented is evidence given by contemporary people, quoted in Icaza's work, and also information taken from Bernal Díaz's *True History*, Motolinía's *Memoriales* and *Historia de los indios de Nueva España*, Brother Jerónimo de Mendieta's *Historia eclesiástica indiana*, and documentation found in the Archivo General de Indias and the Archive of Simancas.   Many of these conquistadores' briefs are preserved in manuscript, unpublished, "in their near totality" in the Archivo de Indias (Icaza 1: vi).   "That information, autobiographic in nature—mostly direct or if not, from family members or persons authorized to give information—tells us things about many well-known or unknown conquistadores" (Icaza 1: vi-vii).

Fortunately, the compiler, Icaza, does not ignore women. He not only quotes them on numerous occasions, but in his introduction makes a most valuable reference to them:

> Except that this information is not arbitrary but true. Noted here are those who were the first women to go over to New Spain, the first cleric who was ordained and said mass, the first nun to take her vows there—a daughter of Licenciado Diego Téllez—and other, similar pieces of information; some of them moving in their primitive naïveté, such as the one about the woman who taught Indian women to sew and embroider in the Spanish manner, and the one about Marina Vélez, "one of the first women who came to this New Spain, bringing up and training at her own expense maidens from the time they were girls."

It is also interesting to find out that among the first woman came the first midwife—Beatriz Muñoz—who must also have had been acquainted with practical medicine in other ways, since "she was of great service in curing the sick who were wounded from the wood and nails of the ships" which Cortés took disassembled from Veracruz to Mexico (Icaza 1: xlv-xlvi).

These pioneer women are mentioned in the examples that follow. It should be noted that mentioned in this listing are only women—widows of the first conquistadores in most cases—who had to take care of themselves. In the list of men, the women with whom they were married also appear, but for reasons of length, that list is not included here. Worthy of mention among these men is the Scotsman Tomás Blaque, "A native of the kingdom of Scotland, legitimate son of Guillén Blaque and Inés Moat...married to Francisca Ribera, who had been the wife of Cristóbal de Canyego" (Icaza 2: 98-99). Uniformly, all these women—thence the existence of this document—were availing themselves of the "grant that later came from His Majesty to the wives and children of the conquistadores" (Icaza 1: 177). It should also be noted how many of these widows remarry two, three, and even four times.

The poverty of the widows and daughters of conquistadores had a double origin: their failure to receive an inheritance from the deceased husband and father; and the elimination of the encomiendas, which was in fact carried out in many places. In the first case, the failure to receive an inheritance from the father-conquistador was due to the fact that not only did the greater part of the conquistadores not leave property but frequently the family inherited heavy debts. In Cuba, Catalina Aguirre at an early date (1528), requested that the "dowry and *arras*" (money given by the bridegroom to the bride) not be impounded from her on account of her husband's debts.[43]

The following list only includes those women—Indian, Mestizo, and Spanish—who were living in New Spain, which is to say Mexico. Nevertheless, this information can give us a general idea of what the situation must have been like in the Viceroyalty of Peru and on the rest of the American continent. The authorities intervened in these matters. Sometimes they married female orphans to soldiers; other times a convent was created to "take them in," or if one prefers, "to jail them for life, against their will." This was a pleasant existence for those women who had a religious vocation, but a death-in-life for those who did not.

A governor of Tucumán [Argentina] sensed the socio-spiritual problem of the conquistadores' orphan daughters and decided to solve it as best he could: "I have found in this city," he says, " and in the others, more than sixty maidens, the poor daughters of conquistadores, without any kind of relief except that provided by God and Your Grace. I have married off some ten of them."[44]

In the document that follows, one can understand in a wider context the difficult situation of many of the women settlers of New Spain. The social, economic, and spiritual implications of the stories of these women merit a much more detailed study, particularly the situation of many conquistadores' orphan daughters who remained unmarried. One should not forget the competition they had from native women, who in the opinion of some, were every bit as handsome as the Spanish women. Very often the Mestizo woman inherited the social and economic status of her father, which facilitated her marrying (Borges 432-34). Nor should one lose sight of how the "value" of these women depended almost exclusively on what their husbands had done in life. In other words, their existence was conditioned not by their achievements, with a few exceptions, but by those of their husbands.

The list of women taken from Icaza's dictionary of conquistadores is the following:

Index of conquistadores and settlers of New Spain who gave personal information about themselves to the first viceroys from 1540 to 1550, as can be inferred from the text of their writings. also included are the reports provided by the immediate heirs or in representation of those who were absent.[45]

Doña Luisa Destrada says

That she is the daughter of Alonso Destrada, His Majesty's former treasurer in this New Spain, and of Doña Luisa, his wife, and the wife of Jorge Alvarado, deceased, who came over to these parts some thirty years ago and took part in the conquest of Cuba, that is, of some of its towns, from whence he came to this New Spain, and later with the Marquis of the Valley [Hernán Cortés], and they were involved in the taking of this city of Mexico and in the conquest of the other provinces of this New Spain, Pánuco, Guaxaca, Teguantepec, Soconusco, and Guatemala, which latter province later rebelled, and he returned to pacify it; and she says that of the towns which her said husband left her,

Suchimilco and Zucar and Chiatla have been taken from her, and others that she possessed in Guatemala; and that she has a son and two daughters, and is in want; and that together with her said husband, three other brothers of his came over to this New Spain and took part in its conquest. (1: 103)

The wife of Pedro Valenciano, deceased discoverer—he left a daughter—says:

That she was the wife of Pedro Garao Valenciano, deceased, conquistador of this New Spain, and that she came over to this New Spain with Pánfilo de Narváez, married to Bartolomé de Porras, who died, and she married said Pedro Valenciano; and that she has the use of one-third of the town which her husband had, which is very little, because she is poor and has her house and family and two married granddaughters, and she is sick and aged; and that she is a native of Ecija, and the daughter of Pero Núñez Mancheño and Catalina de Cerrana. (1: 103)

Isabel de Ojeda does not say

Where she comes from nor whose daughter she is, and says that she was the wife of Antonio de Villaroel, who came over with Pedrarias to the Mainland, and from there he came to Cuba with Diego Velázquez, and from there he came over to New Spain, with the Marquis, with whom he took part in all the conquests of it and of Michoacán and Panuco and Jalisco, for which he was never compensated; and that she was left with a twenty-thousand-peso debt, and that she has in her house nieces and poor maidens yet to be married, and not having the means, has not married them; and out of the need to provide for them, she is in want, and that he was a gentleman and alderman of this city. (1: 106-07)

Leonor Gutiérrez says

That she is the legitimate daughter of Juan Jiménez de Ribera, a native of Las Montañas, who took part with the Marquis in the taking of this city of Mexico and in the other conquests of this New Spain and of Pánuco; and as such he was taken care of from the treasury; and that her said husband had the town of Tiltitlán in encomienda, and that it is in possession of His Majesty, and it was taken away by the Court, and he brought your Royal Warrant so that justice could be done to him over it, and once it was brought he died, and that she, as a woman and a poor person has not been able to deal with that matter, and that she has a son and a daughter by the man mentioned, the daughter yet to be married; and she is in want and she has given information about the man mentioned, and she names persons who say that they know it. (1: 108)

Ana de Segura, the wife of Jerónimo Tría; he has gone to Spain and left a son in this land, married to a daughter of Montaño, the conquistador; she says

That she is a resident of this city, and a native of Seville, and the legitimate daughter of Francisco de Segura, notary public of said city, and of Antonia Maldonada, and that she is the wife of Jerónimo Tría, and first she was the wife of Diego Remón, who died, and she married Juan Catalán, one of the first conquistadores of this New Spain, for which he was given half of the town of Taualilpa in encomienda, and on the death of her said husband, it was taken from her, for which the Marquis [Cortés], seeing that she was poor, gave her the Tlamaco farm, a very small thing, the warrant for which she says she is presenting; and that later   she married Jerónimo Tría, and that she is laden down with sons and daughters, and is in want, and has had and has her house full of her family, and she is presenting the copy of the warrant which she has for the town. (1: 108-09)

Ana Rodríguez, a widow, the wife of Hernando de Jerez, says

That she is a native of Jerez de la Frontera, and the daughter of Pero Flores and Marina Rodríguez, the mother-in-law of Juan de Jaso, the younger, and she came over to this New Spain twenty-four years ago, and that she was the wife of Hernando de Jerez, deceased, who was a conquistador of it, by whom she has a daughter; and that her said husband came over with Narváez and took part in the taking of this city and in the conquests of Motín and Honduras and Pánuco, and that her said husband left her the town of Atlauca, and Your Grace took it away from her; and she brought His Majesty's warrant so that it might be returned to her, and it was never done, and she was married for a second time to Pedro de Funes, who was killed by the Indians on a crag in Jalisco, and that she has very little. (1: 111)

Doña María de León, who was the wife of Pedro Castelar, may he rest in peace, says

That she is a native of the city of Seville, and daughter of Licenciado Pedro de León and Doña Beatriz de Alcocer, his wife, and he came over to this New Spain with four daughters and two sons, and he died shortly thereafter; and that she married Pedro Castelar some fifteen years ago, and the she has been left with a two-year-old daughter; and said Castelar was one of the first conquistadores of Cuba, and in 1520, he came to discover this New Spain, and later he came with Narváez and took part in the taking of this city, and when it rebelled; and in the conquest of this New Spain, Guazacualco and Tustepec, Pánuco, and in His Majesty's service, he lost a ship, and likewise he took part in the conquest of Chiapa and Chamula and Chinantla and Chustitlán, Tapilula and Talpa and Cimatlán and Higueras and the Papayuca Valley, and other provinces that she names; and she identifies the captains and the town of Xicaltepec was given to him in encomienda for these services, which does not produce much; and she says that she is presenting the encomienda warrant, and that she is in want, and her said husband had court positions and lived honorably, she asks that all of this be recognized. (1: 112)

Beatriz López says

That Alonso Arévalo, deceased, was the son of Pedro de Arévalo, a licenciado and María Temiño, his wife, natives of Berlanga, and he came over to Cuba, when the governor there was Diego Velázquez, who gave him Indians in repartimiento, and from there he came with Grijalva to discover this New Spain, and when it was discovered he went over to Cuba and came with the Marquis, with whom he took part in the conquest, taking, and pacification of this city of Mexico and of the other provinces that were conquered before it, and in the conquest of Pánuco and Michoacán and Zacatula and Jalisco and Motín and Milpa, and in their pacifications, because they rose up in rebellion again, and in other parts...and at present there are two sons of his, and he left a little town that produces no more than one hundred twenty pesos, and they are poor, she does not say that she is his wife, nor does she state where she was born, nor whose daughter she is, nor does this report have any more effect. (1: 112)

Inés Alvarez de Gibraleón; her son died; she married Guido de Labazares.

She does not state where she was born, nor whose daughter she is, and says that she was the wife of Francisco Rodríguez Zacatula, who died about a year ago and left a son in her, and that he came over to this New Spain with Pánfilo de Narváez and took part in the taking of this city of Mexico and in the conquest of the other provinces that border it, and in those of the Sea of the North [Atlantic Ocean] and the Sea of the South [Pacific Ocean]; and that since her said husband died, she has had a page with his arms and horses as His Majesty orders; and that the Indians left to her from her said husband—she does not state which ones they are—are of little use, and she has had them since Your Grace came to the land, and before she had not been compensated, and she is presenting evidence showing that her said husband came over with said Narváez and was a conquistador. (1: 113)

Doña Ana de Rebolledo says
That she is from Tudela in Navarre and is the legitimate daughter of knight commander Don García de Rebolledo and Doña Ana de Mendoza, and that she was the wife of Pedro Hernández de Navarrete, deceased, a former resident and conquistador of this city of Mexico, in the taking of which he took part, and in the conquest of the other provinces bordering it, by whom she was left with two sons and to daughters yet to be married, and that she has the use of the town of Acayuca, which was given in encomienda to her said husband by the Marquis in compensation for his services, the tributes or earnings of which town, producing so little, is not enough to support her, and she is left very poor and in need, and that said knight commander her father served His Majesty in Spain, and she does not state how. (1: 115)

Here there appears a daughter of Moctezuma married to a Spaniard. She does not, however, state her name:
The wife and sons of Cristóbal de Valderrama say
That it was twenty-four years ago that their said husband and father came over to this New Spain, and served in the province of Michoacán and Colima and Zacatula and other parts, and has the town of Tarinaro and Ecatepeque; and that she is a daughter of Montezuma, and said towns are very little, and that said Valderrama was from Las Montañas. (1: 116)

. The wife of Cisneros says

That she is called Doña María de Medina and that she is the daughter of Jerónimo de Medina and Doña Roca, his wife, natives of Illescas, and that her said father and Gonzalo Hernández de Medina, her grandfather, served the Catholic Monarchs; and that she came to this New Spain seventeen years ago with her said mother, and two years ago she was married to Juan de Cisneros, deceased, who was a conquistador of this city of Mexico and New Spain and who died serving His Majesty in the last pacification of Jalisco; by whom she was left with four sons and two daughters, all legitimate, and was left with the Indians of Taxmalaca, which were given in encomienda to her husband for the services that he did, which Indians, not being many, are not enough to support her. (1: 117)

Doña Francisca de la Cueva says
That she is the wife of Francisco Flores, who was a native of Encinasola, which is in Extremadura, and a son of Juan Flores, and, she says, he served His Majesty for thirty-five years in these parts, eight of them in the islands and the rest in the conquest of this New Spain and in the provinces of Guatemala; and she is the daughter of Pedro de San Martín and Doña Argenta, his legitimate wife, natives of Ubeda, and she has five children, one male and the rest women, two of whom are of marrying age, and she has little prospect for her support... (1: 118)

Mari Hernández, the wife of Andrés Núñez, deceased...and he went with the Marquis to the island, and he was given the town of Tequisquiac in encomienda, which produces very little; when he died, it was left to her, and she gave it in marriage with a daughter of hers and of said Andrés Núñez, to Gonzalo Portillo, who has them at present, and that she is in want and has always lived chastely and purely, like a good widow. (1: 119)

Catalina de Santa Cruz, the former wife of Luis Sánchez, conquistador.
She is the daughter of Francisco Santa Cruz, conquistador, and the wife of Luis Sánchez, deceased, who was a native of the town of Ledesma, and came over to New Spain in 1520, and took part in the taking of this city of Mexico and conquest of the other provinces bordering it...the town of Pungaravato was given to him in encomienda, and it was taken away from him, and that she is left with two sons and

two daughters, whom she supports with the charity that Your Grace gives her from His Majesty's house, and she is in extreme want. (1: 120-21)

Francisca de Paredes, who was the wife of Pedro del Golfo, says
That she was born in this city [Mexico], and that she is the legitimate daughter of Juan de Paredes and Beatriz Hernández...and she was left poor and is in want, and that her said father had Indians in encomienda and because of his death, they were placed in possession of His Majesty; she beseeches Your Grace, on behalf of herself and her sister, to remember them. (1: 121)

Isabel Gómez, who was the wife of Francisco González, says
That she is the legitimate wife of Francisco González, deceased, one of the first conquistadores of this New Spain and city of Mexico and other provinces, where he died in His Majesty's service, and because he came for that reason, he left her in Seville in great want; and that she came to this New Spain some ten years ago, and brought a daughter and two grandchildren, orphans, and she has said daughter married in Pánuco to Vicencio Corzo, and that she is poor and is in want; she does not state her parents and where she is from. (1: 121-22)

Francisca de Mesa says
That she is a native of the town of Marchena, and the legitimate daughter of Francisco de Mesa and Inés de Herrera, a native of Las Montañas, and her said father was one of the discoverers and conquistadores of this New Spain and city of Mexico, and he entered into the volcano and brought out sulfur for gunpowder, which was a great help in the conquest; and that her grandfather served in the war of Granada and Melilla and other parts, and later was a conquistador of the islands; and that she is the wife of Jerónimo Flores, and she has two legitimate children by another, first husband; and that she had and has in her house six brothers, sons of her father, Mestizos, and great expense, and she came over to this New Spain some twenty years ago with her first husband, and they landed on the coast of Guazacualco, and lost what they were bringing with them; and she names people who say that they know it. (1: 123-24)

Leonor de Nájara, an Indian woman, says

That she is a native of this land and that she was the legitimate wife of Pedro Moreno de Nájara, deceased, who came over to this New Spain with Pánfilo de Narváez, and found her in the conquest, by whom she has four sons and and one daughter, and she is very poor and is suffering from want; and His Majesty's officials are not doing for her what Your Grace ordered. (1: 124)

Catalina de Cáceres, an Indian woman, says
That she was the legitimate wife of Pedro Borges, one of the first conquistadores of this city of Mexico and New Spain, who died and left her with many children; and very poor and suffering extreme want. (1: 125)

Ana Quintera, who was the wife of Antonio Arriaga, says
That she was the legitimate wife of Antonio Arriaga, deceased, who was a conquistador of this city of Mexico and New Spain, Pánuco and Michoacán, Zacatula and Colima and Los Yopes, for which he had towns in encomienda, and they were taken away from him; and he left four daughters, one married, and all of them suffer great want; and that Your Grace has done her the kindness to order that three of them be provided with a house for one hundred pesos, and one of them for fifty per year; and that said Arriaga was a conquistador of Cuba, and he came over to this New Spain with Pánfilo de Narváez, and that he was a native of Berlanga. (1: 125-26)

Catalina de Rodas, she is from Guacachula.
She does not say where she was born, nor whose daughter she is, and says that she was the legitimate wife of Agustín Rodas, who died some eight months ago, and was one of the first conquistadores of this city of Mexico and New Spain, by whom she has four sons and a daughter, all of them poor. (1: 126)

Juana Ruiz says
That she was married to Diego de Olbera, deceased, who was a native of the town of Utrera and the son of Hernando de Olvera and Antonia Saavedra; and that his said father served the Royal crown in the war of Granada, and that her said husband came over to this New Spain with Narváez, and took part in the conquest and taking and pacification of it and of this city; he died some four years ago; by whom she was left

with three sons and four daughters, one of whom married Alonso Calvo, and he left a town that he had in encomienda, which is called Chicobasco, which produces very little and was not enough to support him, for which reason he was always in great want, and she suffers the same, for which reason Nuño de Guzmán gave her Jalapa and Acatlán on the southern coast, which were taken from her by this Royal Court; and she brought suit against it, which is in the Council. (1: 128)

Andrea Ramírez says

That she is the legitimate daughter of Francisco Ramírez, a native of León and Juana Godoy, a native of Córdoba, and that she was first the wife of Juan Tirado, and at present of Juan Blázquez; and that her said parents came over to the islands with the knight commander, a long time ago, and that her father and a brother of her mother came over to this land when Miguel Díaz de Aux came here, and he brought two horses and a boy and two Negroes, and they took part in the conquest of this New Spain, in the taking of this city and of Pánuco, and her uncle in the taking of Guatemala; and that she has five children and is in extreme want. (1: 128)

Catalina Hernández

Diego Díaz says that he is the guardian and takes care of Catalina Hernández and Leonor Hernández, wife and daughter of Cristóbal Hernández, deceased, who was a conquistador of this New Spain and discoverer of it; they are in his care; and that the said wife of Cristóbal Hernández is a native of this land, and poor, and is in want. (1: 129)

Ana de Maya, wife of Juan de Cuéllar Verdugo, says

That she is a native of the town of Cuéllar, and the legitimate daughter of Antonio Maya, one of the first conquistadores of this city of Mexico and New Spain, and of Mari Alvarez, and that she is the wife of Juan Cuéllar Verdugo, and that her said father served His Majesty with his arms and horse; and he first came with Grijalba on the discovery, and that he was killed by the Indians in the war over this city and that she married her said husband, by whom she has a son and four daughters. (1: 129-30)

Leonor García, wife of Francisco García, conquistador, says

That she is an Indian, and was the wife of Francisco García, deceased, who was a conquistador, and left her very poor, because her husband was poor; and she is in extreme want; she does not state where he was a conquistador, nor in fact does she say any more. (1: 131)

Catalina de Herrera, says

That she is the legitimate daughter of Garci-Hernández, deceased, who was one of the first conquistadfores of this city of Mexico and New Spain and its provinces, because he came over with Narváez, and before he came over to this New Spain he left her married in Santo Domingo, and because she became a widow, she came to this New Spain some twelve years ago, where she had her said father and brothers, all conquistadores, and she does not state who they were; and she was married again for a second time to Juan Fuentes, who is likewise dead, and from him two sons and a daughter remained; he served His Majesty with Nuño de Guzmán in the conquest of Jalisco, at his own expense, with his arms and horses, and she was left very poor and is in want. (1: 133)

Malgarida Ruiz, a widow, says

That she is a resident of the city of Ciudad Real, in Chiapa, and was for a long time a resident of Guaxaca, and that she is the daughter of Juan de Acosta and María de Abrego, and a native of the island of Madeira; and that she is the wife of Lorenzo Genovés, who came over to this New Spain with the Marquis of the Valley and took part in its conquest and the taking of this city, and then he stayed to guard it when the Marquis went to encounter Narváez; he had Minxapa in encomienda and other towns which she names; and he is dead and he left a legitimate daughter, who is married in Chiapa to Luis Mazariegos; and she is poor and has no support, for which reason she is in the house of said daughter. (1: 134)

María de Guzmán says

That she is a resident of this city, a widow who was the wife of master Martín de Sepúlveda and the mother of Baltasar de Sepúlveda, her legitimate son...she is in want. (1: 134-35)

María de Zamora says

That she is the legitimate daughter of Alonso Pérez de Zamora, who was a conquistador of this city of Mexico and New Spain, and the wife of Adrián de Benavente, who is at present absent from this city, by whom she has children, and she is very poor and is in want; and her said husband has no trade, for which reason he has gone to seek some help in supporting himself. (1: 141)

Leonor Osorio says

That she is a native of Seville and the legitimate daughter of Gonzalo de Vargas and Leonor Osorio, and that she came over to this New Spain some twenty years ago in the company of the wife of Andrés Barrios; and that she was the wife of Juan de Espinosa, one of the conquistadores of this city of Mexico and New Spain, who died, and she was married again to Francisco de Ribadeo, a conquistador of this city of New Spain, to whom one-fourth of Tlapa was given in encomienda, and at the time he died he had use of and had in encomienda the towns of Aurecho and Papaltepec, *and since at the time His Majesty had not given the grant which there is at present for women, they were taken away from her,* and later she married again, and her third husband went with the Marquis to the island, where he died of hunger; and she was left very poor, so much that she has had to go to other people's houses, and she is in extreme want; and she has three legitimate children, who, not having anyone to stay with, go wandering about. (1: 142)

Antonio de Carranza and Ana de Carranza, mestizos say

That they are children of Pedro de Carranza, one of the first conquistadores of this city of Mexico and New Spain, who had in encomienda the towns of Guatepec and Tepeye, and they were taken away from him without cause, and that said Ana de Carranza es thirteen years old, and they are poor, and Gonzalo de Ecija has them in his house; for the love of God he begs Your Gracious Majesty to remember them. (1: 142-43)

Ana and Beatriz, legitimate daughters of Pedro Abarca.

They say that their father was a native of Calatayud, which is in the Kingdom of Aragon, and that their father took part in the conquest of this city and other towns of this New Spain and of the province of Guatemala; they say that they are poor; the older is eleven years old, and the other nine; they are registered as daughters of conquistadores. (1: 148)

María de Solís says
That she is the daughter of Francisco de Solís, a resident of this city, and she was the wife of Juan de Villagrán, deceased, who was a conquistador of Pánuco, by whom she has two legitimate daughters, and she was left very poor; and that she has a lawsuit against the wife of Diego de las Roelas, over the Indians that the latter has. (1: 148)

Licenciado Benavente on behalf of Antonia de Benavides, his niece, says
That she is the legitimate daughter of Alonso de Benavides, who came to discover this land with Francisco Hernández de Córdoba, and later he was with the Marquis of the Valley, and took part in the conquest of this city; and later he was sent with His Majesty's shipment, when Quiñones and Alonso Dávila went; and the French captured them; and later he returned to this land and received the town of Maxcalcingo in encomienda, and married María de la Torre, her mother, who is now the wife of Dorantes,[46] and who has the town, and she gives her two hundred pesos per year, which is not enough to make a dowry for her and to support her. (1: 151)

Francisca de Silva says
That she was the wife of Alonso Macías, who was a native of Palos, the son of Bartolomé Macías and Leonor Peinada, who came over to this New Spain with Pánfilo de Narváez, and took part in the conquest and taking of this city of Mexico, and provinces, and fifty leagues bordering it, by whom she was left with three daughters and a son, all very poor, because they were not left with anything to support them; and she is in want. (1: 155-56)

Isabel de Monjaraz says
That she is the legitimate daughter of Martín Ruiz de Monjaraz, and that she was the wife of Manuel de Cáceres, deceased, who was a resident of Colima; and that her said father was one of the first conquistadores of this city of Mexico and New Spain, and they came over to it with the Marquis; and her said husband came over to this New Spain with Garay and took part in the Pánuco operation and later in the

conquest of Colima and Tonalá; and that she was left with two children by said husband, and she was pregnant, and she was not left with the help that she needed; and that her said husband was the first to plant cacao in said province, and other trees of Castile, from which much profit has come. (1: 156-57)

Isabel Ortiz, the wife of Antonio Ortiz, says

That she was born in this land, in the province of Taxcala, and the wife of Antonio Ortiz, and first she was the wife of Melchior de Villacorta, one of the first conquistadores of this New [Spain], by whom she was left with two daughters, who are at present married in this city; and her first husband had Indians in encomienda, which were taken away from him by this Royal Court; and she says that she is presenting the deeds for it, and that by Antonio Ortiz she has two other daughters, yet to be married, and all of these daughters, the ones and the others, are poor, and that she is a daughter of an important person of this land. (1: 157)

Beatriz Núñez de Carvallo is married to a son of Escobar, the conquistador, who is called Alonso Niño; she says

That she was the wife of Rodrigo de Paz, a settler, and that she was left poor with four children, and that she is the daughter of Juan de Manila, who was a conquistador of this city and New Spain. (1: 159)

Isabel Jiménez says

That she is a native of the town of Utrera, and the legitimate daughter of Juan de Jerez del Alcantarilla and of Lucía de Ayllón, and that she was the wife of Alonso de Valbuena, who was a conquistador of Cuba, where he had Indians in repartimiento, and from there he came over to this New Spain, and she does not state with whom; and he took part in the taking of this city and conquest of the provinces of this New Spain; and that she came in search of him some three years ago, and learned that he had died in Guatemala, by whom she was left with a daughter nearly thirty years of age, and she has not married her off because of the limited means she has; and both of them suffer extreme want. (1: 159)

Catalina de Escobar says

That she was the wife of Juan Serrano, deceased, who was one of the conquistadores of this city of Mexico and New Spain, and as such, until he died he enjoyed the reward given to him provided as maintenance for the conquistadores; and that he did not leave legitimate children [Did he leave illegitimate ones?], and that she is a native of this land. (1: 159)

Isabel de Zeballos says

That she is the legitimate daughter of Alonso de Zeballos, a native of Medina de Pumar and of María de Leyva, his wife, a native of Ciudad Real; her father was one of the first conquistadores, and he served His Majesty in all the conquests of this New Spain; and later he died; he left two daughters and a son; they are in great want; she was married to Cosme García; she is a widow and poor, with two sons and two daughters, one married and the other a maiden; such is their want that if they did not go to Doña Marina de la Caballería, she would have nothing to eat; she requests and begs, in view of the fact that her father was given nothing in remuneration, being one of the first conquistadores, that compensation be made to her in the repartimiento. (1: 160)

Isabel Gutiérrez

Does not state where she was born, nor whose daughter she is; she is a resident of the city of Los Angeles, and was the wife of Jerónimo de Cáceres, who was a conquistador of this New Spain, and when he died, she married a Juan López de la Cerda, and is at present his wife; he is absent from said city; and that she has a child, and that she came over to this New Spain twelve years ago, and has people in her house. (1: 167)

Doña Catalina Sotomayor says

That she is a resident of Michoacán, *and that she is one of the first three women who came to this New Spain*, because she came here with Pánfilo de Narváez, and she was married here to Juan de Cáceres Delgado, one of the first conquistadores who came over with the Marquis; when he died, she was married again, to Pedro Méndez de Sotomayor, of whom she is at present likewise the widow, and she has a legitimate daughter, and she is in want. (1: 171)

Ana González says

That she is a resident of Colima, and that she was the wife of Juan de Villacorta, one of the first conquistadores of this New Spain, and that she is poor, and a native woman of this land, and that when she was married to the above-mentioned, she had a town in the Valley of Aguatán, and when her husband died, it was taken away from her because at the time the grant did not exist that later   came from His Majesty to the wives and children of the conquistadores; and that later she was married again, to Pero González, and they have come into such poverty that they have nothing to support them except alms that are given to them. (1: 177)

Ginesa López says

That she is a native of the town of Palos, and the legitimate daughter of Diego de Lepe and Catalina Vanegas, and that she was the wife of Juan Picón, who was a conquistador and discoverer of this New Spain, who left her after being married to her for five weeks to come to serve His Majesty; and she came over to this New Spain five years ago; and that *she is in want having as she does twelve Spanish women in her house*, all poor; and also that her said husband was a conquistador of other provinces of this New Spain, which she mentions. (1: 181)

Doña María de Mendoza says

That she is the legitimate daughter of Alonso de Mendoza, later Robles Rengel, and that her said father came over to this New Spain with Pánfilo de Narváez, and took part in many conquests in it, and in the siege of this city, from which the Marquis sent him to His Majesty in Spain to give him an account of this land, and he died upon his return; and she was left poor, because her said father was never remunerated with more than one municipality; and that on said voyage he spent everything he had; and she is presenting a warrant from our lord the prince, in which Your Grace is ordered to favor her and help her in whatever comes up, both her and the person she marries, which warrant is with this original. (1: 181)

Guiomar Marmolejo says

That she is three years old, and that she is the legitimate daughter of Antonio Marmolejo, conquistador of this city of Mexico and New Spain, and served His Majesty in all that; and that her guardian is Alonso del Castillo. (1: 182)

Catalina Garrida

Bartolomé Garrido says that he takes care of Catalina Garrida, the daughter of Diego Garrido and Elvira de Arévalo, his wife, and that said Diego Garrido came over to this New Spain with the Marquis of the Valley, who was the governor of this New Spain and as such he had a repartimiento of Indians in said province, whom Francisco Preciado has at present; she asks to be remunerated as the daughter of a conquistador. (1: 182-83)

Juana González, widow

Does not state where she is from , nor whose daughter she is, and says that she was the wife of Juan del Puerto, who was a conquistador of this New Spain, who died fourteen years ago in Pánuco, and had the town of Tanquera in that province, and it was taken away from him; and that she is a widow, poor and old, and she is out of the way, in the mountains, and is in want; and that her said husband distinguished himself on a brigantine on the lake. (1: 183)

Mari Jiménez says

That she is the legitimate wife of Francisco de Portillo, deceased, one of the first conquistadores of this New Spain, by whom she was left with, and she has five children, three male and two daughters; and that she is the poorest widow left in the land; and she has written proof of what her conquistador husband was like, and the secretary has it; and that he likewise left other bastard children; and she is in extreme want. (1: 183)

Mari Angel, the wife of a conquistador, says

That she is a resident of this city of Mexico and a native of the city of Toledo, the legitimate daughter of Pedro Zapata and María de Guzmán; and that she came over to these parts eighteen years ago, married to Captain Francisco de Paradinas; he came over to these parts to serve His Majesty, as he did in Spain; he died and left four children, two male and two female, and she has them in this city; she was married a second time to Bartolomé López Cabea; he was one of the first conquistadores and settlers of this city and New Spain, and was in this city at the time that the Indians threw the Spaniards out of it; he had a repartimiento in Veracruz, in Pánuco, and because of his end and death, they were taken away from her; she begs that until the repartimiento is made, she be provided with some support as the wife of a conquistador, because she is in want. (1: 184)

María Corral

Does not state where she was born, nor whose daughter she is, and says that she was the wife first of Diego de San Martín, one of the first conquistadores and discoverers of this New Spain, who died, and left two legitimate children, and she was married a second time to Antonio de Gutiérrez, also a conquistador of this New Spain, who also died, leaving no children, having the town in encomienda, half of the town of Imizquiaguala, and Your Grace agreed that the said half should be possessed by her and the mother of said Antonio Gutiérrez, who died, and because of that, the part belonging to the latter was given over to His Majesty, so that she was left with only the fourth part, which she holds at the present time; and that she was married for the third time to Juan de Vargas, who left her with a son and a daughter; so that she has four children; and said fourth part of said town is very little, and she cannot support herself with that, her first children being as they are children of a conquistador, and that she has been in New Spain for more than twenty years. (1: 184-85)

Ana Méndez and her children; she says

That she was married to Pedro del Río, one of the conquistadores who came over with Narváez, and who served in the conquest of the city of Mexico and its vicinity, and Michoacán, and Guatemala, where he had Indians, and left them to ask for some in Mexico; since he was not given any, he came with his wife to Peru, where he served His Majesty in the matter of the chieftains and the lofts, and in all the incidents there; and that he was never compensated, because he died before La Gasca divided up the land; and that her children were left poor and without help; two of them are in Salamanca, studying, and the third in Peru with their mother, who is married to Chief Constable Estudillo. (1: 185)

Doña Marina, wife of the Treasurer Alonso de Estrada

She does not state her place of origin nor who her parents were; she is the legitimate wife of Alonso de Estrada, who was His Majesty's general treasurer in this New Spain, and its governor, who always served the Catholic King, and later His Majesty in Flanders, and from there he sent him to Málaga with the post of admiral, and from there he sent him to the island of Sicily, where he was engaged in matters of his Royal service more than three years, and returning from there, he served him in the communities, in very important matters, and when they were completed, he sent him as treasurer to this New Spain, and he came to it with his household, wife and children, in the year twenty-three; and he served in said post and gave a very good accounting of the Royal treasury, and he governed this land in the name of His Majesty very well, and he saw that the provinces of Chiapa and the Cipotecs were conquered, and that the three towns which are presently there were settled, where he spent much of his wealth in order to supply those who were going there, and he did not take anything for himself, and he served a good term; and she has four daughters, three of whom are married, to the treasurer, and Francisco Vázquez and Jorge de Alvarado, to whom her husband gave everything he had and two sons and eleven grandsons; and that she is a great settler, and has been; and she was left in great want, for which reason she has not brought her oldest son to this land; and now she is sending for him; and she has a maiden daughter yet to be married; she particularly pleads to Your Grace for her and for the son; and she has the town of Tehualhuaca, which provides her with very little; she asks that she and her children be remunerated for her husband's service. (1: 219-20)

Cecilia Lucero says
That she was the wife of Diego Jaramilla, a native of the city of Badajoz, who is now deceased; and he came over to the islands fifty years ago, and took part in all the conquests and pacifications of them, and later, some twenty-four years ago he came over to this New Spain, and served His Majesty in everything that came up at that time; and he always had his house full, with much family, arms, and horses; and he received the town of Zumpango in encomienda, of which at present she has the use; and she has two grandchildren, children of Valdés. (1: 220)

Doña Beatriz de Zayas says
That Your Grace is aware of who she is, and that Martín Peralta was her husband, and how his parents and grandparents served the Catholic Monarchs, and how his mother was a servant of Queen Isabel, and was married in Granada after it was conquered, to his father, who for the services he performed, being a nobleman, was knighted and was given the mayoralty of Santa Fe, and how said Martín de Peralta, in both court

positions and in the other things he was entrusted with served His Majesty very well in this land, in all loyalty; he left her poor and in need, with three unmarried daughters and a twenty-two-year-old son; and that she only has a small town, Tipuzque, which is not worth even two hundred pesos; she begs that all compensation be made with this repartimiento, to her and her children, *by which Our Lord God and His Majesty will be served, in consideration of the quality of their persons and whose children they are.* (1: 221)

Doña Catalina de Albornoz, the wife of Bazán, says

That she was the wife of Pedro de Bazán, a native of Jerez, near Badajoz, who died six months ago; and he came over to this New Spain some twenty-five years ago and served His Majesty in the conquest of Jalisco, when it was discovered and Colima and in the [Pacific Ocean] and Chiapa and Guazacualco; she names persons who she says know that, and in other provinces of this New Spain; and that he left a legitimate son, and that she has in encomienda the town of Pungarabato, and she says that she is presenting the deeds for it; and besides that, he also had other towns and always had his house full of his servants, arms, and horses; and that on his way to Castile, the French stole everything that he had, and that, the debts having been paid, very little remains to her; and that she is the niece of the accountant Albornoz; and that said Bazán left in Castile two other legitimate daughters, and that said town is worth five hundred pesos per year. (1: 222)

Ana Ruiz de Berrio says

That she is the wife of Juan de Cuéllar, who died some nine months ago, and served His Majesty in the conquest of Cuba, from where he came with the Marquis to discover this New Spain; and he took part in the conquests of its provinces and the taking of this city, for which the towns of Iztapaluca and Quimichtitlán and Chimalhuacán and Chiaba, of which at the time he died he only had Iztapaluca, which produces very little, and of which at present she has the use; and she was left with nine children, five daughters and the rest sons, who were left poor. (1: 222)

Doña Francisca del Rincón says

That she is the legitimate daughter of Licenciado Ruiz de Medina, who was a public prosecutor in this Royal Court, and that he served His Majesty in said profession, and that she came over to New Spain twelve years ago with her said father and other sisters of hers; and that she was the wife of Lope de Mendoza, deceased, who served His Majesty as a captain in Higueras and Honduras, for which he was given in encomienda the town of Paciyuca, which he left to her and of which she has the use at present; and in keeping with her quality, and because of the clergy whom she supports, who are in the town, and because it produces very little and she has paid off many debts, in the amount of more than four thousand pesos, for her support, she is in want. (1: 222-23)

The wife and children of Tomás de Lamadriz; she says
That she is a resident of Guaxaca, and a native of Lamadriz, and the daughter of Gonzalo de Castañeda; and that she is the wife of Tomás de Lamadriz, who came over to New Spain twenty-three years ago, and died and left her with three daughters and the town of Tequiastlán was given to him in encomienda, which is at present for the use of her and her said daughters. (1: 224)

The wife of Marín Cortés
Is a resident of the city of Los Angeles and the wife of Marín Cortés, who was a native of Murcia and the son of Pedro de Abellán and Beatriz Marín, and came over to this New Spain twenty-three years ago, and took part in the conquests of the provinces of the Grijalba River and Yucatan and Guatemala and Higueras; and he was the first to give training in the production of silk in this land, and for that purpose he had a contract with His Majesty to produce it in part in the town of Tepexi, for twenty years, and during this time half the tributes of the town go to him, in which contract she remained and is now; and that her said husband left a son and a daughter, legitimate and very poor and indebted, for which reason, and from the limited earnings they have from said town, they are in want. (1: 224)

Doña Juana de Zúñiga says
That she is the legitimate wife of Juan Rodríguez de Villafuerte, a well-known nobleman, and consequently she is also; he was a conquistador of this city; and he came over to this New Spain with the Marquis, as a field officer; and he served in other pertinent positions in other conquests of this land, and as a captain of the brigantines; and he went to Michoacán as a captain of men at arms, and he went as a general

to Colima and Los Opelcingos; that he left her poor and needy and with many debts, and the Indians that he left do not produce much, and she and her daughter are poor. (1: 224-25)

Inés de Corneja says
That she is a resident of the town of San Ildefonso de los Cipotecas and the legitimate daughter of Pedro Asensio, one of the first conquistadores of this New Spain and Guatemala, and that she was the wife of Juan Becerra, deceased, who came over to this New Spain with Luis Ponce, and he was a conquistador of the Cipotecs, Mixes, and Chontals; and that she has the use of the town of Ayacastepec, which is a Mixe town, due to the end and death of her said husband, who had it in encomienda; he was a native of Toro. (1: 231)

Isabel de Escobar says
That she is a resident of Pánuco and a native of the city of Seville, and the legitimate daughter of Francisco de Párraga and Florentina de Escobar, and the wife of Diego de las Roelas, deceased; and that her said husband came over to the Mainland with Pedrarias and took part in many of its conquests, and in the discovery of Peru, with Almagro; in remuneration for which he received in encomienda a town in Pánuco, called Tempual; and he sent to Spain for her; and she came over to this New Spain eleven years ago, and she has under her care and in her house two nephews; and that the said Indians that she has are poor and produce very little, and do not manage to support her. (1: 236)

Catalina Mejía says
That she is the legitimate daughter of Melchior Pérez and of Francisca Jerez; she says that she has in encomienda the town of Coyupustlán, which is in the area of Guadalajara, by warrant of Francisco Vázquez de Coronado; she requests that her repartimiento be settled in this town, or where it may please Your Grace. (1: 240)

Doña Inés Cabrera says
That she is a native of the town of Noñes and the daughter of Pedro de Torrecilla, a native of Córdoba, and that she was the wife of Juan de la Torre, deceased, and that six months after this city was conquered, she and her said husband came with their household, children, and family to settle here, and that at his expense he sent a Spaniard with arms and

horses to the conquests of Michoacán and Nueva Galicia and Pánuco, and he did not go in order to guard the city; and that ten years earlier he had served in the conquests of the islands of Hispaniola, Cuba, and Jamaica, and he always had his arms and horses, for which reason the Marquis gave him in encomienda the town of Tutitlán, the warrant for which she says she is presenting; and because it is not much, he later gave him Iztlauca in encomienda, and since her husband died and at the time the grant did not exist that there is now for wives and children, the former Court took them away from her, for which reason she has lived in need due to the expense she has had with her children. (2: 35)

Francisca de Valenzuela

Does not state her place of origin, and states that she is the wife of Pedro de Salamanca, and the daughter of Gregorio de Valenzuela, who was a servant of the Marquesses of Mondéjar, father and brother of Your Grace, with whom he went to Algeria in the fleet that he took some thirty years ago, where he was captured and was for a long time prisoner in the power of Barbarossa, and that she came to this New Spain six years ago, married, and brought a daughter and a son by another husband that she had, and the daughter yet to be married, and that she is very poor and is in great want, and Bernaldino Vázquez de Tapia and Antonio de Carvajal know of it.

Beatriz de Chaves

Does not say where she is from nor whose daughter she is, and says that she was the wife of Juan Lope de Aguirre, deceased, who came over to the island of Hispaniola and Cuba more than forty years ago, in the conquests and pacifications of which he served His Majesty, and he had distinguished occupations and positions, and when the Marquis came to conquer this land, he wished to come with him, but because of the need for him there, he was not allowed to come, and later he came over and went and took part in the conquests of Higueras and Cipotecas, and had Indians in Guazacualco, which were taken from her when he died, and he left her many debts; and she came over to this land more than thirteen years ago and is in the house of Juan de Jazo, and has no resources for her support, and her husband always maintained a good deal of honor and family, and did distinguished service for His Majesty. (2: 57)

The wife and children of Lope de Saavedra; she says

That said Lope de Saavedra came over to this New Spain twenty-four years ago, with an appointment from His Majesty to administer the property of the deceased in the province of Pánuco, where he took part in many incursions, and where he had Indians; and later he came into this government and had the post of inspector of many provinces, and Treasurer Estrada gave him the town of Papantla in encomienda, now held by Andrés de Tapia, and he served in the pacification of Tultitlán with some people that he took under his command, and he left two sons and two daughters, and that she is a native of Cáceres, the daughter of Gonzalo Gómez de Saavedra and Doña Leonor de Orellana, and she is in want. (2: 60)

Inés de Sigüenza, a widow, says
That she is the wife of Licenciado Gamboa, a physician, who came over to this New Spain with her and with his household and six maiden daughters, and when he arrived her he died, and they were left very poor, and if it were not for the alms that is given to them by order of Your Grace, they would have suffered from very extreme want. (2: 60-61)

[Here appears the "first" master seamstress in the Indies.]
Ana López says
That she is a resident of this city, and a native of Seville and the legitimate daughter of Alonso López and Elvira Sánchez; and that she came over to this New Spain twenty-three years ago in search of Martín Román, her husband, who she knew had died in Peru, and that she is the first woman who trained and showed the Indian women how to sew and embroider, and she has always lived from the work of her hands, with the needle, honorably; and she has in her house five orphans whom she has brought up and trained, yet to be married; and she has married off two others, and that she is by now a woman advanced in days [?] and cannot work as she used to do, nor does she have the means to carry out the desire she has to marry off said orphans. (2: 61)

Beatriz Hernández says
That she is a resident of this city and the legitimate daughter of Francisco Sánchez Moreno and Ana de Portillo, and she came over to this New Spain twenty-five years and two months ago, after this city was

conquered; and that she is the wife of Pedro del Golfo, the son of Antón de Carmona; he came over to this New Spain twenty years ago, and he has six legitimate children and his house full, and his arms and horses and family, and that earlier she was the wife of Juan de Paredes, one of the first conquistadores of this New Spain, by whom she was left with two children, whom she has living at present, and that she is in want; she beseeches Your Grace, as a wife and representative of her husband because he is absent, to remember them in the repartimiento. (2: 61-62)

Francisca de Zambrana says
That she was the wife of Alonso Giraldo, deceased, who came over to this New Spain twenty years ago and took part in the conquest of many of its provinces, and he left two sons and a daughter, whom she has married in Culiacán, and that she and they suffer from extreme want, and that her said husband died of hunger on the island [At this time, it was still thought to be an island] of California, and because he was very honorable person, the former governors always gave him municipalities, and he had in encomienda the Indians now possessed by Diego Rodríguez, a resident of this city; and that she is very poor. (2: 64)

María de Pineda says
In effect, that she is a native of Seville, and the legitimate daughter of Juan de Pineda and Leonor Hernández, and that she was the wife of García de Lerena, deceased, who was a native of this city of Burgos, and the son of Juan de Lerena, and that he was a resident of this city, who came over to these parts as soon as this city was conquered, and took part in the conquest of Pánuco and in all the others that came up later, with his arms and horses; and that she has a record of it, and he had the town of Tetiquipac, which the Treasurer took away from him for no reason at all, and by a judgment of this Royal Court it has been ordered returned to her; and that she has five legitimate children and is in want, because all of the slaves that her husband left to her in the cloth works died in the epidemic. (2: 67-68)

The wife of Rengino, Inés de Torres
Inés de Torres says that she was the wife of Rengino, deceased, who came over to this New Spain with Your Grace and died poor in this city, and left her three sons and a daughter yet to be married; he served His

Majesty from 1508 on in the islands, where he had honorable positions, both in the courts and in other things, and that she and her children, because they are poor, suffer from want. (2: 68)

The mother-in-law of Juan Cermeño says
That she is a native of the town of Palos; the legitmate daughter of Antón Martín Ciruelo and Marina Alonso de Cerpa, and that she was the wife of Juan Ruiz, and that she is the mother-in-law of Juan Cermeño; and that her said husband came over to this New Spain some twenty-four years ago and took part in the conquest of Pánuco, where he had Indians in repartimiento, and they were taken away from him for no reason at all, and that she has two legitimate daughters, one a maiden and the other the wife of said Juan Cermeño, and she is poor. (2: 70-71)

Catalina Rodríguez
She was married to Juan Moreno, one of the first conquistadores; he had Indians in the province of Guaxaca, in a place called Alpizagua; they were taken away from her by Treasurer Alonso de Estrada; later she has lived here and she lives poorly, in great need. (2: 72)

Francisca López says
That she is a native of Puebla de Montalbán, which is in the Kingdom of Toledo, and is the legitimate daughter of Teresa López, and she came over to this New Spain six years ago, and she is a widow and has a daughter yet to be married, and that she is poor and has no other help but that of God and Your Grace. (2: 75)

Juana Rodríguez
She does not state where she was born nor whose daughter she is, and states that she was the wife of Martín Pérez, deceased, and that she and her said husband came over to this New Spain twenty-five years ago; and he took part in the conquest of Pánuco and Michoacán and in other provinces in the vicinity of this city; for which he was given the town of Xalancingo in encomienda; and that he died eleven years ago; and they were taken from her by this Royal Court and put into a municipality, for which reason she is poor and is in extreme want, so much so, that good people are helping her get along in life. (2: 96)

Juana Agustina says

That she is a native of the city of Seville and the legitimate daughter of Alonso López and Inés Hernández Brava, and that she was the wife of Diego Sánchez, deceased, who came over to New Spain twenty-one years ago, and she fourteen years ago; and by him she has four sons and two daughters, all legitimate, and besides she has under her care another son and another daughter, both illegitimate; and that her said husband left her many debts, and she is very poor and is in want; and that her said husband served as best he could and was under command. (2: 98)

Ana de Argumedo says
In effect, that she was the wife of said Ginés Doncel, deceased, with whom she came married from Castile to the island of Hispaniola twenty-eight years ago, and he always served His Majesty, being a captain of the fleets that were sent to the Mainland, in which service he was killed by the Indians; and because of the expenses he had in that, he left her very poor, with one son and one daughter whom she has married off in this city, to Hernando Morales; and that she came from said island of Hispaniola three years ago, and is in extreme want. (2: 100)

Luisa Méndez says
In effect, that she is a native of the city of Seville and the legitimate daughter of Hernán Méndez and Constanza de la Roca, his wife; and that she came over to this New Spain sixteen years ago with Juan González Gallego, her husband, who died here; he served His Majesty by cultivating the fields and other farmlands that he has in Teguantepec and had done at the time that wheat began to be produced in this New Spain; and he opened the road that goes to Veracruz; and that she is married to Alonso de Baeza, a resident of Puebla, who has gone to Guatemala; and that she is poor, in great need. (2: 100-01)

The wife of Juan Destacio
Does not state where she was born nor whose daughter she is, and states that she was the wife of Juan Destacio, who died in this city at the age of sixty years, which he spent in the service of His Majesty in the discovery and conquest of the islands of Hispaniola and Cuba, from where he departed with Narváez to come to the conquest of this New Spain; and there being a need there for him, for munitions matters, he was ordered to stay; and in that he served as much as if he had come over with the others; and later he came over to be one of the first to

settle this land and took part in the conquest of the valleys, where as in Cuba and Hispaniola, besides serving in the wars, he served through his trade, with the forge, for which reason Nuño de Guzmán gave him a town in encomienda, which he later took away from him, and two Negroes have it at present; and he left her six children; she begs to have her Indians given back to her in this repartimiento, although they do not amount to much. (120-21)

Catalina de Garay

She does not state where she was born nor whose daughter she is, and she states that she was the wife of Juan de Lizana, deceased, who died eleven years ago, one of the first conquistadores of this New Spain, because he came over with the Marquis, and as such, he was given in encomienda the towns contained in a warrant which she says she is presenting; and as her said husband died, they were put in possession of His Majesty; and that she has four legitimate children by the above-mentioned, and that they were all left poor. (2: 162-63)

Inés Hidalga

She does not state where she was born nor whose daughter she is, and states that she was the wife of García de Mérida, deceased, who came over with Diego de Camargo, a captain of Garay, to Pánuco, where he was defeated; and he came to Villarica, where he helped to win and conquer that whole region, from whence he came and took part in the taking of this city and its provinces, for which reason Indians were given to him in encomienda, and he possessed them, and upon his death they were put in possession of His Majesty, because at the time the grant that there is at present had not come about, for which reason she was left poor, and she lives in great poverty and want. (2: 164-65)

Leonor Díaz, a widow, says

That she was the wife of Diego Yáñez, deceased, one of the first residents and settlers of the city of Los Angeles; and she and her said husband, with their household, came to this New Spain fifteen years ago, and have always resided in said city; and that she has four daughters and three sons by her said husband, one of the daughters being married, and that they are all in want. (2: 174-75)

Leonor de Villanueva says

That she was the wife of Juan de Manzanilla, deceased, who was a resident of the city of Los Angeles, and a conquistador of this New Spain, by whom she was left with a daughter; and she has been left poor because her husband left her with many children from his first wife, and the Indians that he left do not produce much; and she has been a widow for two years and is in want; and that she is the daughter of Pedro Villanueva, a conquistador of this New Spain. (2: 175)

Beatriz Hernández, a widow, says
That she is a resident of the city of Los Angeles, a native of Guadalcanal [Spain], the legitimate daughter of Alonso Martín Calvo, from Azuaga, and Ana Hernández; and that she came over to New Spain eleven years ago, and is a resident of said city, and that she was the wife of Ruy García Docón, who died there, and she was left with a son and a daughter, and she was left very poor, and is in want. (2: 181)

Beatriz de Robles, a widow
Is a resident of the city of Los Angeles, and says that she is a native of Mérida and the legitimate daughter of Juan de Robles and Inés González de la Gemya, and that she came over to this New Spain about nine years ago, and that she is widowed and poor, and is in want; and that her said father served the Catholic Monarchs in the wars of Granada and was a nobleman. (2: 183)

Ana Hernández says
That she is a resident of the city of Los Angeles and a native of Guadalcanal [Spain], and the legitimate daugher of Pero Hernández and Isabel Méndez, and that she came over to this New Spain eleven years ago with his children, three sons and two daughters, which daughters she has married off in said city; and that she is poor and is in want. (2: 183)

Marina Vélez de Ortega says
That she is a resident of the city of Los Angeles, and a native of Guadalcanal [Spain], and the legitimate daughter of Antón Ruiz de Ortega and Catalina Martín, and that she is the wife of Cristóbal Martín Camacho, a native of Moguer, who came over to this New Spain with Garay, and served His Majesty in some of its conquests, and she does not state which, *and that she is one of the first women who came to this New Spain, and one of the first residents of said city of Los Angeles,*

where she has always had in her house five orphan maidens, bringing them up and educating them since they were girls, at her expense, among whom she has a legitimate daughter of Juan Gómez de Peñaparda, conquistador of this New Spain; and that they are all very poor, and she with them, and she is in want.

Isabel Benítez says

That she is a resident of the city of Guaxaca, and she does not state where she was born nor whose daughter she was, and states that she is the wife of Juan de Peñalver, deceased, who was a conquistador of the provinces of the Cipotecs and Mixes, among the first, for which reson he was given the town of Aguila in encomienda, which due to the wars and uprisings that there were was abandoned, and in recognition of this, Your Grace always did him the favor of providing him with municipalities; and that she has three children by her said husband, and she was left poor and is in want. (2: 211)

Beatriz González says

That she is a resident of Pánuco and she does not say where she was born nor whose daughter she is, and says that she is the wife of Benito de Cuenca, one of the first conquistadores of this New Spain, who has two children, and who came over here with Captain Pánfilo de Narváez, and took part in the taking of this city of Mexico, where helped heal the wounded, and later he served in the same capacity in the province of Pánuco, and because the Indians that her said husband had in encomienda were very few, and poor, and not very productive, they are in debt and in want; she asks to be remunerated, since he took part in the war. (2: 219)

María de Vargas says

That she is the daughter of Juan Martínez and Isabel de Vargas, who came to this New Spain about twenty-three years ago, and as one of the first settlers, he was given towns of Indians in encomienda, and upon his death they were taken away from her, because at the time the grant from His Majesty had not come about; and that she was the wife of Hernando de Sierra, deceased, by whom she was left with two sons and a daughter, all of them poor, as is well known; he was deputy treasurer in Veracruz and one of the first settlers of this New Spain. (2: 234)

Leonor López says

That she is a resident of this city and that she came over to this New Spain twenty years ago, she brought a son and a daughter; his name was Juan López; he took part in the pacification of Nueva Galicia, where had a repartimiento; and he was married, and he was killed in the battle that occurred, in which Cristóbal de Oñate was captain, and then his wife and children died, and the town that he had was put under His Majesty's control; she is in want, with a twenty-five-year-old daughter; she begs to be remunerated.
(2: 235-36)

Catalina Guillén says

In effect, that she is a native of the city of Jerez de la Frontera and the daughter of Francisco Guillén and Doña Isabel de Villavicencio, and that she was the wife of Francisco de Carvajal, the son of Baltasar de Mendoza and Doña Leonor de la Cerda, residents of Cáceres, and that her said husband came over to this New Spain seventeen years ago, and was a resident of this city for fourteen [years]; he died and left a legitimate son and an illegitimate daughter yet to be married and he left many debts. No resources at all to support her, and she is in great want.
(2: 238)

Sabina de Esquivel says

That she is a resident of La Purificación, Nueva Galicia, and that she was the wife of Martín de Rifarache, who died three years ago; he came over to this New Spain after this city of Mexico was conquered, and served His Majesty in the conquests and pacifications of the provinces of Michoacán and Zacatula and Los Opelcingos and Colima and Zatlán and Jalisco, and Nueva Galicia, with Nuño de Guzmán, and later in the last pacification of said province, with Your Grace; and that she was left with a legitimate daughter by her said husband, and three other illegitimate children, and she was left poor and in debt and in great want. (2: 250-51)

Doña Catalina de Salazar says

That she is the daughter of Gonzalo de Salazar, and that it is well known that when her husband was on his way to these parts he died and that she is here, *and she brought with her two sons and a daughter, with the intention of remaining and marrying them in these parts; so that they will serve His Majesty as their forbears have done.* (2: 290)

Ana Osorio, the daughter of Rodrigo de Baeza says
That she was born in this New Spain and that she is the legitimate daughter of Rodrigo de Baeza and Mari López de Obregón, and she states the same qualities and merits for her said father to the letter, that Barolomé de Obregón and Luis de Obregón and Gaspar Carrillo, her brothers, say and delare in the three statement that they have put forward. (2: 325)

Inés Alvarez de Contreras says
That she is a native of Alcalá la Real, was married in Castile to Pedro de Valdivia, a nobleman, who died in Algeria in His Majesty's service, and she was left poor with one son and one daughter; and that she has lived in this New Spain with my said son, whose name is Andrés de Valdivia, so that he may serve His Majesty here as his father did, and this is well known; and her son is going to the pacification in Peru; they are in great want. (2: 347)

With Inés Alvarez de Contreras the list of women mentioned in Francisco A. Icaza's *Diccionario de conquistadores y pobladores de la Nueva España* comes to an end. The information is most valuable, not only from the historical point of view, confirming as it does the permanent presence of women in New Spain from earliest times, but also from the sociological point of view, since in some cases we become privy to the social and economic circumstances that these brave women had to endure.

After having read so many cases of the wives of conquistadores, and of their "needy" children, it is worth meditating on the image of the conquistador that is current today. That individual is almost always characterized as arrogant, thirsty for gold and bent only on returning to Spain as soon as possible to enjoy his riches and claim social status. But we can see that this was not the case. It was a minority who was in fact able to reap more than poverty, tragedy and troubles. Their wives, some of them Spaniards, other natives, and their children, many of them Mestizos, are witnesses of the extreme harshness and economic privation of those times. These women were, in fact, the foundation on which the Spanish-speaking peoples were supported.

CONCLUSION

This study has been a "passing glance" at a period that was very rich in events of all kinds, in a good share of which women played a lead role—women of all human and social types, but women just the same. My intention has been, at the very least, to arouse the interest of those who are curious to know more about their culture, and in this case, about an indispensable part of that culture, the contribution of women.

It is not good for us to let ourselves, out of conformity, be led by those historians and chroniclers who shape our past according to their own interest, leaving things out and putting things in at will, and in the process wiping out the highly important intellectual and social contribution of Hispanic women in the Americas. This misrepresentation has occurred and will continue to occur; and, rather than to accept things freely, it is our duty to search for information where it may be found, so as to have a better understanding of who we are and where we come from. The documents are there which show how Spanish and Indian women, gave their lives—with courage, love, and generosity—for their own interests and the interests of those close to them, working, loving, at times insulting their male companions to give them encouragement in the face of adversity, in the most extraordinary enterprise known to our times: the Iberian expansion, encounter, and colonization of the Americas, Africa, Asia, Oceania, the Atlantic and the Pacific, the Mediterranean, Northern Europe and a good part of Italy, during the fifteenth and sixteenth centuries. This formidable territorial expansion, never before seen, was accompanied by a very rich literary production, comparable in importance only to the geographic achievements accomplished by these two Iberian peoples. Five hundred years after these events occurred, this history and these events are the heritage not only of Spain and Portugal, of what was the ancient Roman province of Hispania, but of all the nations and peoples of the world who were directly or indirectly affected by all that went into this contact between continents.

It is symptomatic that Spain, which is so abundant in these kinds of outstanding individuals, should have paid so little attention to personages whom many other nations would have held up as perennial examples of valor and sacrifice. I call it symptomatic because it is always the same heroes and literary and historical topics that are always mentioned: the Cid, the Great Captain, Cardinal Cisneros, the Catholic Monarchs. Nevertheless, many other historical figures are worthy of attention, especially during that unique moment of the encounter and colonization of the Americas. Latin American society is the result, in part, of an idealistic effusion that came over Luso-Hispanic society and then disappeared not long afterward, passing into the hands of much more pragmatic, realistic nations who were able to reap the economic benefits of those deeds.

This study has been nothing more than an attempt to "discover" the history of women in the encounter of the Americas. I hope to have stimulate sufficient interest so that others may go deeper into the infinite ramifications of so important a presence.

NOTES

1.   Alonso del Castillo, survivor of the failed Pánfilo de Narváez expedition, was one of Alvar Núñez Cabeza de Vaca's companions. Another of them mentioned in Icaza's *Diccionario* was Andrés Dorantes (Icaza 1:182). It is worth mentioning that Alvar Núñez Cabeza de Vaca married María Marmolejo, a Spanish woman of converted Jewish origin who could very well have been a very close relative of Antonio Marmolejo and his daughter Guiomar (See the critical edition of *Los naufragios* by Enrique Pupo-Walker (Madrid: Castalia, 1992) 29. The fact that Alonso del Castillo, one of the three survivors, had been her guardian makes one think that there was possibly some relationship.

2.   Isabel de Guevara, "Carta a la princesa doña Juana," July 2, 1556, letter 104 of *Cartas de Indias*, Biblioteca de Autores Españoles, Vol. 265 (Madrid:Atlas, 1974), 619.

3.   Quoted in Julián Juderías, *La Leyenda Negra* (Madrid:Editora Nacional, 1967), 267.

4.   Cortés did not burn his ships, since if he had done such a thing he would not have been able to get any benefit from them; what he did do was to "bring them up on the coast" (Cortés, *Cartas de relación de la conquista de México* [Mexico:Espasa-Calpe Mexicana, 1985], 35) so that they could not be used by those who wished to return to Cuba.

5.   This point need not be considered better or worse than any other, nevertheless, if to a certain extent it could be called "incomplete."

6.   See Archivo Ducal de Alba, "Cédula real concedindo a las indias casarse con castellanos". Valladolid, 5 de febrero de 1515. Caja 247, Legajo 1.

7.   Doña María de Toledo. Virreina de Indias. *Carta a la emperatriz quejándose de los aposentadores* (no date). Real Academia de la Historia, Colección San Román, Caja 8. Núm. 47.

8.   Stress mine.

9.   Antonio de Pigafetta, *Primer viaje alrededor del mundo* (Madrid:Historia 16, 1985), 55.

10.   "Magallanes". Royal Academy of History. Colección de Don Juan Bautista Muñoz. Mss. A/103. fol. 142.

11.   See also: Anónimo, *Historia de las Amazonas*. Biblioteca Nacional de España. Ms. 1537.

12.   A *palmo* is a measurement of length "equal to about 21 centimeters, and it is supposed that it is the length of a man's hand open and extended from the end of the thumb to the end of the little finger." *Diccionario de la Lengua Española* (Madrid:Real Academia Española, 1970). The English span has the same origin and is equal to about 23 centimeters. *The Random House Dictionary of the English Language*, 2nd ed. (New York:Random House, 1987).

13.   Stress mine.

14.   The text in quesiton is the following: Michele da Cuneo, in *Raccolta colombiana*, vol. 2, 2, p. 96: "A dí 2 de octobre intrassimo ne la Grande Canaria, la noche seguente vellificamo et a li 5 del dicto entrassimo a la Gomera, una de le isole dicte Canarie; nel qual loco se io vi dicessi quello habbiamo facto de triunfi et tiri de bombarda et lanzafochi, sarebe troppo longo. E questo fu facto per cagione de la Signora de dicto logo, de la quale fu alias il nostro signor Amirante tincto d'amore." [On October 2, we reached Gran Canaria. The following night we set sail, and on the 5th of the same month we reached Gomera, one of the so-called Canary Islands. It would take too long for me to tell about all the successes, the cannon shots and the fireworks that we set off in that place. It was all done on account of the lady of that place, to whom our Admiral had taken a fancy in other times.] (Cioranescu, 120). To attempt to create an entire romance on the sole basis of these lines written by Cuneo and preserved in a document the authenticity of which has been questioned, is to stretch the evidence to unsuspected limits.

15.   She also inherit a substantial will from her father Don Luis de la Cueva. Archivo General de Simancas, Guerra y Marina, Legajo 3, Doc. 228.

16.   See my study of this aspect: Juan F. Maura, *Alvar Núñez Cabeza de Vaca o el arte de la automitificación* (Mexico:Frente de Afirmación Hispanista, 1988).

17.   See Elizabeth Salas, *Soldaderas in the Mexican Military* (Austin:Univ. of Texas Press, 1990).

18.   See my critical edition of the *Naufragios* (Madrid:Cátedra, 1989), 55-56.

19.   Torre Revelló, 264.

20.   "Conversos" were the Spanish Jews who had to change from their Jewish religion to the Catholic in order to remain in Spanish terrritory.   Even so, during the first generations, this background was considered a stigma.

22.   See also Carta real a fray Miguel Ramírez, obispo de la Fernandina y abad de Jamaica, para que conceda libertad a los indios. Segovia, 15 de octubre de 1532. Archivo Ducal de Alba, Caja 170, Legajo 55.

23.   Quoted in Spanish in Rachel Phillips, "Marina/Malinche: Masks and Shadows," *Women in Hispanic Literature: Icons and Fallen Idols*, ed. Beth Miller (Berkeley:Univ. of California Press, 1983), 97. The quotation here, with an omitted phrase restored, is from Margaret Sayers Peden's trans. of Octavio Paz, *Sor Juana or, The Traps of Faith* (Cambridge, Mass.:Belknap Press, 1988), 12.

24.   Spindles, or distaffs (Lope writes *ruecas*) are staffs with a cleft end used in spinning. The distaff is a traditional symbol of femininity. (*Random House Dictionary*).

25.   Stress mine.

26.   Stress mine.

27.   Cortés Alonso, 978.

28.   See the excellent study by Enrique de Gandía, appearing in his edition: Ruy Díaz de Guzmán, *La Argentina* (Madrid:Historia 16, 1986), 7-48.

29.   Roberto Ferrando, introduction to Fernández de Quirós, 29-30.

30.   O'Sullivan-Beare, 223.

31.   File 937 (1507-38), Ducal Archive of Medina Sidonia.

32.   Fredo Arias de la Canal, preface to Francisco Ruiz de León, *Hernandía, triunfos de la fe y gloria de las armas españolas: Poema heroico proezas de Hernán Cortes (1755)* (Mexico:Frente de Afirmación Hispanista, 1989), 74-75.

33.   Arciniegas, 111.

34.   One example is María de Alvarado, Lope de Vega's Amarilis, who wrote her work in the farthest reaches of the Peruvian Andes. See Menéndez y Pelayo, 84.

35.   Juan Ruiz, *The Book of True Love*, trans. Saralyn R. Daly (University Park:Pennsylvania State Univ. Press, 1978), stanza 892, 229.

36.   Royal Warrants of the years 1502 and 1503, Academia de la Historia, Muñoz Collection, quoted by Fernández Duro, 15.

37.   Juan de Solórzano Pereira, *Libro primero de la recopilación de las cédulas reales, cartas y provisiones y ordenanzas reales*, foreword by Ricardo Levenne, Publicaciones del Instituto de Historia del Derecho Argentino, vol. 5 (Buenos Aires:Imprenta de la Univ. de Buenos Aires, 1945), book 1, law 10 "Spanish men can marry Indian women, and vice-versa, at will," vol. 2, p. 138, quoted in Villafañe, 129.

38.   Manuel Serrano y Sanz, *Apuntes para una biblioteca de*

escritoras españolas desde el año 1401 al 1833, Biblioteca de Autores Españoles, vols. 268-71 (Madrid:Atlas, 1975), 268: 19.

39. For a better understanding of the character of this exceptional woman, see, among the many studies published, Fredo Arias de la Canal, *Intento de psicoanálisis de Juan Inés y otros ensayos sorjuanistas* (Mexico:Frente de Afirmación Hispanista, 1972), 47.

40. Serrano y Sanz, 270:47. See also J. T. Medina, *Historia del tribunal del Santo Oficio de la Inquisición de Lima (1569-1820)* (Santiago:Imprenta Gutemberg, 1887), vol. 2, 34-41.

41. Serrano y Sanz, 270:361-62. Of fundamental importance for in-depth study of many of these Hispanic American female writers is Beristain de Souza's Bilbioteca Hispano-Americana.

42. Francisco A. de Icaza, *Diccionario de conquistadores y pobladores de Nueva España*, 2 vols. (Madrid, n.p. 1923).

43. Royal Warrant, Valladolid, April 1, 1513, in *Colección de documentos inéditos de Cuba* (Madrid: Real Academia de Historia, 1885) vol. 4, part 2a, 49-50.

44. Letter from the governor of Tucumán to the king; Tucumán, March 10, 1586, in *Documentos históricos y geográficos relativos a la conquista rioplatense* (Buenos Aires, 1941), vol. 1, 120-21.

45. Icaza 1: lix. Volume and page references for the biographic entries are to the two volumes of Icaza's *Diccionario de conquistadores* and will be found in parentheses in the text.

46. This Dorantes is none other than the one who accompanied Alvar Núñez Cabeza de Vaca on his journey through lands of North America. A reference to him appears in this same *Diccionario* 1:195-96, as follows: "And in 1527 he went to Florida as a captain in the fleet that Narváez took, where they became lost; and he spent nine years as a slave of the Indians, going naked and serving them in that way; and at the end of that time, by land, with many hardships, he managed to arrive in this New Spain, eleven years ago; once he arrived he married a widow, who

had been the wife of a conquistador of this New Spain, whose name he does not state, who left a town called Maycalcingo."

BIBLIOGRAPHY

Manuscripts

Archivo Ducal de Alba. Caja 170. Legajo 55. Caja 247. Legajo 1, Doc.2.

Archivo Ducal De Medina Sidonia. File 937.

Archivo General de Simancas. Guerra y Marina, Legajo 3, Doc. 228.

Biblioteca Nacional. Historia de las Amazonas, mss. 1537.

Real Academia de la Historia. Colección Muñoz. Legajos. A/103, A/105. Colección San Román. Caja 8, Núm. 47. A/106, A/110.

Articles

Acosta de Samper, Soledad. "Las esposas de los conquistadores." *Boletín de la Academia de la Historia del Valle de Cauca*, 25, no. 108 (1957): 140-154.

Barris Muñoz, Rafael. "Entorno a Alvar Núñez Cabeza de Vaca." *Boletín del Real Centro de Estudios Históricos de Andalucía* 1 (1927): 42-61.

Borges, Analola. "La mujer pobladora en los orígenes americanos." *Anuario de Estudios Americanos* 29 (1972): 389-444.

Cortés Alonso, Vicenta. "Los esclavos domésticos en América." *Anuario de Estudios Americanos* 24 (1967): 955-983.

Iglehart, Id. "La intrépida monja alférez." *Américas* (Jan.-Feb. 1982): 9-11.

Hanke, Lewis. "Free Speech in Sixteenth-century Spanish America." *The Hispanic American Historical Review* 26, no. 2 (1946): 135-149.

246 *Juan Francisco Maura*

Johnson, Julie Greer. "Bernal Díaz and the Woman of the Conquest." *Hispanófila* 28, no. 1 (1984): 67-77.

Konetzke, Richard. "La emigración de mujeres españolas a América durante la época colonial." *Revista Internacional de Sociología* 9 (1945): 123-150.

___, "El mestizaje y su importancia en el desarrollo de la población hispano-americana durante la época colonial." *Revista de Indias* 7, no. 23 (1946): 7-44.

Miró Quesada, Aurelio. "Ideas y proceso de mestizaje en el Perú." *Revista Histórica* 28 (1965): 9-23.

Pinto, Carlos. "La mujer española en Indias." *Revista de Derecho Historia y Letras* 13 (1902): 397-403.

Pittaluga, Gonzalo. "Las mujeres, el trigo y la quina." *Revista de América* 6, no. 16 (1946): 77-80.

Ratcliffe, Marjorie. "Adulteresses, Mistresses and Prostitutes: extramarital relationships in Medieval Castile." *Hispania* 67, no.3 (1984): 346-350.

Romero, Mario Germán. "Mujeres de la conquista en Don Juan de Castellanos I." *Boletín Cultural y Bibliográfico* 5, no. 10 (1962): 1293-1304.

___, "Mujeres de la conquista en Don Juan de Castellanos II." *Boletín Cultural y Bibliográfico* 5, no. 11 (1962): 1432-45.

Sánchez, Joseph P. "The Spanish Black Legend: Origins of Anti-Hispanic Sterotypes." *Encounters* 1 (1989): 16-21.

Sancho de Sopranis, Hipólito. "Datos para el estudio de Alvar Núñez Cabeza de Vaca." *Revista de Indias* 27 (1947): 69-102.

Tío, Aurelio. "Doña Leonor Ponce de León la primera puertorriqueña." *Boletín de la Academia Puertorriqueña de la*

Historia 2 (1971): 7-22.

Torre Revelló, José. "Esclavas blancas en las Indias Occidentales." *Boletín del Instituto de Investigaciones Históricas* 6, no. 34 (1927): 263-271.

Villafañe, María Teresa. "La mujer española en la conquista y colonización de América." *Cuadernos Hispanoamericanos 59*, no.175/176 (1964): 125-42.

Books

Alfonso El Sabio. "Las Siete Partidas." *Antología*. México: Porrúa, 1982.

Arciniegas, Germán. *América, tierra firme*. Buenos Aires: Sudamericana, 1966.

Arenal, Electa and Stacey Shlau. *Untold Sisters*. Albuquerque: University of New Mexico Press, 1989.

Arias de la Canal, Fredo. *Intento de psicoanálisis de Juana Inés y otros análisis sorjuanistas*. México: Frente de Afirmación Hispanista, 1972.

Aristotle. *The Politics*. Trans. T.A. Sinclair. New York: Penguin Books, 1981.

Bell, Aubrey F.G. *El Renacimiento español*. Zaragoza: Ebro, 1944.

Bolton, Herbert E. *Coronado: Knight of Pueblos and Plains*. 4th ed. Albuquerque: The University of New Mexico Press, 1991.

Boyd-Bowman, Peter. *Indice geobiográfico de más de 56 mil pobladores de la América Hispana* I. 1493-1519. México: Fondo de Cultura Económica, 1985.

Boxer, C. R. *Women in the Iberian Expansion Overseas, 1415-1815*. New York: Oxford Univ. Press, 1975.

Bragdon, Henry W., Samuel P. McCutchen, and Donald A. Richtie. *History of a Free Nation*. Glencoe, Ill.: Macmillan/McGraw-Hill, 1992.

Branch, E. Douglas. "The Story of America in Pictures," *The New Webster Encyclopedic Dictionary of the English Language*, 1980 ed. New York: Avenel Books, 1980.

Cantarino, Vicente. *Civilización y cultura de España*. Macmillan, 1988.

Casas, Bartolomé de las. *Historia de las Indias*. 3 vols., México: Fondo de Cultura Económica, 1965.

Carvajal, Fray Gaspar. *La aventura del Amazonas*. Madrid: Historia 16, 1986.

Cervantes Saavedra, Miguel de. "El celoso extremeño," *Novelas ejemplares*, vol. 2, Barcelona: Juventud, 1962.

Cervantes de Salazar, Francisco. *Crónica de la Nueva España*. 2 Vols. Madrid: Atlas, 1971.

Cieza de León, Pedro. *El señorío de los incas*. Madrid: Historia 16, 1985.

Cioranescu, Alejandro. *Colón y Canarias*. La Laguna: Goya Artes Gráficas, 1959.

Colón, Hernando. *Historia del Almirante*. Madrid: Historia 16, 1984.

Cortés, Hernán. *Cartas de Relación de la conquista de México*. México: Espasa-Calpe Mexicana, 1985.

Crow, John A. *The Epic of Latin America*. New York: Doubleday, 1946.

De Bry, Theodore. *Discovering the New World*. Ed. Michel Alexander. New York: Harper & Row, 1976.

Delgado, Jaime. "La mujer en la conquista de América." en *Homenaje a Jaime Vicens Vives.* vol. 2, Barcelona: Univ. de Barcelona, 1967.

Díaz del Castillo, Bernal. *Historia verdadera de la conquista de la Nueva España.* México: Porrúa, 1983.

Díaz de Guzmán, Ruy. *La Argentina.* Ed. Enrique de Gandía. Madrid: Historia 16, 1986.

Dillard, Heath. *Daughters of the Reconquest.* Cambridge: Cambridge Univ. Press, 1984.

Documentos históricos y geográficos relativos a la conquista rioplatense. vol. 1, Buenos Aires: 1941.

Elvas, Fidalgo de. *Expedición de Hernando de Soto a la Florida.* Madrid: Espasa-Calpe, 1965.

Enciclopedia universal ilustrada europeo-americana. Madrid: Espasa-Calpe, 1958.

Erauso, Catalina. *Historia de la monja alférez escrita por ella misma.* Ed. Jesús Munárriz. Madrid: Ediciones Hiperión, 1986.

Ercilla y Zúñiga, Alonso de. *La Araucana.* Santiago: Nascimento, 1932.

Fehrenbach, T.R. *Fire and Blood.* New York: Macmillan, 1973.

Feijóo, Benito. *Antología.* Madrid: Alianza, 1970.

Fernández del Castillo, Francisco. *Doña Catalina Xuárez Marcaida: Primera esposa de Hernán Cortés y su familia.* México: n.p., 1920.

Fernández Duro, Cesáreo. *La mujer Española en Indias.* Madrid: Viuda e Hijos de M.Tello, 1902.

Fernández de Navarrete, Eustaquio. "Bosquejo Histórico sobre la novela española." Biblioteca de Autores Españoles, *Novelistas posteriores a Cervantes*. Madrid: M. Rivadeneyra, 1854.

Fernández de Navarrete, Martín. *Colección de los Viajes y descubrimentos*, 3 vols., Biblioteca de Autores Españoles, 75-77. Madrid: Atlas, 1954.

Fernández de Piedrahita, Lucas. *Historia del Nuevo Reino de Granada*. Book 3. Biblioteca Popular Colombiana, Bogotá: Editorial ABC, 1942.

Fernández de Quirós, Pedro. *Descubrimiento de las regiones austriales*. Madrid: Historia 16, 1986.

Fuentes y Guzmán, Francisco Antonio de. *Historia de Guatemala o Recordación Florida*. Madrid: Luis Navarro Editor, 1883.

García Berrio, Antonio. *Introducción a la crítica literaria actual*. Madrid: Playor, 1983.

García Sebastián., and Felipe Trenado. *Guadalupe: historia devoción y arte*. Sevilla: Editorial Católica, 1978.

García Serrano, M. Victoria, Annette Grant Cash, Cristina de la Torre. *¡A que sí!* Instructor ed. Boston: Heinle & Heinle, 1993.

Garcilaso de la Vega, El Inca. *Obras del Inca Garcilaso de la Vega* 4 vols., Biblioteca de Autores Españoles, 132-35. Madrid: Atlas, 1963.

Gibson, Charles. *The Aztecs under Spanish Rule*. Stanford: Stanford Univ. Press, 1964.

Gobernantes del Perú: Cartas y papeles, Siglo XVI. Ed. Roberto Levillier. vol 3. Madrid: n.p., 1921.

Gomes de Brito, Bernardo. *Historia trágico-marítima*. Buenos Aires:

Espasa-Calpe, 1948.

Gómez Gil, Orlando. *Historia crítica de la literatura hispanoamericana*. New York: Holt, Rinehart and Winston, 1968.

Granzotto, Gianni. *Christopher Columbus*. Trans. Stephen Sartarelli. New York: Doubleday, 1985.

Groussac, Paul. *Mendoza y Garay*. 2 vols., Buenos Aires: Academia Argentina de las Letras, 1949.

Guevara, Isabel. Letter to Princess Juana. July 2, 1556. Letter 104 in *Cartas de Indias*, Biblioteca de Autores Españoles, 265. Madrid: Atlas, 1974.

Haring, Clarence H. *The Spanish Empire in America*. New York: Oxford Univ. Press, 1947.

Herrera y Tordesillas, *Historia General de los hechos de los castellanos en las islas i tierra firme del mar océano*. 9 vols., Madrid, 1601-1615.

___, *Historia general de los hechos de los castellanos en las islas, y Tierra-Firme de el Mar Océano*. 5 vols., Asunción: Guaranía, 1945.

Hudson, James and David Goddy. *Scholastic World Cultures, Latin America*. New York: Scholastic Incorporated, 1987.

Icaza, Francisco de. *Diccionario de conquistadores y pobladores de Nueva España*. 2 vols. Madrid: n.p., 1923.

Juderías, Julián. *La Leyenda Negra*. 15th ed. Madrid: Editora Nacional, 1967.

Lafaye, Jacques. *Quetzalcóatl y Guadalupe*. México: Fondo de Cultura Económica, 1977.

Levi Provençal, E. and Emilio García Gómez. *Sevilla a comienzos del siglo XII: El tratado de Ibn Abdūn*. Madrid: Moneda y Crédito, 1948.

Levillier, Roberto. *El Paititi, El Dorado y las Amazonas*. Buenos Aires: Emecé, 1976.

Lizarraga, Reginaldo. *Descripción breve de toda la tierra del Perú Tucumán, Río de la Plata y Chile*. Biblioteca de Autores Españoles vol. 216. Madrid: Atlas, 1968.

Lockhart, James. *Spanish Peru 1532-1560*. Madison: Univ. of Wisconsin Press, 1968.

León, Fray Luis de. *La perfecta casada*. México: Porrúa, 1980.

Lope de Vega, Felix. *Fuente Ovejuna*. Ed. Francisco López Estrada. Madrid: Clásicos Castalia, 1969.

___, *Fuente Ovejuna*. In *Life is a Dream and Other Spanish Classics*. Ed. Eric Bentley. New York: Applause, 1985.

López de Gómara, Francisco. *Historia de las Indias*. Biblioteca de Autores Españoles, 22. Madrid: Atlas, 1946.

Lummis, Charles F. *The Spanish Pioneers and the California Missions*. Chicago: A.C. McClurg, 1930.

___, *Los exploradores españoles del siglo XVI*. Barcelona: Araluce, 1959.

Majó Framis, Ricardo. *Vida de los navegantes, conquistadores y colonizadores españoles*. 3 vols., Madrid: Aguilar, 1963.

Maltby, William S. *The Black Legend in England: The Development of Anti-Spanish Sentiment, 1558-1660*. Durham: Duke Univ. Press, 1971.

Márquez Sterling, Carlos. *Historia de Cuba desde Cristóbal Colón hasta*

Fidel Castro. New York: Las Américas Publishing Co, 1969.

Martínez, José Luis. *Pasajeros de Indias.* Madrid: Alianza, 1983.

Mártir de Anglería, Pedro. *Décadas del Nuevo Mundo.* Madrid: Polifemo, 1989.

Maura, Juan Francisco. *Alvar Núñez Cabeza de Vaca o el arte de la automitificación.* México: Frente de Afirmación Hispanista, 1988.

McAlister, Lyle N. *Spain and Portugal in the New World 1492-1700.* Minneapolis: Univ. of Minnesota Press, 1984.

McKendric, Melveena. *Woman and Society in the Spanish Drama of the Golden Age.* Cambridge: Cambridge Univ. Press, 1974.

Medina, José Toribio. *Historia del tribunal del Santo Oficio de la Inquisición de Lima (1569-1820).* vol. 2, Santiago: Imprenta Gutemberg, 1887.

___, *Descubrimiento del río Amazonas según la relación de Fr. Gaspar de Carvajal con otros documentos referentes a Francisco de Orellana y sus compañeros.* Sevilla: Imprenta de E. Rasco, 1894.

___, *The Discovery of the Amazon according to the account of friar Gaspar de Carvajal and other documents.* Trans. Bertram T. Lee, ed. H.C. Heaton. New York: American Geographical Society, 1934.

Mendes Pinto, Fernão. *Peregrinação.* 7 vols., Oporto: Portucalense Editora, 1944.

Menéndez y Pelayo, Marcelino. *Historia de la Poesía Hispano-Americana.* Santander: Aldus, 1948.

Morales Padrón, Francisco. *Teoría y Leyes de la conquista.* Madrid:

Ediciones Cultura Hispánica, 1979.

Muñoz Camargo, Diego. *Historia de Tlaxcala*. Madrid: Historia 16, 1986.

Newark, Tim. *Women Warlords*. London: Blandford, 1989.

Núñez Cabeza de Vaca, Alvar. *Naufragios*. Ed. Juan Francisco Maura. Madrid: Cátedra, 1989.

Obregón, Mauricio. *Colón en el mar de los caribes*. Bogotá: Tercer Mundo, 1990.

Ortega Martínez, Ana María. *Mujeres Españolas en la Conquista de México*. México: Vargas Rea, 1945.

O'Sullivan-Beare, Nancy, *Las mujeres de los conquistadores*. Madrid: Compañía Bibliográfica Española, 1956.

Ots Capdequí, José María. *Instituciones*. vol. 14 in, *Historia de America*. 25 vols. Barcelona: Salvat, 1959.

Paz, Octavio. *El laberinto de la soledad*. México: Fondo de Cultura Económica, 1959.

___, *Sor Juana or The Traps of Faith*. Cambridge, Mass.: Belknap Press, 1988.

Pérez de Villagrá, Gaspar. *Historia de Nuevo México*. Madrid: Historia 16, 1989.

___, *Historia de la Nueva México, 1610*. Trans. and ed. Miguel Encinas et al. Albuquerque: Univ. of New Mexico Press, 1992.

___, *History of New Mexico*. Trans. Gilberto Espinosa. New Mexico: Río Grande Press, 1962.

Perry, Mary Elizabeth, *Gender and Disorder in Early Modern Seville*. Princeton: Princeton Univ. Press, 1990.

Phillips, Rachel. "Marina/Malinche: Masks and Shadows." *Women in Hispanic Literature: Icons and Fallen Idols*. Ed. Beth Miller. Berkeley: Univ. of California Press, 1983.

Pigafetta, Antonio de. *Primer viaje alrededor del mundo*. Madrid: Historia 16, 1985.

___, *Primer viaje en torno al globo*. Buenos Aires: Espasa-Calpe Argentina, 1941.

Poem of the Cid. Trans. W. S. Merwin. New York: Las Américas, 1960.

Powell, Phillip Wayne. *Tree of Hate*. New York: Basic Books, 1971.

Pumar Martínez, Carmen. *Españolas en Indias*. Madrid: Anaya, 1988.

Quesada, Vicente G. *La vida intelectual en la América Hispana durante los Siglos XVI, XVII y XVIII*. Buenos Aires: La Cultura Argentina, 1917.

Restrepo Tirado, Ernesto. *Historia de la provincia de Santa Marta*. 20 vols., Biblioteca de Autores Colombianos. Bogotá: Editorial ABC, 1953.

Romero de Terreros y Vinent, Manuel. *Ex Antiquis: bocetos de la vida social en la Nueva España*. Guadalajara, Mexico: Editorial Jaime, 1919.

Ruiz, Juan. *The Book of True Love*. Trans. Saralyn R. Daly. University Park: Pennsylvania State Univ. Press, 1978.

___, *Libro de Buen Amor*. México: Porrúa, 1972.

Ruiz de León, Francisco. *Hernandía*. Ed. Fredo Arias de la Canal. México: Frente de Afirmación Hispanista, 1989.

Salas, Elizabeth. *Soldaderas in the Mexican Military*. Austin: Univ. of Texas Press, 1990.

Sánchez, José. *Hispanic Heroes of Discovery and Conquest of America in European Drama*. Estudios de Hispanófila 47, Chapel Hill, N.C. Madrid: Clásicos Castalia, 1978.

Sánchez-Romeralo, Antonio and Fernando Ibarra. *Antología de Autores Españoles Antiguos y Modernos*. New York: Macmillan, 1972.

Schmildl, Ulrico. *Relación del viaje al Ríó de la Plata*. Madrid: Historia 16, 1985.

Sender, Ramón J. *La aventura equinoccial de Lope de Aguirre*. Madrid: Editorial Novelas y Cuentos, 1962.

Serrano y Sanz, Manuel. *Apuntes para una biblioteca de escritoras españolas desde el año 1401 al 1833*. Vols. 268-71, Biblioteca de Autores Españoles. Madrid: Atlas, 1975.

Tapia, Francisco Xavier. *Cabildo abierto colonial*. Madrid: Ediciones Cultura Hispánica, 1966.

Todorov, Tzvetan. *The Conquest of America*. New York: Harper & Row, 1982.

Toro, Alfonso. *Un crimen de Hernán Cortés. La muerte de doña Catalina Xuárez Marcayda*. México: Patria, 1947.

Torquemada, Juan de. *Monarquía Indiana*. México: Porrúa, 1975.

Truslow Adams, James. *The Epic of America*. New York: Garden City Books, 1933.

Tudebode, Peter. *Historia de Hierosolymitano Itinere*. Trans. John Hugh Hill and Laurita L. Hill. Philadelphia: The American Philosophical Society, 1974.

Ubieto et al. *Introducción a la Historia de España*. Barcelona: Teide, 1984.

Unamuno, Miguel. *Del sentimiento trágico de la vida*. México:

Espasa-Calpe, 1982.

Valle Inclán, Ramón María. *Tirano Banderas*. Madrid: Imprenta Ribadeneyra, 1927.

Varner, John Grier and Jeannette Johnson Varner. *Dogs of the Conquest*. Norman: University of Oklahoma Press, 1983.

Vázquez, Francisco. *Jornada de Omagua y Dorado*. Buenos Aires: Austral, 1945.

Vega, Jesús y María Luisa Cárdenas de Vega. *América Virreinal: La educación de la mujer (1503-1821)*. México: Jus, 1989.

Vigil, Mariló. *La vida de las mujeres en los siglos XVI y XVII*. Madrid: Siglo XXI, 1986.

Villagutierre y Sotomayor, Juan de. *Historia de la conquista de Itza*. Madrid: Historia 16, 1985.

Villalón, Cristóbal. *El Crotalón*. Vol. 2 of *Orígenes de la novela*. Ed. Marcelino Menéndez y Pelayo. 5 vols., Buenos Aires: Editorial Glem, 1943.

Weber, Max. *The Protestant Ethic and the Spirit of Capitalism*. New York: Charles Scribner's Sons, 1958.

Welty, Paul T. *The Human Expression, A History of the World*. New York: Harper and Row, 1985.

Wilgus, A. Curtis, *Colonial Spanish America*. New York: Russell and Russell Inc., 1963.

Winks, Robin W, et al. *A History of Civilitation*. Englewood Cliffs: Prentice Hall, 1988.

Wright, I.A. *Early History of Cuba 1492-1586*. New York: Octagon Books, 1970.

Zavala, Silvio. *Estudios Indianos*. México: Edición del Colegio Nacional, 1948.

___, *Las instituciones jurídicas en la Conquista de América*. México: Porrúa, 1971.

___, *La Encomienda Indiana*. México: Porrúa, 1973.

INDEX